THE
LAURA ASHLEY
─── BOOK OF ───
HOME DECORATING

THE
LAURA ASHLEY
—— BOOK OF ——
HOME DECORATING

ELIZABETH DICKSON AND MARGARET COLVIN
FOREWORD BY
LAURA ASHLEY

OCTOPUS BOOKS

First published 1982 by
Octopus Books Limited
59 Grosvenor Street
London W1.

© Octopus Books Limited 1982
Reprinted 1982

ISBN 0 7064 1478 0

Produced by Mandarin Publishers Limited
22a Westlands Road
Quarry Bay, Hong Kong

Printed in Hong Kong

CONTENTS

LAURA ASHLEY AT HOME

No two homes in the world are the same, because everyone likes to put things together in their own way. When planning our Home Furnishing collections, I take into account the factors which are common to most homes, such as the part played by history and a love of domestic arts. Most of us live with one or more pieces of furniture from other times, old books, china and pictures, and this greatly influences our choice of prints for the collections. We aim to make them as timeless as possible.

For me, the more faded and mellow the interior, the more beautiful it is. I long for a newly-decorated room to "settle down". Hand-made patchworks, needleworks, rag rugs, lots of lace and white starched linens (together with old-fashioned smoothing irons) are all bliss to me. I have lived with slate floors for preference, strewn with gum boots, dogs and children and at the same time somehow managed to maintain the ritual of the dining room and the complete peace of comfortable bedrooms. These things turn a living environment into a home.

Many of the photographs in this book have been taken in my family homes. These have ranged from Welsh Victorian to 17th century tailor's establishment, from remote Welsh hill farm to Regency London house, and now an 18th century French chateau. Every one of these homes has been a joy to decorate, although I am more of an applicator than a decorator, tending always to go for effect rather than a perfect finish. And although I love the simple cottage look, I have also flamboyantly attempted elaborately swagged curtains and festoon blinds, with results which could politely be described as amazing. I believe in the end it's not the stitches but the feeling that counts!

This book has been designed to help bridge the gap between the shop shelf, laden with an enormous choice of items for the home decorator, and the bare rooms or old decor of your home. Should you have curtains or blinds, wallpaper or paint? Which prints and colours should you choose? The first part of the book is packed with rooms decorated in a variety of styles to inspire you. Or you may know exactly the effect you want, but be at a loss as to how to achieve it, in which case the second part of the book tells you how to decorate and make the soft furnishings shown in the first half. We at Laura Ashley hope the book will give you many hours of happy browsing and help you transform your house into a happy home ...

Laura Ashley

Above left: Laura and Bernard
Ashley's 18th century home in
Picardy, France.
Above: The library, with decorations
chosen by Bernard Ashley.
Right: A view of the salon showing
the beautiful original mouldings
above the fireplace and doors.
Above far right: The dining room
and (above centre) a table laid for
more informal breakfasts in the old
card room. As these photographs
show, Laura Ashley's timeless prints
and soft colours look as good in
elaborate, formal surroundings as
they do in a simple rustic cottage or
urban family home.

THE SECRET OF STYLE

The way in which you arrange and decorate your home is the natural and outward expression of your individual style. Your very own style is closely integrated with your outlook on life, and so therefore it becomes a definite reflection of your personality, just as your handwriting gives a hint to the reader of what kind of person you are.

Again, just as your tone of voice conveys to the listener how you are feeling today, or the expression in your eyes reveals a glimpse of your true spirit to the careful observer, so the manner in which you choose to design your surroundings allows insight into your character.

Your style may be borrowed partly from another person's way of doing things, simply because you admire or gently hanker after their way of life or talents. Or you may be a cheerful copycat of the way someone else has organized their domain and their individual style of dress. This means that you may be overlaying your ideas with a veneer of somebody else's, whether a barely detectable skin, or a glossy and easily cracked glaze.

There is no harm in that, provided that you do not let your own ideas on designing, decorating, dressing or even cooking and serving a meal remain totally inactive. If you let your own style lie completely inert, then the untapped energies will wither away, as does neglected love or a plant that is starved from a lack of light and water. Your style needs to be nurtured and polished, like all talents.

Practically no style can be entirely new: pretty well everything we look at and make is in some way derivative of something earlier. The tidy proportions of the child's wooden playpen are on the same classic lines as the basic structure of the ancient marble Parthenon, are they not?

You may decide that you have an urge towards something much more tricky than playing straight copycat to someone else's appealing ideas in dress or surroundings. This is the absorbing business of a pursuit to capture the elusive, intangible atmosphere that another person succeeds in spinning about themselves. With a few exceptions, to try to pin down that certain something, that magical ingredient another individual possesses and then reproduce a carbon copy for oneself is just a waste of time. It is far better to see or hear something one likes and try to interpret it in another medium.

DEVELOP YOUR OWN STYLE

Where someone with style is likely to succeed, is with his expression through another medium of an atmosphere or experience the first person expresses. For instance, the talented composer will produce through his score his own interpretation of the essential qualities in a poet's verses. Or a fashion designer translates the colours and the spirit of a painting, which has influenced her, perhaps even subconsciously. This will be far more successful and satisfying than trying to reproduce style exactly as it is presented without any strain of the admirer's imagination.

What then is this quality (difficult to define), which we name as style? It is something that abides while fads, trends, fashions and notions shift or fade into oblivion. As a distinguished fashion designer, probably the very greatest, and someone who knew a thing or two about the art of living, is reputed to have said: 'Fashion passes, style remains.'

Let us try to pinpoint the essentials. First, style is constant. Trends hurtle along as if they were bright comets pelting by, perhaps to reappear to some, who happen to be in the right place at the right time, to view again decades later, and perhaps in the course of time to burn out and disappear entirely. Fashions are taken up and dropped, some disappearing without a whimper into obscurity, and others faithfully recurring in an upwards spiral.

Each time a fashion reappears, its interpretation is slightly different, and appropriate to the relevant decade, rather as a ballad can be sung in a different tempo, and with a fresh meaning, as it is passed down from the repertoire of one generation to the next. The same experience is presented again and again with a new face for the new recipient to feel and evaluate.

For an example, take one of the popular design elements of this decade, which is the revival of the method of dressing windows with festoon blinds. For several years the plain holland blind was almost synonymous with shiny laminated surfaces, chrome and glass furniture. Straw roller blinds and café curtains then turned up in ginghamed bistros and in young couples' kitchen-dining rooms. This half-the-window café curtain style was part of the standard home decoration scheme, along with the Tiffany style lamp and all the trimmings of fake art nouveau, down to the purple painted front door. Now, pad along to the watering-holes and living areas of the chic, look up at the windows, and, lo, the ruched blind which stems from an earlier century is well and truly reinstated, with its deep frill, plus a glimpse from the street side of the window of the required piping in a different colour. The shape looks complex to make.

If you want to learn how to make these ruched blinds (otherwise known as festoon or Austrian blinds) then turn to the instruction section on page 97 and find out all about the topic for yourself. Anyway, for years the feminine festoons were deemed fusty by some.

Left: The robust pine cupboard makes a handsome alternative to contemporary assembly-line kitchen storage units for keeping glass and utensils. The green and white scheme conveys a restful ambience. A ceramic plant-shaped candlestick echoes the leafy patterns on wallpaper and lampshades. The rustic appeal of the butcher's block table, wood-handled cutlery and pine floor is offset by the crisp formality of the pleated shades and linen mantelpiece runner.
Below: Objects that cost little but look good. Jolly shapes like a horseshoe upturned for luck and a chandler's lantern plus the deft composition combine to unlock the secret of forming a good collection.

Now they are all the rage again: the wheel has come full circle.

THE KEY TO STYLE

But where does this talk of ruched blinds fit in with the subject of style? The connection lies in the way the concept is interpreted by the user. A voluptuous fashion like the one referred to would look out of place and very uncomfortable in a brisk masculine type of office. Frills nudging up against the computer terminals? Hardly – it would be almost as incongruous as a person clad in spacesuit top with Victorian lacy drawers and wellies. But imagine a high-ceilinged bedroom with light from large north facing windows and solid traditional furniture. The room badly needs something to soften its austere atmosphere. Combine ruched blinds with dress curtains of lace, for a light diffusing, feminine effect and you have achieved style.

If you feel you do not possess a definite sense of style and plan to go ahead and develop one, then sit down first and collect your thoughts. Are you sure there are not several interesting ideas ticking away in your brain, just longing to get out and express themselves?

Never be afraid of experimenting with different styles in order to develop your own.

FIND INSPIRATION ALL AROUND

Never give up trying. Keep your eyes open; be aware; observe. Study the interiors in genre paintings in galleries – the details in paintings that depict scenes from everyday life whether contemporary or from an earlier generation can sometimes be an inspiration. Ferret about in antique shops and never be afraid to ask what you do not know. Try to notice how the people whose sense of style stimulates you arrange their own possessions.

Visit historic houses, scrutinize the way that the pictures are hung, how the collections are grouped and the pieces of furniture arranged.

How is your sofa arranged in relation to the space in the room? Does it look inviting to sit on or is the total seating arrangement rather static? Are your colours mixed to create an atmosphere of warmth or detachment? And do you like the feel of the textures you enjoy the sight of? Study how objects succeed or fail in their relationship one to another. See how fresh garden flowers, or wild, like cow parsley, harmonize with old English chintzes, whereas the stubby cactus will jar – the latter, on the other hand, looks good with geometric prints or the bold stripes of a cotton Mexican rug.

Try to keep a fresh eye. If you can retain a sense of wonder like a young child, then you do receive visual images much more clearly, and keep them bright in your mind's eye for far longer.

Try this exercise. Look at an object as if you are seeing it for the very first time, with what one might call the virgin sensibilities. Practise this, and you find that you will be able to revalue the things – trees, a garden gate, a jug – that are already very familiar to you. Imagine the enthralment of someone very young and small seeing at eye level, in the early morning, a drop of dew cradled inside a half-open umbrella of lupin leaves. Each time you make a fresh, innocent discovery like this, you evolve and

Left: Rose-red lacquer paint for walls and a narrow arched window create a study corner. Postcards of early skyscrapers echo the turret shape and the cast iron wall bracket reaffirms gothic tracery. A green wood cupboard stores more bric-a-brac.
Right: Cheerful tones of warm reds, orange and a clear yellow, spiked with lime, for the bedside manner. Flowers bloom on the walls, the chairseat, the wooden Russian dolls, gipsy shawl, petal wreath and within the pine frame. The curvy glass shade enhances a vigorous colour scheme.
Far right: The walls of a flagstone-floored room are washed pink with curling garlands of leaves and fruit stencilled in misty, opalescent tones. This backdrop lends a romantic, softening edge to the furniture. The Victorian deck chair covered in chenille is placed beside a mahogany-topped pub table.
Below right: Curtains skirt the recessed shelving to make an easy solution for hide-away storage, and hessian upholstery puts the formal upright chairs into a country perspective.

how of finishing off the job in the way that a professional does.

This book is also about another aspect of style: achieving a certain splendour on a budget. This is the art of making decisions about where you are prepared to compromise in your own interior decoration. What luxuries or objects will you forgo in order to save for what you want to have eventually? What are your priorities? One person was too busy and not sufficiently in funds to choose the right wallcovering for her new home for two years. Family, job, dog and dry rot all jostled first for attention. Consequently, the evenings when she did get round to inviting friends to eat were illuminated by candlelight, since she had not finalized whether the lighting was to be spots or a standard lamp, and the walls were a roseate pinky plaster, unrendered, of course. Yet with the addition of a big bowl of roses in the centre of the table and the silver polished, she found herself on the receiving end of compliments about pink-walled Italian villa interiors. It is worth waiting for what you want. If you long for blue and white china, then do not be deflected into settling for something plastic instead of waiting for the willow pattern. Find a stylish way of bridging the time gap: say a china junk shop plate for each of you, perhaps each of a different design, but pretty enough to eat off happily every day.

TAKE PRIDE IN YOUR SURROUNDINGS
Pride in the way we look after our homes is not just a monotonous routine of cleaning under the beds. Pride in surroundings is keeping the place looking fresh, but lived-in, in extracting real use out of objects rather than adopting the attitude of treating them as long redundant effigies. This will take you a long way towards achieving style. Lack of pride in your home

consolidate your own sense of personal style.

Another aspect of style is economy of line and design. Beauty can certainly be portrayed ruffled, flounced and exotically draped, but the first step towards style is to pare back to the essentials before piling on any extraneous additions.

In the restoration or decorating of houses this does mean mentally and often literally stripping a place back to study the shell or the bones. It means scraping away perhaps five layers of paint applied over generations, or dismantling a wall to reveal an original fireplace hidden away for years. All this is similar to the commonsense notions of clearing the decks before washing up the dishes, or moving the furniture out of the room before you have a blitzkrieg of a spring clean. Or sartorially speaking, it parallels the maxim that if in doubt about the way you look, then subtract the accessory you have added, rather than des-

perately piling on the bits and bobs. Of course, you can go frilly and add the razzmatazz if you so wish, mixing tartan with paisley prints and candystripes, but approach with caution.

If you are bored with the way you have decorated a room you may want to know how to remedy the situation without having to start entirely again and we hope you will find some ideas among the pages here. Or perhaps you are looking for the answers to all sorts of light-hearted but nevertheless burning questions. How can you give the garden chairs a new look? When should you pipe or would it be altogether more fun to flounce? Just what is a corona and how do you drape it?

Supposing that there is a form of decoration that is new to you, say the art of machine patchwork, or how to attach fabric coverings to the wall surface, then refer to the second half of the book and you will find out how to set about your project, plus the extra know-

soon becomes neglect, and one step from that is to decay.

The doyen of interior decorators, the late John Fowler, whose work included more than one generation of royal households, had one golden rule for people when they first set up home. 'Pig it', he would say. In other words, never be afraid to wait. After all, it is you who are going to live there. Find out about your home before you decide on any details of decoration. Make friends with the place! Consider what colours you really do notice through the downstairs windows, and what materials will harmonize with them. Observe where the sunlight falls. Make life easy for yourself and the people who live with you. Are you tidy or messy? Do you need lots of coathooks or would the clothes be better shut into a cupboard? Is there room to line up the wellington boots by the door, or do you never wear them?

Style is discrimination: deciding what features of the house you are going to keep, and knowing what is worthless and to be discarded. Style is implementing any careful restoration that is needed before adding the extras. Style is looking at the colours of nature to see what shades go together: look at a pheasant's feather or the tones of seashells.

Remember that good home decoration is like putting together the right clothes or balancing the right ingredients for a simple, satisfying meal: the enterprise requires some money, usually a good deal of time and certainly patience. This book is designed to help you make the best use of your potential as a home decorator.

Of all the objectives you may have in your life, the ability and the determination to create a warm, welcoming and attractive home is one of the most worthwhile and precious.

ALL ABOUT KITCHENS

Below left: Modern, laminated fitments, a ceiling hung shelf unit, a spotless cream floor and a pale leafy bough wallpaper that rampages over all the walls and even the ceiling: all these combine to give this fully fitted kitchen a sophisticated colour scheme with creamy tones perfectly matched even to the row of crocks on top of the wall cupboards. The window has a pair of tailored Roman blinds. Right: The space has been reclaimed from a pantry in a French château to make an efficient up-to-date kitchen leading off the main dining room. The china and glass in constant use are stored on open, new pine shelves, and the cooking and work table is the centre of operations.

The kitchen is the central force around which most households spin. Now this axis can either be a jolly space where everyone rushes in and helps themselves to whatever it is they want, or it may, over years of habit, have become the cook's autonomous power-house, where only the most intrepid of compulsive biscuit tin rummagers will dare to tread.

ALL SYSTEMS GO

This resilient core of kitchen from which the vital household energy generates is the place where the stove burns, raw ingredients are coaxed into meals, the waste disposer digests, and the steam rises. All human life is here, as often as not decked out in rubber gloves and cotton apron, but there can be room for gladrags too. All sorts of clothes are worn in the kitchen, including wellington boots if the draining board and sink unit is not fitted out with a wide enough lip at the near side, so that the washing up water slops over onto the floor – an occasional design drawback.

The kitchen of tomorrow is a room that will warmly serve many purposes: it will have to, as the home becomes increasingly more expensive to heat and living costs force us to live in a smaller, simplified space. As it is, the room here and now calls the tune as the most important, lived-in and appreciated space in the home. It is, potentially, a space for daring experiment.

Of course, not everyone is tethered to the stove, as if by some mystical earth mother's umbilical cord. Many folk view without interest the chains of office bestowed on he or she who presides over the *batterie de cuisine*. The significance of the kitchen, its layout and its position in the home, largely depend on one's lifestyle and social attitudes towards food and its preparation. A person may have already passed the middle years without learning how to boil an egg, yet be content to go merrily on with no more advanced knowledge than how to decant the birdseed. At the other end of the scale, you find some who have been schooled in the domestic sciences before reaching the age of majority, and who are already in possession of many well-tried gems of kitchen lore.

If you enjoy a degree of emancipation in your life with meals more often out than in, the kitchen may be lodged in your consciousness as some vague adjunct to the rest of your house or flat, a place seemingly full of sharp edges that you graze yourself on as you manoeuvre a path towards the black coffee. The colour scheme and layout will be irrelevant as they are seen only through a crusty fog of hangover. And then in the evening the kitchen work surface becomes the bar top, useful for fiddling with circular ice cubes, slicing lemon and as somewhere to dump dirty glasses before you sally forth to dinner.

RELENTLESS ROUTINE

On the other hand, the kitchen can be a splendid rallying point in the house where the clatter starts with a grunted communication about poached versus scrambled, then rapid departures all round to school, work, shop; the action continues with spin, chop, wash and so on, to reach, perhaps, a short lull after lunch while kitchen and owner rest on their haunches for a few moments. The yoke is soon slipped back on again for the next shift, whirling into full gear so that by the time that keys are heard in front door locks, the place is coasting along rapidly towards the evening meal, with yet more preparations in hand for the next day. Meanwhile children toil over homework in one part of the room, hamsters have been rescued from behind the floor brush, and neat packages have been retrieved from the vault of the deep freeze. In such a family setting it would be easy to slip into the habit of wearing a dressing gown all day long, sitting among the crumbs and marmalade all morning with feet up by the long pine table.

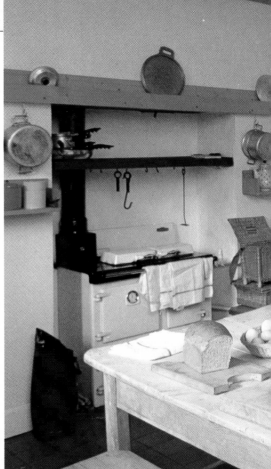

When you consider how to devise a kitchen and how best to make the space work for the occupant, it is sensible to think about how much time the person will spend there – and what, on the whole, the quality of that time will be. In order to receive the greatest benefit from the kitchen, the user must be able to impose a certain amount of self-discipline. And a discipline, however harsh, is easier to sustain if there is a stable framework to function in. A woman who grapples with the long hours of isolation she is likely to find thrust upon her when she rears small children is going to spend much time kitchen-based. In order not to let her spirits waver, or to help boost her morale on the days when the sink seems particularly deep, the kitchen should be designed to be as integrated as possible with the rest of the home and outside world. Whatever the size and style of kitchen, one factor remains constant for all women with young children of pre-school age: they want to be positioned near their

Four glimpses of kitchen life, where the different rooms are very definitely the heart of the home.
Far left: The dresser shape is formed by a set of pine shelves hung on open brickwork above a sturdy sideboard with deep drawers for storing cutlery and table linen. The terracotta and cream china is displayed against a backdrop of naturally harmonizing brick tones.
Left: The centre of family life, a large farmhouse kitchen in Wales where a lamb may stray in through the back door in spring and cats drink milk from their saucers by the Aga. The wicker cat travelling basket and picnic hamper make a simple composition with a row of shiny, time-honoured aluminium pans, cabbages and china pots.
Below left: A series of awkward connecting spaces now spread agreeably into one large kitchen and family area, floored and walled in gleaming modern tiles of warm terracotta and cream tones. There are two main tables, one which acts as a surface for the preparation of food, an island between the sink and stove and the storage on the other side, plus doing the job of sideboard. Then a straight-legged pine table is used for dinner, playing card or board games and doing jigsaws or homework.
Below: The stove is fitted into the old brick range and the combination of open brickwork walls both whitewashed and left plain is particularly soothing and pleasant to live with. Note the door with attractive stained glass panels and how the tall, rather narrow window appears even more so with the decorative arrangement of tall, thin bamboo birdcage and green plants.

mother during all their waking hours, irrespective of whether she is dealing with pans of boiling water, up to the wrists in flour, or trying to sandwich in an hour's study for exam finals.

GOOD-NATURED KITCHENS

Whatever the lifestyle and aspirations of the user, whether home-based or out of the house for a proportion of the day, the kitchen should be a pleasant place to return to, if it is to play any major role as a location in the household. A reassuring atmosphere is one that both soothes because of the quiet, unchanging order and sense of down to earth stability about the place, and at the same time sends the spirits soaring with the cheerful, cared-for appearance of attractive decoration and clean surfaces. Just one comment, in passing, on the subject of people's quirks and foibles about kitchen hygiene. It is curious how someone will invest substantial sums in planning and furnishing a kitchen and yet soldier on with the same clutch of ancient, cracked wooden spoons for cooking. Often enough, the cause is that it is easy not to notice the deterioration of an object in constant use, and while one is sympathetic to anybody who reaches for a kitchen utensil with the same automatic reaction as a Pavlovian dog triggered by bells, it really is worthwhile taking time off to stand back and take a thoroughly objective view of the state of play in the kitchen.

Left: Straw blinds, neutral cool tones, not a trace of food or mealtimes, and plenty of shiny, spotless stainless steel; such a hyper-efficient kitchen is the one-person domain of a busy career woman who cooks for relaxation.

Right: A minute kitchen leading off the formal dining room of a terraced London house. The room is so designed that it will look in keeping with the green dining room next door. Coloured stencils on cupboards and boxes give a rustic chalet look. The same simple motif decorates the blind. The blue criss-cross wallpaper consolidates the neat and well-arranged space, and the blue in the design is used on the blind borders.

Far right: Underneath the arches, a cavernous cellar niche makes masterly use of space, housing shelf and cupboard storage unit. Bright butter yellow surfaces create an illusion of warm sunlight in a Greek island kitchen.

Below: On a winter's day in this town kitchen, all is orderly, well-lit and welcoming. Advent calendars are stuck on the glass panes, a shopping basket sits under the worktop and the dishes are stored away from the dust.

WHERE THE HOUSE HEART BEATS

The heart of the house is the room to which most people gravitate, and so consequently this becomes the most informal area. Whereas the bedroom is the sanctum in a night-owl's crash-pad and a soundproof recording room is the pulse of life for others, or the allotment shed a paradise for the keen gardener who prefers earth to any room indoors; so the heart of the house for a family or communal group is a large, comfortable kitchen. The image of the ideal family group gathered around the hearth is, of course, one that is eternally warm and desirable. So, if you are moving house or remodelling your existing one, then you would do well to consider carefully the attractions of eating the main meals in the kitchen with enough room for relaxation, child's play and jobs like ironing as well: all reasons for earmarking the room with the best space and outlook downstairs to the kitchen, as long as the plumbing and linked areas, such as hall or corridor, permit.

This area benefits from the same sort of annual or specifically-timed reappraisal that the professional shopkeeper gives to his premises with standard procedure stock-taking, or when someone makes an inventory of their possessions for insurance or letting purposes.

There is a distinct revival in this decade for the comforting farmhouse style of wood-panelled and tile or brick floored kitchen, a consolidation of the open-plan kitchen and dining area, which first caught on as a lifestyle some years ago in the knocked-through ground or basement floors of converted 19th century houses. Part and parcel of that metamorphosis in design and layout which brought the activities of cooking and eating into one large, light and unpretentious room, was the first real public appearance of the now ubiquitous stripped pine dresser downstairs, with the brass bedstead a mandatory item upstairs, and the metal-legged coffee table proclaiming status in a space somewhere in between.

THE PLEASURES OF WOOD

In the contemporary kitchen anything wooden is likely to be ornamental as well as functional: part of an overall eclectic mix of rich textures, fretwork, canework, carving, plus decorative extras such as etched or stained glass panels, stencilled or hand-painted furniture, and complemented, possibly, by a wood burning stove in the adjoining sitting area, studio or library. With the resurgence of solid comforts and traditional values in the kitchen space, with the room established as an attractive place to sit in, comes the popularity of the range style of cooker. The brightly enamelled modern version of the Aga cooker is so good to look at that it is worth planning a decorative scheme around it.

The mode of decoration described above is a natural progression from the cottage style of plain pine arranged in a kitchen with plain walls

– agreeable to live with and simple to maintain, but a look adopted and so exploited in advertisements, shops and eating places that one longs for something more. The desire emerges to experiment with a mood that invites a dash of fantasy to mix with all that rather hard-seated, pure and spartan reality.

SAFETY FIRST

Wood is marvellous for good looks and durability, but do remember that as the amount of wood used in kitchen planning increases, so does the risk of fire.

All kitchens, everywhere, are all the more safe if they are fitted with a hand-sized fire extinguisher which everybody in the house is fully confident of being able to use in an emergency. The hem of kitchen curtains must be drawn well away from the kitchen hob or matches. Saucepan handles must be turned away from the floor, facing inwards on the stove, and so safely out of the grab range of inquisitive small hands.

If sharp knives are secured by their blades to a magnet panel, then the latter should be wall-mounted, well away from children. Also, over-hanging tablecloths are a temptation to the very small to clutch when they are exploring the world from ground level. One yank on the cloth corner, from a child winching itself into the standing position, and the contents of the table laid for the next meal go flying. Pet bowls should be placed well out of the mainstream of traffic to avoid the chance of being tripped into (and cats' tails escape being trodden on) and preferably put outside the back door. Animals and children of all ages should be trained to keep out of the traffic lane linking stove, sink and work surface during peak hours, such as the critical moments before weekend meals when tempers often become strained.

Left: This kitchen of unstained ash furniture rich in moulded panels, fretwork and canework was made by knocking together a small kitchen and dining room. Now the cooking area is separated from the rest of the space by a proscenium arch, and the visual interaction of the different areas and the textures of natural materials create a comfortable family room. The design of this room is executed in style, yet the plain cast iron casserole dishes, steel utensils and plain china are simple and unpretentious. The chopping block has a two-day drawer. Below left: Thanks to elaborate shelves hung over the Aga, the two together resemble an old range. Below: View of a rustic family kitchen in a London house where the basement rooms were gutted and reconstructed into a beautiful spacious area with pink painted walls and garland stencilling. The 1920s glass hanging lights are decorated with images reminiscent of children's story books of half a century ago, and these naive, enchanting designs were an inspiration for the stencil treatment. The dresser is arranged with splendour in a variety of pale harmonizing colours.

Anyone who is constantly in the company of the very young while ferrying loads of food and dishes about is sensible to keep firmly in flat shoes: a precaution against somersaulting down cellar stairs or tripping over the rug if you are carrying a tray full of dishes and unable to see the youngster on all fours at your feet. Keep a first aid box in the kitchen strategically placed near a worktop and keep a duplicate tube of burn ointment in a drawer as near as possible to the stove.

If your larder or kitchen storage is designed with the upper shelves out of arms' reach, or set back behind an appliance like a tall fridge-freezer, then be sure you have a ladder, or stool with a built-in step, which can be assembled in a trice, instead of hopping onto the worktop to retrieve a jar from the upper reaches. Likewise, standing on a chair which can easily skid from under you, especially on a wet or polished tile floor, is a dangerous short cut which is not worth the risk when it comes to washing down kitchen walls or spring cleaning the shelves.

On the other hand, to sit rather than stand when engaged in kitchen chores or ironing is a positive aid to well-being since it lessens the strain on back and feet. Quite one of the most pleasant moments of quiet relaxation in cooking is the slow, measured and leisurely process of making mayonnaise by hand, sitting in a comfortable kitchen chair, or even on the back door steps on an early evening in summer, a drink at the ready to sip while the emulsion thickens.

A chair or stool for sitting in while ironing or using the kitchen worktop needs to be taller than the standard upright chair. A stool is fine for breakfast bar meals, except that many people find the lack of back support offers an insufficient amount of comfort and relaxation for more than the minutes snatched for a quick bite. High stools are inadvisable seating for young children who may, so far off the ground, easily topple backwards.

SAFE AS HOUSES: BASIC SECURITY

From safety to security. Intruders are much more likely to approach from the rear of a house than the front, and so be sure that your back door is suitably reinforced if the frame is not very strong and that you have efficient secure bolts. A catflap should be positioned well out of possible reach of the keyhole, in case anyone attempts to unfasten a door which is locked from the inside.

Right: Another view of the stencilled kitchen. The dining section of the room has ample space for a large table and a wicker armchair in the bay. The window is dressed with ruched lace blinds, echoing the colours of the stencils.

Below right: The objective in this spacious room is to provide a family room with a battery of the basic necessities for cooking, plus a place to eat and relax in. The Mediterranean style is epitomized by the pink washed walls, as warm looking as the outside of a Tuscan villa; functional utensils zestfully on show, floor tiles and a few large pieces of furniture complete the picture. The original chimneypiece is now tiled as a setting for the hob. Heart wood cutouts add a restrained touch of whimsy to the pine cupboards which mask the central island, an unusual and pretty form of display. The butcher's block is fitted with an electric power point for the food mixer.

Below: View of the sink side of the room seen from the hob. The green tiles now used as a splashback were rescued from the floor of a demolished Victorian conservatory.

The person who is often alone and whose kitchen window overlooks a garden or another easily accessible place such as a stairwell with a fire escape, will feel more secure if a light is fixed to the outside house wall, over the kitchen windows or back door. The power can then be switched on from a point within the kitchen, and if the lamp is correctly positioned, this will allow the maximum amount of light to flood the immediate vicinity. For the same reasons, a householder whose home is in a neighbourhood which has a high crime rate, should be discouraged from growing an abundance of shrubbery, which might shelter an intruder, around the back door or windows on the ground floor at the rear of the house.

Here the plot is to take a basic scheme of red and white and co-ordinate the mix throughout a multi-activity space, but with the assurance that all aspects of the room turn out to be efficient both in looks and feel, and very easy to run. The result took the owner five weeks' worth of evenings.
Far left: Close-up of the kitchen fitments: louvred cupboards and wooden storage units are painted with red gloss and the walls covered with tiles.
Left: Cherry red appliqué on the lined place-mats and napkins match the enamel tea pot and neat tie-backs for the curtains.
Below left: The stark lines of roller blinds at the windows are softened with scalloped edges.

If you possess a sofa deemed to be on its last legs, about to be pensioned off to make way for a bouncy new one in the drawing room, or replaced with unit seating of various permutations for the living area, then there may be room to line the sofa up against the kitchen-dining room wall, if you have a really large space. This is an interesting alternative to sending the sofa out to grass in a child's room or off to the auctioneers, since the young may be content as they are, without the addition of more pieces of care-worn furniture, and a kitchen sofa makes the room an even nicer place to put your feet up in — as all the family and animals are bound to agree. If you feel energetic, give the sofa a coat of new colours,

BRING THE GARDEN INDOORS
There is an everlasting lyrical quality about a row of terracotta flower pots on a kitchen window-sill filled with geraniums, especially when there is also a pair of wooden shutters or sprigged muslin curtains. Stoneware marmalade and Stilton cheese jars, which come in a natural beige colour with a band of brown at the top, look miraculously pretty in spring if they have been planted with crocuses: the proportion of plant to pot is just right. Plants hung from the ceiling in baskets made of wicker, terracotta pots, glass fish bowls or any container you can recycle such as a redundant cake tin, are a winning idea provided the gazelle-like agility needed for sustaining the lofty watering routine fits in with your life. Also, be sure the plants in your hanging garden have saucer-like containers between pot and supporting strings or network, so that drips from a generous watering do not rain down

onto the head of the potato-peeler below. Fast climbing plants like jasmines and some pelargoniums are fun to grow in the kitchen where you can see a change in them almost every day.

MAKE USE OF SPACE
A large kitchen may possibly be easier to run with an island unit. This can be fitted with hob, working surface, sink or simply kitted out with the necessary power points for operating portable gadgets like electric mixers. The island makes a functional looking, useful stepping stone, too, between work areas against opposite walls. Towel rails and useful cup hooks can be screwed onto the side walls of the island, and similarly you can sling all manner of baskets, dried flowers and other objects on ceiling hooks. Rise and fall lamps are the most adaptable of central kitchen light fittings and recessed lamps in the ceiling are unobtrusive.

Right: View through to the south-facing window over the sink and worktop end of the kitchen in this Edwardian house. Two rooms have been knocked into one general cooking, eating and sitting area. In the evening the table is an attractive informal setting for supper. The remaining section of the connecting wall is papered, and the ceiling covered in tongue and groove pine boarding. The floors were on different levels, and so the kitchen end is tiled and the living space floored in cork to make a warm, cosy surface for child's play.
Below: The sitting area at the far end of the room. The frame of the wall mirror is fabric covered and the old sofa refurbished with loose covers.

matching the loose covers to the window blinds, curtains or chair tabs and even going so far as to re-cover grease marked recipe books in a matching or harmonizing paper.

A refectory table works well in a kitchen-dining room with an assortment of different upright chairs if you do not have a collection of matching ones. Or you could partner the table with the good looking addition of rush-seated ladderback chairs – or even use a baroque style of reproduction dining chair. These ideas are more appropriate to a large space than a cramped kitchenette in a flat, or a kitchen that is shaped like a passage and is the linking space between the main room and a utility room, or is just an awkward small space – fine for two

but not so easy if several of you are sharing.

In tiny spaces a round table is compact and blinds take up less room than curtains. Surfaces look better arranged in an unbroken line.

Table top cooking equipment has practical advantages, the first being that the hostess can spend more time with her guests. Microwave ovens, spit-roasters and the time-honoured fondue making equipment all ensure that food can be cooked *in situ*, with participation for all in the feast. Electric filter coffee-makers, toasters and a thermostatically-controlled deep-fryer means that you can have a leisurely breakfast or light lunch all cooked at arms' length.

Mechanical items are dear, sometimes with hidden drawbacks. So make a plan of campaign before you buy some streamlined chrome-edged automaton which purrs obediently for a few weeks and then breaks down, only for you to learn that there is an absence of after sales service in your area. First, what sort of mecha-nical items will fit in with your lifestyle? For example, do you shop daily or mount military expeditions to a supermarket once in a blue moon? Do you live mostly on Chablis and brie or do you enjoy complicated cookery? Do you need a machine that shreds, minces and performs other culinary feats to keep pace with your turnover of home made patés for the family freezer? Check whether there is sufficient space for machinery before you buy, and whether calling in builders to make any extra room needed will be worthwhile in the long run. Scrutinize small print stating guarantees, and if you buy a smaller gadget such as a mixer or liquidizer, then lodge it and its family of accessories near the spot where it will be most in use.

Finally, a bottle rack can also store tins neatly, a notice board pins down items like timetables and a wooden plate-rack looks pretty and friendly.

A GOOD PLACE TO EAT

Our eating habits today are as versatile as the spaces we eat in and the items we eat off. The old guard was well-defined: somewhere for everyone and everyone well fed in their place. That is to say, the wealthy ate in an impressive dining room or hall with finger bowls, bells and double damask, the minions ate below stairs around a scrubbed kitchen table, and children polished off their tapioca pudding in the far away nursery wing. Some households are still run on grand, old-fashioned lines with the cooling roast beef carried down echoing passages that link the servants' quarters with the domain of the master, but for the rest of us, life is less formal and less leisurely. Yet our meal times and eating patterns are now more flexible and more varied than they have ever been before.

A MEAL FOR ALL REASONS

We now have a far greater range of cooking appliances, items to eat off and utensils to eat with than in the past. All sorts of new frontiers are crossed: if you have not time for or refuse to do the washing up and feel like spending money on disposables, then you can go ahead and serve champagne in beautifully designed and coloured paper cups with napkins to match, or if you have a passion for pink you can buy stainless steel cutlery with pink nylon handles. There is a wider choice of well designed tableware in the shops; but before

Above: Separate tables for a very self-possessed young lady who has her own breakfast spot reserved for her by the window of the conservatory. After the repast her park bench seat and wire table can be folded flat to store away. The thick white lace border is an easy and attractive idea to copy when you want to romanticize the look of a plain linen blind, and in this room it looks charming with the white painted furniture. The pink and white theme follows through down to the cutlery and decorative china. The cottagey teapot thatched with a pink lid wins the heart of even the most reluctant of young breakfast eaters.
Below: The converted coach house of a castle in Ireland where several are to be gathered together at the refectory table for an informal lunch party.

you set out to buy, you have to decide what sort of texture and style you would like to live with, and whether you are going to buy plates to complement a dinner service you have been given or inherited, or whether to use the plates from the older generation for decorative purposes only and go out and buy something completely new.

The social attitudes to meal times have changed. Now we telephone for a takeaway meal and serve the food straight from the foil containers as we flop down in front of the television, or we eat on the move, having stopped at the fast food place for a hamburger in a bag. Then there are outdoor meals charcoal cooked on barbecue equipment, and more equipment for cooking meals at the dining table indoors. The advantage of table-

top cooking is that your guests can join in with the cooking in a very informal and convenient way, or the hostess can prepare the chops on the spot to exactly the liking of each individual.

During the school holidays, or at any time when there are different numbers at home for different meals, then any meal becomes a movable feast, and can be a form of glorified picnic.

SUCCESS IN PRESENTATION

Meals are served for an infinite number of occasions, but whether it is an egg on a tray for one, a children's party or a buffet supper for fifty people, there is one consideration which remains constant, and this is that the food should not only taste good but be presented in a tempting and attractive manner.

Above: If you have planned a breakfast conference, then why not make the table look as glamorous and pretty as a party when you go through your agenda over the cornflakes and coffee? Or, if you already have a formal dining room for large numbers, then you could use a corner of the room for a smaller, circular table around which to enjoy a weekend family breakfast. The combination of green and apricot colours makes a good muted background to food. The pelmet over the window is draped with sprigged cotton into a series of voluptuous deep swags, echoed by the ruched blinds, ruffled tablecloth and cushions.

The art of good presentation is, of course, a topic that can be discussed in entirely subjective terms, but any decoration should be kept simple. Time is well spent when a cook minutely chops parsley to add it as a last minute persillade to a delicious stew, or uses the complete stem and feathery leaves of parsley to form part of a table centrepiece – parsley with pale cabbage roses in a silver bowl looks very fetching – rather than garnishing a butterdish with a sprig, in the mistaken belief that a simple slab of pure, fresh butter looks humble and positively naked without a fussy addition.

FINDING ENOUGH ELBOW ROOM
When you live in a place where priority in the main rooms is given to activities other than formal dining, then you will need to improvise. You can probably eat in the corner of your main room, and with luck choose the corner nearest to the kitchen, or adapt your way of living to use the kitchen as the main eating area. In a flat where there is little enough space anyway, you can sometimes convert part of the hall or passageway. If you do use a space such as this you want to check whether there are any draughts, and if so to provide a solution like a low banquette seating arrangement, or a simple framework, such as two bookcases that jut out from the wall on either side of the table and seating, thus outlining a snug space. Also, if you use part of the traffic area for eating in, it is

often an improvement to hang a large mirror opposite or behind the table, or even to cover that part of the wall with ceiling to floor mirror tiles, in order to dispel any feeling of corridor gloom. In any dining room space, a mirror is an attractive way of maximizing the glow of candlelight and the festive gleam of silver and glass.

NOCTURNAL STYLE
If you are out during the day and produce most of your meals at home in the evening, then bear in mind as you plan your dining area, whether a whole room or a corner, that it will be most often in use after dark. This means that the space will have, visually and in its atmosphere, a

Far left: Over the top decoration with a full tented ceiling and pinch-pleated curtains opened during the day to frame French windows, and at night closed to screen the far wall. The baroque mirror gives an illusion of a more spacious, lighter room.
Left: For devotees of the dark and shiny look: a corner of a Paris apartment, where the lamp-base, tableware and the rattan chairs are black and gleaming lacquer-bright.
Below left: A meticulously arranged town house dining room, decorated in browns and beiges. The chair covers in beige linen union are matched by the curtains reflected in the mirror.
Right: A vigorous start to the day with a breakfast corner for two by the window. Table mats, napkins, egg and tea cosies all make a special feature of this table. The red overcloth can be easily removed, leaving the floor-length cloth underneath as a permanent cover.
Below: This tablecloth has the top circle cut to fit exactly the surface of the table and the full skirts are gathered and then piped around the perimeter. The restrained geometric print is well offset by the rustic bowls and rush mats.

different weight and tone from the other rooms in your home: an opportunity to use dark and dramatic colours that come alive with artificial lighting. A fabric tented ceiling, which is not as difficult to achieve as the results would appear, is a very glamorous way of dealing with a dark dining space, because it creates a definite atmosphere of intimacy and mystery. When you sit round a table with a background of fabric around and above you and all in a dark design, then you feel enclosed in a space of comforting cave-like warmth – a pleasant transition from the mood of arriving for a meal and having drinks in the more brightly-lit drawing room or main room first.

If you have an ugly window in your night-time dining area, then treating the glass as part of the wall, and hiding it with the same material as the ceiling rather than attempting to enhance it, is a useful aspect of the canopy idea.

A formal dining room offers a calm stopping-place where the members of the household can gather and relax during a meal in an orderly space away from the clutter of the rest of the house. The symmetrical arrangement of furniture and objects in a formal dining room are a timeless reminder of traditional values that are comfortable to return to in a busy, uncertain life, and they are as reassuring as the tick of a grandfather clock.

When you plan your dining room think about a room with a few pieces of large furniture, because both a dining table and a sideboard are going to take up space and likely to be in a dark wood which is dominating to look at. Add upright chairs, but after those, little more. Think of your room as a courtyard where people meet and a few objects make the focal points.

One benefit of having a separate room for dining is that much of the work which goes into producing a meal can be done methodically well in advance. This is easier than pre-planning for a meal where the main table-top for eating at is part of an open-plan area linked to the kitchen, or another space teeming with constant activity. You can get a formal dining room ready down to almost the final details with the safe knowledge that a table laid for a supper party the night before, if you are going to be busy during the day, will not curtail the rest of a household's activities. All of this adds up to greater peace of mind for the hostess when the moment comes for her to light the candles and bring her guests to the table.

These pages show examples of four different rooms which are used only for eating, and where comfort, formality and a sense of order are given full rein without being dictated to by a linked kitchen or an adjoining sitting area.

Left and opposite page above: Polished table and dining chairs, varnished wood floor and dark coloured walls, a sturdy old wood dresser, blue and white china and an open log fire – these are the hallmarks of a country dining room, comfortably spacious and in a style of decoration that is straightforward and unpretentious. The brick red painted walls and highly polished copper and brass contribute to a feeling of warmth, and act to soften the severity of the dark furniture in a space that might otherwise feel chilly when the fire is unlit. The glazed cotton chintz curtains with convolvulus flower print and ruched blinds have a pattern and colour scheme that makes a fitting frame to the view of the tall trees and ivy-clad walls outside. The end window has a variation on the same Austrian blind treatment, and the white painted woodwork is complemented by the shape and plain print of the hardboard pelmets.

Try to allow space for a surface that is heat-proof or otherwise geared to cope with hot dishes, such as an electric heating tray. Also, try to have a surface that is at a comfortable height for carving on, which is slightly higher for most people than conventional table tops. Soft strip lighting over frames illuminates pictures, a flexible rise and fall lamp over the table pleases most people, and coasters are the sensible way to prevent wine stains and drips.

If a cloth is put onto a valuable polished table then a stout protective wad, such as an army blanket, should be put beneath the cloth.

When the kitchen is next door, a trolley is useful. And a partitioned ornamental screen – decorated lacquer looks good with damask and mahogany – or a simple screen in baize, can be placed to mask the view and stop the draughts from the door that connects an elegant dining-room with an untidy but functional kitchen.

A hatch is another way of bridging oven with table. The squat shape of a hatch can be hidden from view by a blind made of material toning with the colours of the walls, and which pulls down when the hatch closes. You could have a blind incorporating part of a stencilled or *trompe l'oeil* painting that takes up the wall surfaces. Imagine an ingenious fantasy of painted birds, flowers and a walled garden. The gate appears precisely where the hatch is: so when the blind, painted with the gate, is pulled up you appear to have an exit from the garden.

Opposite below right: A detail of the red dining room showing the blind and curtain designs.
Opposite below left: This smart dining room shows how the same print used for walls and soft furnishings can unify a room, and to what extent the choice of a white background maximizes the light. Potted palms are placed on either side of the French windows, and the green borders outline formality.
Above left: Golden yellow and white makes a springlike yet formal setting to a meal laid for four.
Above: A grey and white curtain with tie-back matches exactly the tones of the moulded wall panels.

BUILDING AN EXTENSION

If you are becoming seriously cramped for space because the size of your household has grown in numbers since you moved to your house, either with your additional children and household pets, or because an elderly relative has come to live permanently with you, or because there is a change in your lifestyle so that you now work from home with an office or studio under the family roof, then you will be researching the different ways in which to find the space that can most satisfactorily encompass your needs. It is still usually a great deal less expensive to add on an extension to your home, even in these times of fierce escalating costs for anything custom built, than it is to move to a new house.

Transferring yourself, family and belongings to another home, adapting to a new area, starting decoration from scratch again, and finding a new place for everything – all of this is extremely time consuming, and extremely expensive.

LIVING IN A GLASSHOUSE

When you build on an extension, the new part evolves as part of an organic household. That is to say, you simply overspill into the new space within an area with which you are already familiar, and very sensibly you also increase the value of your home at the same time.

One way of adding extra space is to make yourself an elegant and useful conservatory. The conservatory, orangery and greenhouse all

stem from the wintering shed for delicate plants which was established in the Renaissance. By the Victorian era, the conservatory had spread from botanical gardens and aristocratic estates to the newly-formed town suburbs, and the pretty glasshouse added onto a 19th century villa was used as an ornamental sitting room and a highly decorative suntrap with arranged walks and specially dug beds for growing exotic plants. Conservatories were all the rage until the fashion for open windows and informal cottagey gardens took over from the scenes of languid ladies among the rattan furniture.

Conservatories are now enjoying something of a late 20th century revival, and they have the great advantage of maximizing the use of

More room for eating and sitting about in, as well as an unusual space for a town house in which to entertain. An old Victorian conservatory is given a new lease of life with a lick of white paint and attractive furnishings to make the space into a most versatile dining room, that feels and looks equally inviting day or night.

Far left: A room which provides the romantic back-drop to a candlelit dinner underneath the stars. The original doors which lead from the conservatory to the garden are on the side which faces to the south. Inside doors lead from both the drawing room and the newly installed kitchen, so making this a perfectly placed focal point for an extra dining space. Cotton blinds look soft as gossamer against the nightlight, and the room is lit with candles on the window ledge and table, and in the wire hanging baskets. The lightweight metal chairs are made more comfortable for relaxing in with rectangular seat-pads of fabric-covered foam and frilly cushions.

Left: The same room by daylight. The space doubles as a fine garden room where arum lilies and other potted plants are cultivated, and a quiet study detached from the rest of the active household.

Below: Two details of the interior decoration to show how the garden colours of the fabric happily bridge the area from inside to out with blinds, table-mats, napkins and cushions in pink and leafy green. The china and candles in summery pinks also add to the effect. The floor is quarry tiled.

natural light as well as allowing you to rear a garden spared the natural hazard of weeds. A conservatory need not feel like a poor relation to the house, merely tacked on as an after-thought, as its shape can respect the architecture and look quite correct from the outside. You can double-glaze the glass and have radiators to produce warmth for winter months, with sophisticated ventilation to keep the place comfortably cool in summer.

In keeping with the conservatory style of decoration are iron spiral staircases, rattan, wicker and wrought iron furniture often in gothic shapes, stained glass, lanterns and lace. The 'eternal peace of the conservatory' is how one early ducal patron of this form of space aptly described the atmosphere.

The appeal of a garden is more than a space in which to rear plants, a satisfying and joyful place to work where the labours can bring tremendous rewards, or where hours can be passed in gentle pottering with the most amount of effort applied to deadheading the roses.

Since ancient times, the garden has been a haven and a solace in which to sit, contemplate, eat, study or simply snooze.

FURNISHING THE GARDEN
Whatever we choose to put into our garden in the way of furniture, or larger structures such as summer houses, gazebos and sheds, the additions should be in sympathy with the rest of the environment. This applies whether the home is a flat that opens out onto a narrow strip of city balcony enlivened by a row of runner beans curling up the railings plus a deckchair and a single folding table, or the house is a stately country seat with follies, a marquee on the lawn for midsummer's night and a wooden bridge of Oriental design linking the jetty with the island on the lake.

GARDEN DWELLERS
Living out of doors at its most simple means something to sit on and eat off within easy walking distance of the stove and sink.

Basically, furniture for outside needs to be either completely weatherproof so that it can be left out all year round, or light, easy to move and collapsible so that everything can be easily folded, transported, dismantled and stored. Rattan, wicker and cane furniture are appropriate to outdoor life but need to be brought under cover overnight or at first sign of rain as they rot in the wet.

Garden furniture was first made in marble and stone and the philosopher Epicurus is believed to be the inventor of furniture for outdoors with the marble seats his students sat on in his gardens. Stone furniture often looks very massive and monumental for most of the gardens of today's more modest proportions, and we are likely to favour the unpretentious deck chair or simple wooden bench made of wood like iroko, which when left out turns to a pleasing grey as time passes.

Although the early garden dwellers were the peoples of warmer climates, it was the English who created much of the fantasy look in outdoor furniture in the 18th century. To complement the graceful country houses, orangeries and banqueting pavilions, exotic birds like peacocks and swans all contributed to the leisurely outdoor living of the aristocracy. Chairs then were made of twisted wood, with their twigs and leaves still left on the branches, and seats were fashioned with shell shapes for grottoes and dells. With the advent of mass manufacture, ornate cast iron furniture painted white and dark green became an elegant feature in the conservatory lit by Japanese lanterns. In England, these glasshouses became

a *de rigueur* adjunct to the houses that were being built in the fast developing suburbs for the newly rich. The Crystal Palace epitomized the trend for a fantasy glass space where the occupants could enjoy a warm temperature and glamorous surroundings even when snow lay on the ground.

Today we use adaptations of the early fantasy wood furniture for outside, just as we still furnish our gardens and terraces with the timeless wooden garden seat. The current interpretations of the Chinese design and rococo shapes of the elaborate 19th century chairs, with all their embellishments, look well in the garden settings of old houses, and they can be brought indoors at the end of the season for use in the hall or dining area. You can make chair tabs and cushion back rests for the chairs with slabs of foam covered in fabric and ribbon tied at the corners, and so give a garden armchair or bench a winter dress to wear inside.

COLOUR IN THE GARDEN
In cooler climates, the best colours for garden furniture are greens, yellow, blue or natural tones. Small print cottons, plain linens and wide stripe fabrics are especially suitable. So, too, are the harmonizing tones of some Indian cottons or the sobriety in rich tones of a Persian carpet for cushion colours.

You can establish different woods for the furniture and bits and pieces that accompany the pleasurable business of living outdoors. Think of the rich subtle tones of an Eastern tent, the tiles of a Persian courtyard garden and you have one school of thought. Think of floppy chintz cushions, creaking wicker seats or *chaise longues* with a parasol and you have another outdoor scenario. Think of watching cricket from a deck chair with a linen cloth for the tea table, or tartan rugs and wicker hampers for a picnic out of the back of the car and you have yet another style.

GARDEN LIGHT
Lighting for outdoors at its simplest is soon put together with lanterns and night-lights hung from trees (or even from a washing line slung across the verandah or your back yard).

Spotlights can be fixed to a wall and switched on from indoors and ships' chandlers are worth browsing in for ideas on lighting that can do battle with the elements. Outdoor lighting can be romantic as well as practical and one does not have to go to the lengths of ancient Rome and have a cascade of urns filled with flaming torches flanking the stone balustrade in order to achieve a glamorous look. Simple candlelight is lovely provided you have some sort of shield from the breeze.

If you have a terrace or a roof garden in a town apartment you can make the most of the space with a striped awning which winds down in summer and so provides you with another, if rather costly, extra room. An inexpensive table can easily be made with a slab of marble or wood screwed onto the top of one of the elaborate cast iron sewing machine table bases which are sometimes found in junk shops.

CHILDREN'S CORNER

Any discussion on outdoor living must include some consideration about where the children are going to play. A Wendy House is easily dismantled and an inflatable pool is a good investment for a family with very young offspring. A pool or sandpit should be positioned within easy reach, earshot or sight of the adult in charge. If you build a sandpit choose a spot where the resulting young storm troops with damp sandy feet will not tramp over good carpet indoors. Simple climbing

frames are good looking and fun for the young, and these constructions are all the better for being left in their natural colours. And, of course, there is something eternally lyrical about a garden swing or a hammock which is slung from the strong branches of a couple of trees in an orchard.

If you consider building an adjunct to your house you may decide on a conservatory, or a garden room with a solid roof and glass walls. Either way, these are appropriately furnished with the pieces of wood already described Cast iron or aluminium furniture with a weatherproof epoxy coating and rattan or bamboo seats and sofas are particularly sympathetic to exotic palms, all sorts of geraniums, vines and jasmine.

If you have the budget and there appears to be no way in which you can add on a glasshouse extension to your home (even by

putting the conservatory onto a flat roof), then you might think of adding a separate structure such as a freestanding summer house. And even the most humble of wood potting sheds can be a delicious retreat from the pressures of a noisy family. Or, for sheer indulgence you can add a domed wire gazebo which stands on four mesh legs over which to ramble old fashioned roses, with wire chairs and tables to match the pergola or gazebo folly.

And, so, to the final details. When you furnish your patch of the great outdoors, think also about gardening aprons, the watering can and outdoor boots. A hessian apron with deep pockets is easy to make and you can have a hessian pinboard or 'walltidy' with pockets in the garden room to match. Traditional equipment in soft, cool colours all adds to the general attractive look and soothing appeal of outdoor living.

THE VERSATILE LIVING ROOM

In many households the transitional space that links the kitchen to the living room, or whatever title you give to the main social and recreational part of your home, is the area where you eat. The dining-living area is often one large room which has two sections, each a kingdom of its own, but at the same time well integrated. The line separating the two is marked either with fabric, a solid or sliding wall, a change of floor level or some other divider whose design attests the ingenuity of the owner.

First, let us deal with the relationship of the kitchen with the nearby eating space. In converted houses the dining, living and cooking areas are often located on the first floor, where two rooms have been knocked into one, and a tiny kitchen is linked to the rear side of the house next to the dining space. This allows the place for seating family or guests before and after meals to be in the room at the front of the house. Such a plan releases the basement, which originally housed the kitchen, to be used as a separate flat, home office, play or utility area or whatever. The arrangement of dining and living room so linked is often the formula in an apartment with the kitchen adjoining, in a form of open-plan, or with a kitchen directly across the passage.

In a household where there is a formal dining space linked to the kitchen a good plan is to consider how much of the kitchen quarters your guests will see when they are seated at the table. Can they see the clutter of the kitchen area from the dining table and if so, what resourceful scheme can unify the down-to-earth kitchen and civilized, elegant dining space in one harmonious sweep?

LINK ROOMS IN STYLE OR COLOUR

If a kitchen window can be glimpsed from the table, then the simplest way out is to enhance it with a pretty blind in a co-ordinating colour scheme. You could have, for example, a green and yellow cotton chintz in the dining room for curtains and festoon blinds, with green painted walls, yellow napkins and mats, and green kitchen blinds, perhaps in the same festoon style, piped in yellow. It is best if the section of the kitchen on view is not the part where plates are stacked or sink and pedal bin are shown in their glory. Adjacent to the dining room with the mahogany table which you see in the photograph on the left, is a kitchen which is on full view when the dirty plates are carried through and the next course brought

Two examples of how to link the spaces of one big area which is divided into dining section at one end, with drawing room or general family relaxing area at the other end.
Far left: The larger design of the orange and green chintz in the far room balances the the severity of the tiny green print. The original doors are newly stripped pine.
Left: Light, bright and very flexible: here is an example of the use of blues to make a room that is cool and soothing to live with. The divider is a full sweep of curtain and the bent wood chairs have matching tabs.
Below: A corner of the sitting area seen left.

SCREENS AND DIVIDERS

A divider which suggests a secret, veiled or hidden view introduces an element of mystery, and the translucent effect of a sheer fabric screen allows a changing pattern of filtered light. Other methods of dividing living and dining areas are to build a wall which just stops short of the main structural side wall in the room, or to have a decorative folding screen. This could be an Oriental lacquered one, or one covered in fabric similar to the main room colour scheme, or one of those deliciously nostalgic Victorian paper collage covered screens. Or, in somewhat Moorish style, build a fretwork dividing partition which can be painted in a bright scarlet to go with an Oriental style of decoration. Or if you are low in funds, make a divider from garden trellis and batten another panel of it painted in the same colour to the outside of the kitchen door. If a side of a kitchen cupboard can be seen from the dining space, then one pretty idea is to carry through the trellis idea: fix a piece to the cupboard panel and then clip on a series of wire rings to hold pots of geraniums.

in. The decorative scheme in this tiny kitchen with barely enough room to swing a tea-towel in is shown on page 17. The simple roller blind and the pine woodwork have been decorated with a sturdy, bright and cheerful stencil motif which carries through the same green as the dining room scheme, and the flowers in the stencil echo the same shade as the large scale green and orange floral quilted chintz in the linked drawing room beyond. Thus the mood sweeps from the grown up formality of a very traditionally decorated room in the front of the house, through a spacious dining area done up in a similar conventional manner, to a jaunty kitchen with an atmosphere more of chalet than country house. The dining into living areas in this room are linked by the original foldback shutters but in the early 1920s apartment seen in the photograph with the blue colour scheme the divider is a curtain. Other ideas for dividing eating and sitting spaces are some form of glass bead curtain, or curtain of translucent fabric, or an inventive gathering of tall palms.

Below left: A compact studio flat with an adjoining open-plan hallway. Over by the window, a round table makes a focal point for mealtimes and can be quickly cleared to take on the role of work surface. Ready for quick exits, or making up the numbers for a supper party are the foldaway and stack-flat chairs. The stark paper blinds, chaste and pure looking, and the wired paper balloon shade make a gesture of uncluttered order in a rather busy room.

Left: The other side of the same white walled room showing a deep shelved recess and seating plan.

Above: Dovetail corner where sofas meet beside the plant and flower-filled occasional table. The cushions in clear spring colours of pink and green are seen in detail with their neat ruffles, tulip-flowered borders and contrast colour piping.

Below: An elegant study area is formed when the cloth is removed from the circular table, one flap folded down and the table moved from the window overlooking the roof-garden to a place against the wall. The stripped pine washstand houses an indoor garden.

Above right: Bright and breezy, a living room painted in guardsman red and white sends the curtains off for a holiday in the long, light summer months and turns the fireplace into a frame for plants or fresh flowers.

Right: When the long winter evenings gather in, the fire and the candles are lighted and back go the full-length curtains onto their wooden pole and rings.

RELAX THE RULES

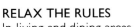

In living and dining areas there are rules which can now cheerfully be broken. Just as the dining room is no longer considered an absolutely necessary room, separate and sealed off from the main living room and kitchen, and the kitchen-dining and dining-living areas are often all rolled into one, so rules about what is used with what are blurred at the edges.

For instance, there are many new materials now which can comfortably blend with the old, provided the components in this coupling are handled with style. Shiny surfaces like chrome, vinyl, gleaming rich coloured acrylics, or lacquered metal can live next to the familiar looks and textures of crisp linen, green baize, rosewood and cut crystal. Modern, angular glasses can mix with the soft patina of antique rat-tail spoons, and the graceful silver soup ladle can be lined up on the table ready for action next to an electric carving knife. And now that cardboard throwaway cups and plates are so stylish and beautifully coloured, provided you have the determination and élan you can serve champagne in pink spotted picnic mugs, and produce the pudding in frilled paper plates, if this is your sort of party, and you do not plan to do any washing up.

The same goes for all those rituals about festive decorations. Why confine a gorgeous sea of bunting to street parties and similar patriotic occasions? And if you love all the coloured streamers draped across the pelmets of the living room curtains for a children's party, then why be bound by convention to take them down after the last of the guests has left, balloon in hand? The upholding of seasonal traditions with an outward display of festivities is seemly, and something that many people enjoy getting wholeheartedly involved in, and they look to the festivals of the past for an inspiration and a reassurance, so the show that is put on is to be respected. However, there is no reason why, for instance, the custom of hanging up holly, ivy and mistletoe should not be extended into a year-round continuum if you feel like doing so.

One household, free of qualms about Twelfth Night superstitions, so relished the look of jolly hollyberries, and were so reluctant

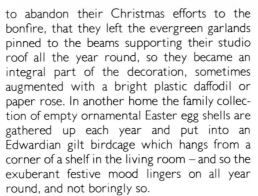

to abandon their Christmas efforts to the bonfire, that they left the evergreen garlands pinned to the beams supporting their studio roof all the year round, so they became an integral part of the decoration, sometimes augmented with a bright plastic daffodil or paper rose. In another home the family collection of empty ornamental Easter egg shells are gathered up each year and put into an Edwardian gilt birdcage which hangs from a corner of a shelf in the living room – and so the exuberant festive mood lingers on all year round, and not boringly so.

One most original way of spinning out the appeal of a ritual decoration throughout the calendar is in an artist's kitchen where he has interpreted the triangular cloth pennants of bunting into the same shapes made up from patchwork, and then used a length of these to form the pelmets in his cottage kitchen and living room. The tablecloth and curtains are also in patchwork, producing an overall bright gypsy caravan effect, with a collection of secondhand materials. To enter into this carnival spirit, the living room pianola is brightly painted.

MAKING A MEAL OF IT

When dining and living areas are connected it is very important to make sure that there is a slot for keeping all the mealtime items that are constantly in use, but which you want to avoid carting to and from the kitchen every time you

eat. A wall cupboard or some other form of hideyhole needs to be organized to store the pepper and salt, cereal packets and jam jars that furnish the table daily, otherwise the temptation in anyone's busy life is to leave the table uncleared of the debris. Unlike the contents of the drinks tray, with a handsome decanter or two and a row of neatly lined bottles, all looking as at home in a corner of the room as they would in the butler's pantry, items like spare sugar lump packets and paper napkins need to be kept hidden, to prevent the room from becoming untidy.

In an Irish castle where the architect knew a thing or two about magnificent proportions and spaces on a generous, larger-than-life scale, the drawing room with its stately panelling and handsome windows is cool and serene in tones of beige, with a luxurious fitted wool carpet and no overcrowding of furniture.

Below: The general effect is spacious, yet there is a very cosy seating arrangement for six over by the window. Views of misty countryside and wide sky are an important facet of the decoration, and the windows are at their best left unadorned by fabric but flanked by original shutters.

Below left: Natural light fills the room and is reflected in the mirror panels. A spotted flounce softens the lines of the standard lamp.

THE FLOWERING OF AN IDEA

Finally, flowers. A bunch of flowers massed in one container makes a much more positive statement than a few stems distributed in a series of vases around the room. Of course, floral arrangements are a very personal matter, but simple and effective is the idea of bunching one group of flowers together – either by species, like a group of multi-coloured sweet peas, or by colour – for example, an arrangement of white roses with a whisper of green foliage. An exception to the idea of one vase of flowers as the focal point is the visually pleasing and

Right: A generous flower bouquet print splashed on the trellis background softens the dark formality of mahogany period furniture in this small narrow room. The chintz is co-ordinated with the criss-cross motif on the walls and with the rich burgundy background interpretation for the fitted cushions on the window seats. The piping on cushions and curtain tie-backs is in the same deep red. This use of space would be a sound idea for a reading or writing area in the corner of a large hall.

Far left: Another example of how a deep rich red, this time in a brighter tone, lifts the sombre note of dark wood furniture. Marbled tones of crimson shade a traditional reading lamp and rich leather covers the buttoned chesterfield and armchair.

sometimes whimsical arrangement, whereby several small containers are grouped together and each is filled with plants; the finished effect is like a botanist's study. For example, arrange half a dozen small containers like egg-cups, sherry glasses, creamers or a mixture of them collected together on a ledge to show off the first spring petals, or a collection of wild flowers. Or, when no fresh flowers are available, then a collection of different leaves, grasses or dried flowers can look very attractive especially when their colours harmonize with the rest of the room's decoration.

A MATTER OF PROPORTION

A suggestion about the siting of the flowers: when you put them on an occasional table which is placed between two facing seating units or on a table where you sit, keep the arrangement below eye level. Conversation can be tricky to sustain when the flow of brilliant chat and the meaningful glances have to high-jump over a big centrepiece of lofty delphiniums. The same applies to the dining table when the talk must volley over candelabra whose chunky proportions would be more fitting in a cathedral. Large table ornaments need to be placed so that they stand at strategic points between guests, but not directly in front of their gaze.

THE DRAWING ROOM

There have been general areas in the home for recreation and sitting in since we first emerged, blinking in the sunlight, from caves.

A withdrawing chamber, or ante-room to the main chamber where the head of the household retired to, was first heard of in the 15th century. By the middle of the 19th century the drawing room had become a very important and spacious room. This grand space was a focal point in the house and was considered as being a room essentially feminine in character, and therefore in the interior decoration, whereas the dining room was regarded as a male stronghold, with the darker furnishings, heavier furniture and richly patterned carpets reflecting a more masculine spirit. The drawing room would usually have had walls in light pastel colours or flowered wallpaper, and the comfortable sofas and armchairs would have been covered in large patterned floral chintzes.

The fine drawing room became a backdrop to much coming and going in the Victorian era. Here, afternoon tea was dispensed all the year round except on really warm summer afternoons, and it was in this room that the household and their guests gathered before dinner to make a stately progress towards the dining room, and where the gentlemen joined the ladies after the evening meal.

THE SITTING ROOM

In residences built on a grand scale, the morning room was situated close by the drawing room; the former being an informal meeting spot, somewhere to assemble near the log fire after breakfast. This room, however, was decorated in a less impressive manner and more in the spirit of a family sitting room today. Today there are still morning rooms or sitting rooms as well as formal drawing rooms, and a study or library as well in big houses. In more compact houses you are more likely to find one main space in use as a sitting room, with a second room, if there is sufficient space, designated as the office from which a home based business is run. It can be a studio, private study or a television room.

Left: A town sitting room with a muted mix of green and browns in controlled casualness. The rough cotton floor rug, wicker baskets and linen covers for the chair make naturally related textures.

Below left: Detail of a corner in the same sitting room.

Right: A contented and well lived-in space for family gatherings, reading, writing and listening to music. One door leads to the hall, another to a small conservatory overlooking a country garden. Bargello covers settle down comfortably with a Persian carpet, Indian silk cloth, blue repp and cotton print. The traditional arrangement of the furniture includes a footstool that acts as both low table and extra fireside seating. A vase of creamy roses is placed below a Dutch oil painting of pale flowers, and on the mantelpiece a white porcelain horse rears below the primitive painting.

Below right: A more predictable and sober style of decoration in the drawing room of an early Edwardian terraced town house. The ornaments and pictures are all arranged with meticulous care and the central table is a highly polished wood butcher's block. A Portuguese wool rug carries through the various colour tones and motifs of the stained glass window panel and the tiles decorated with flowers in the marble fireplace.

children's playroom.

In some households, the television set is a hefty, dominant model, in which case it may be preferable to have it based in another room altogether such as a bedroom, so that several members of the family can watch a programme while they are snuggled under the duvet, and the others are able to enjoy a conversation in the downstairs room. In some families, the most popular place for the set is in a corner of the kitchen where you can eat supper while you watch.

PLAN YOUR DESIGN

Once you have decided which room or area of the home you are going to allocate to living, sitting and general recreation spaces, then you will next embark on a plan of how to arrange the room so that it feels right, looks good and can conveniently accommodate all the many activities for which you have earmarked it.

First of all get your plan down on paper. Make a list of all the activities for which you need the room. Listening to music, reading, card games, playing with children, entertaining friends, sewing: the possibilities are legion. Once you have drawn up your list it will help to clarify for you what you will use of your existing pieces of furniture.

Next, list any items that you definitely intend to house in the room – such as a prized collection of inlaid boxes, some impossible white elephant of a piece of furniture which you may have inherited, or your telescope complete with stand if the family happens to be besotted with star-gazing. Now work out how you can position the furniture so that it allows

PROGRAMMING THE TELEVISION

Tempers tend to fray less in families where the television set is in a different area from the main living room, because when the head-quarters of the box are in the main room there is likely to be argument about who is watching what programme and when. Also, when a television programme is in full swing, the set does tend to prevent any other conversation. So, if there are often visitors at the house who spend their time in the sitting room, or when the room is the scene of several quiet family activities going on simultaneously, such as reading, writing and doing homework, then it is better if the television is a lightweight portable that can be easily transplanted to the

for the different activities as well as accommodating the other things you have decided to put in the room. After an inevitable amount of adding and subtracting you will decide what extra bits of furniture you need to get the place functioning properly. At this point refer to your budget – with luck you will have been able to set aside some funds for redecoration and new furnishings. Decide on the furniture needed, then finally get down to planning the decoration, your starting point for the exercise being any furnishings you are already committed to such as the fitted carpet which was part of the purchase price of your new home.

LINK SPACES WITH COLOUR

When it comes to colour schemes there are several basic considerations to keep in mind. The first of these is to remember that the colours of paint or wallpaper in the connecting spaces such as the hall and staircase will help to make the entire area seem more spacious, airy and uncluttered if they harmonize with the colour tones of the living areas. For example, a hall wallpapered in a sand and white print might lead to a book-lined object-filled living room, where the lively atmosphere is offset by the calm and serenity of painted walls the colour of buttermilk.

Again, if the living and kitchen spaces are linked then it may come as a visual jolt to paint one area a completely different colour from another. If you, at any rate, start out with the two spaces painted in the same colour, or one just a tone lighter, then you can be adventurous later. There is little point in galloping into long term decisions about colour schemes for the whole home. If you are in doubt about what sort of room you really want, then paint the whole place a rich parchment shade, anywhere in the easy-to-live-with honey and buttermilk tones: you can then experiment at leisure. Your cream colour can act as an undercoat later, and you will be far better off than if you paint all the walls scarlet, and six

months later wake up one day to the realization that red is a colour that makes you feel hot and bothered, rather than chic.

TEAM UP THE COLOURS

When you plan your colour scheme, pin swatches of the different fabrics and pieces of paper covered with the paints you will use to a large sheet of paper, say a couple of feet wide. You will find this a more efficient and objective way of getting the balance of weight and tones, and contrasting colours that you feel really happy with, rather than relying on your memory.

If you like rich, glowing colours but find it hard to establish the subtleties of tone, one

invariably good and safe solution is to use the tones of colour in an Oriental carpet for your reference. Here you will find the exact shades of greeny grey and maroon combined with deep blue that you have been looking for. Or another solution which sounds obvious enough, but is good if you are in any doubt, is to use nature as your reference. Study the plumage of a pheasant and you will find a rich combination of colour tones glowing in harmony. In the same way the tones of lichen on bark are naturally right, and striped tulips will inspire you to put bright colours together in shades that magically do not grate.

Cream and beige tones mixed with matt textures such as linen, smooth tweeds and fine

Left: A sitting area arranged with severity in the neat groupings and trim lines. The related hues of the pale ceiling, rug, cushions and low stool add to the feeling of cool sophistication in this American drawing room. The French windows are partly covered with gathered curtains.
Below: A room of similar proportions in a Victorian house in Wales where the ample space is used as a family room. A conglomeration of various chairs, a haphazard mix of cushions and a carpet with bright dominant pattern all jostle along together in their expression of informal family life. Chocolate brown paint is used to give the illusion of a lowered ceiling.

slub silks or glazed surfaces such as porcelain, combined with a pale deep pile carpet and masses of creamy flowers, all bring together a mood of sophistication and urbanity in a drawing room. All very serene and glamorous to look at, but entirely unsuitable when the occupants include young children, friendly dogs and family cats that like to have a good claw sharpening session on the backs of the chairs. Also, one person's opulent gesture in tones of beige may be another person's interpretation of cold porridge. You should enjoy your surroundings!

Dark colours such as green walls, polished wood floors covered in rich, soberly patterned rugs, and tones of deep blues and burgundy all spring to life at night, and so contribute to an exciting atmosphere for a drawing room mostly in use after dark. This colour scheme is also thoroughly sensible for family life: animals are less likely to be dismissed from their snoozing places on ancient dark upholstered buttonback chairs, a wicker dog-basket lined with an old tartan travelling rug looks in keeping under the table against the wall, and a paisley shawl looks happy next to a papier-mâché lamp or old armoire. If you do have a large family room where there is plenty of traffic near a door leading to the street or back garden, then choose a dark carpet. This will show less marks from dirt and spillage. Also, if your room houses a piano be sure not to place anything heavier than sheet music on the top of the frame: a flower vase can topple, and so damage the inside of the piano with water.

The time-honoured English style is a form of interior decoration that has its roots firmly in the tradition of the grand country house style of living and has evolved slowly over nearly two and a half centuries of life in the shires. The general look is one of restraint and elegance, that happily keeps going into an old and rather threadbare state without the occupants being concerned about the keeping up of appearances. As the colours fade, so they become even more in tune with the misty shades of the garden, and well-worn, laundered chintz is impervious to the wet paws of sloppy spaniels.

The flat for singles, the town apartment for the country couple, the first home for newly-marrieds, the elegant bolthole, the independent flat for grandmama: these are just some of the single space but multi-activity areas that can be decorated in style and allow plenty of room for mobility.
Left: A most desirable one-room space is the lofty studio, with the garden brought indoors and hanging with cheerful abandon over the wall of the sleeping area up in the gallery. Movable spotlights are fixed to a track along one of the beams. Natural tones coupled with white calico covers and the very minimum amount of furniture make this into a restful space with an atmosphere conducive to concentration or lounging around in peace. Light from the dormer ceiling windows, reflected on the pale yellow wall, suggests a morning full of sunlight.
Below: Another view of the same living space.
Opposite above: A dual purpose room in a Paris apartment kept in neat order with geometric prints, candy striped curtains and tall drum lamps on either side of a convertible sofa bed.

Opposite centre left: In the same room as the picture above. The theatrical looking daybed, all curves and scrolls in white painted cast iron and bursting with cushions in the same blue, yellow and pale olive green, converts in a matter of seconds to a comfortable bed for occasional overnight visitors.
Opposite below right and left: Bright lighting ideas for a bed-sitting room seen here in both daytime and evening dress. The pendant lamp has a switch at the door and the romantic forest green wall lamp is the last to be turned off after bedside reading. The daybed pillows have green slip covers, matching the mattress cover and turning the bed into a sofa during the day. More deft use of space and lighting is the metal coolie lampshade, again in dark green, poised over the television table to give soothing light at night. Thriving at the side of the window is a fast climber plant. Flowered borders on the wallpaper, curtains, cushions and lampshades neatly tie together the whole decorative scheme. In the foreground is a classic cane and bent-wood rocking chair.

This particular style which is as much sought after as it is elusive in its ability to be very easily copied, is rather like the correct garment for the country. For example, just as an English gentleman's tweed jacket is a well cut garment made in a fine material of great softness, and in colours that are pure camouflage in the moorland, so it also never looks too new. In the same way, the English style when well carried off in the drawing room or boudoir, looks as if nothing much has changed in generations. The country house style has nothing harsh about it, and the colours borrow as much from the subtleties of the herbaceous borders and rose garden, as they do from the distant hills that extend beyond the view from the cushion-filled window seat. The rich shades of porcelain and silks once brought back from an expedition to the East are here too. The style also takes in its stride the eccentricity of the English, such as oyster shell back grotto chairs and fantasy summer houses.

HALLMARKS OF COUNTRY HOUSE STYLE
Pointers to this way of decorating a living room which gives a pleasantly informal country air to a town house or city flat are books and plants piled on circular or octagonal tables with cloths that reach down to the ground, often with the hems fringed, plain lampshades with possibly Chinese porcelain vases mounted as lamps, ample comfortable seating, coconut matting or plain fitted carpet possibly with the addition of Oriental or cloth rugs. The colours that suit this style of decoration are moss green, yellow, apple, blues and apricot. Plants are massed in china or wicker planters, there are tapestry bell-pulls, tasselled tiebacks of two-tone twists of silk or cotton rope hold back the curtains, and a pier glass or convex mirror reflects the light from the window.

THE DECEPTIVELY SIMPLE, EASY LOOK

In a discussion on the very subjective topic of style in the living areas of the home, which surely must compete with the kitchen for the most used space in the house, one can summarize by saying that the single most important quality in the room arrangement, whether it is a Gothic style drawing room with a soaring ceiling, or a turretlike nook whose uneven walls you have transformed with gloss paint over sheets of anaglypta, is the ability to make somewhere feel both personal and lived-in without it being either over-cosy or shabby.

Part of this ability lies in being able to resist the urge to tidy up every time someone leaves the room. All members of the household will be happier if they know they can relax within the four walls. A chilly, faintly forbidding atmosphere soon pervades any place where you know that each time you return to the room during the course of a lazy weekend, you will find to your dismay that the cushions have been plumped up and arrayed in a geometric formation, the newspapers have been folded into a neat pile, or the magazines put into waiting-room precision. There is a fine balance between what is cosiness and the freedom to move around without knocking over half a dozen bits of china on the spindly rosewood, and what is definitely cloying, where you are surrounded by a studied arrangement of objects.

KIT OUT A GRANNY FLAT

If your living room is very small it is a good idea to stick to one or two different colours or several tones of one colour. Never put a lot of bright colours together in one small room: the result can look restless.

If you have an elderly relative living with you in your house, you will want to allocate space for a granny flat – or at any rate a granny-room. The ideal is to create a small environment that feels independent, and at the same time allows the person to retain their own special atmosphere; their own choice of decoration if possible, and some of the cherished pieces of furniture that will be a happy reminder of some of the best moments of the

Turn down the covers, and the seating area in a study or sitting room becomes an extra sleeping space of deepest comfort.

Far left: An efficient work room where the steel Directoire bed is plumped up with an army of fat square cushions by day, and turns into a snug and cosy hideaway by night.

Left: A detail of the room seen below: a recessed shelving unit with storage cupboards underneath.

Below: A comfortable sitting room by day, which by night tidily transforms itself into a bedroom when the extendable sofa base is folded out.

Bottom: The sofa corner ready to sleep in.

past. The room should be able to house the memorabilia without everything being too easily knocked over, and there should be enough space for the occupant to be separate from the rest of the household if she wishes, but at the same time you should be able to remain in close contact, so that the person feels loved and needed. The interior decoration should continue the style the occupant is familiar with instead of being a new venture.

A granny flat, even if just one large room, does need cooking facilities, as in most bedsitting rooms. A simple solution is to have a screen to partition off the kettle and wash basin or sink, or a set of doors on glides, or a screen of shelves that doubles as storage.

Left: Think big in a small and really rather eccentric space, and tile off an eating area. The mulberry and pink colour scheme and minimum amount of furniture in a space with little natural light makes a memorable corner for dining in. The central lamp and candles lend a soft glow to the pinks, and plants are grouped in the window and corners.

Below left: Prints within prints: matching and contrasting wallpapers are used as part of the flower vase theme series of pictures, hung for a smooth visual transition from the dining area back to the corridor space. The muted tones of the tweed rug on the chair and bowl of pot-pourri add a cottagey charm in an apartment far from the countryside.

Right: Two views of an open and shut case kitchen. Behind the doors, a cupboard is converted to a tiny cooking and washing module with the inside of the shelves painted a contrasting green. Add white shelf units on either side of the shutaway kitchen and the total construction becomes an interesting feature in this red and white bedsitting-room. The all-purpose trestle table can be used for both dining and working.

Below right: Retire to the sewing corner – and know you can leave the work in progress. A sturdy old kitchen table, jollied up with several coats of crimson paint and varnished, fits into an alcove corner of the sitting room as if it were tailor made. The hollyberry red and green colour scheme continues with a glass shade, cushions and rug.

SMALL SPACES

The first general rule when you are confronted with the need to make good use of a small space is to think big. Tell yourself that small is indeed beautiful. This will not, of course, send the walls sprouting in all four directions to make new shapes, but it will give you the confidence to tackle the area and begin to envisage its possibilities of function. Although corners are the traditional places for sulking in, they also turn into the focal points that attract happy attention. And tight corners are not necessarily just something you get trapped into and which require much foxy cunning to escape from. The small space is the place to use, when your back is up against the wall for just that bit more room.

Think of the myriad examples of neat small lairs that work well and with basically the same components as their large size cousins. Think of the domestic dog kennel, cat-box, dovecot, dolls' house, beehive, igloo, lighthouse, sandcastle, even a cuckoo clock. Think of places where wildlife lives: set, warren, nest, antheap. One linking factor is that these miniature habitats all work well without superfluous bits of space. The natural ones are all well camouflaged, cosy and well-fortified retreats. The man-made ones decoratively and on the whole efficiently serve their purpose, though you may have to take the front off the dolls' house to get at the contents, and the sandcastle exists only until the tide comes in.

A HOME FOR PLANTS

In your home there is less danger of the elements sweeping away your space and you can turn sunlight, warmth and even a damp atmosphere to good account. For instance, if you crave a garden and do not own one you can translate a small area, provided it is screened from draughts and receives some natural light and warmth, into a tiny conservatory. Or, if you do have a garden, use the indoor space for a plant nursery with herb pots, a terracotta strawberry pot, and seedboxes – ideal for protecting young plants. You can organize a small area where there is a skylight or enough natural light from the side windows into a children's corner with sprouting avocado stones, bulbs balanced on water jars so they can see the roots growing, busy lizzies and other satisfactory fast-growing and rapid climbing plants, not forgetting the plates of mustard and cress beds. Place the assorted green plant life on shelves, preferably of glass because this adds to the total outdoor effect, then add a barometer and a microscope if you have them, a work surface and somewhere to keep botany books, and you have a small junior laboratory. Or forget the instruments, add a rattan chair and you have a comfortable resting spot; but however you use the plant space go right ahead and keep the watering can where it remains visible. Hide it away, and it can become soon forgotten. The traditional watering can in zinc with a large rose for spraying is a very elegant shape, and you can buy attractive bright enamel painted cans now to match your overall colour scheme.

Small but usable spaces are often located in oddly-shaped but fun-to-decorate attics or turrets at the top of the house, perhaps with porthole or other unusually shaped windows, or in the cellar.

A small space can be given the same wall-covering as the rest of the area if you want to pull the shape into a whole, or done in co-ordinating tones if it is linked to the main space. Or you can establish a separate mood by isolating the space from the rest, such as painting the wedge-shaped under stairs space lighter than the hall. Remember that even the smallest eyrie has potential.

CONNECTING SPACE

The entrance hall, landing and passages are the areas of your home where there is the most amount of traffic and these circulation areas sometimes look and feel like city ring-roads – that is to say, they are efficient well-beaten tracks where the surroundings lack distinction and there is little invitation to linger.

Halls, and the spaces that connect them, are the pig-in-the-middle spaces in a home, and they tend to miss out on the attentions that are lavished on the rooms that they connect. Unlike these specific areas, halls and passages often lack the alive atmosphere that you sense in a kitchen dining-room, for example, where people relax, reflect and notice their surroundings. However, they do offer great potential and the ways in which they can be planned and decorated are worth careful thought.

Halls are where first impressions are made, yet they are also often treated as afterthoughts in decoration because people find them rather daunting to work on. In fact, you can have great fun with the scope they offer for experiment. If you crave for a particular dining-room wallpaper but the cost is too high for the number of rolls required, then a small hall might be a spot where you can indulge your whims.

In older houses there may be space which can be reclaimed from the hall to enlarge other much-used areas; such as removing the wall that divides hall from front room to create a larger open living area, or creating a lobby in the hall with some form of framework filled with books or plants. If there is a south-facing passage along an outside wall or unused space around the back door then you have the possibility of adding a conservatory.

The shape and function of your hall are determining factors in how you decorate it. If you enjoy a rural existence then you need floors that are easily cleaned in order to cope with muddy feet, whether they are from wet shoes at the front door or gumboots round the back. In a country household where the family includes large bouncy dogs, the house is easier to run if the hallway furniture is sturdy and sufficiently uncluttered to encompass the swish of a dog's tail.

You may have a house with a finely proportioned hall, impressive staircase and doors that lead off in all directions, in which case you have before you the basic ingredients with which to compose a scheme of decoration in the grand country house manner. If you have a cottage with uneven floors and low, beamed ceilings you can convey an aura of well-ordered seclusion or cramped discomfort to the visitor from the moment the latch door opens. Or yours may be an apartment where the front door is linked to the back room by a tunnel that defies the decorator's imagination.

LIGHTING THE WAY

When your hall and staircase are shadowy or dark you will want to introduce as much light as possible for both comfort and safety. The

Four focal points on landings, halls and passages. Left: The indoor patio look makes an informal low eating area, conversation corner, business meeting room, or simply a waiting place and comfortable rendezvous for a cup of coffee. The bamboo armchairs have covered-in boxy sides which prevent any draughts from the staircase whistling round the ankles. Bright touches like the painted tray and planter on the dresser really zip together the choice of red as the main colour with a smart black for contrast.

Far left below: Fresh white paint can make an amazing difference. Barley sugar twist legs on the upright chairs spiral in harmony with a wicker table, also revamped with fresh gloss. The seat covers are refitted with the same tulip print as the painted stencil on the wood. The picture on the wall echoes the vibrant colours of the geometrically patterned rug.

Below left: The simplest way to invent a cupboard or basic clothes hanging space: skirt a hallway alcove with an attractive, widely gathered, pretty print curtain.

Below: Burgundy red and white colour scheme, jovial wicker garden chair and table and stripped pine all combine to create an attractive corner for the upstairs telephone extension, and lend a gentle, friendly character to the landing.

ideal is a light that can be switched on at the front door, plus hall and landing lights that are operated from a two-way switch both upstairs and down. Children can be very apprehensive about a dark staircase, and a lamp alight in the hall is a sensible idea, from late afternoon in the winter when the children return from school, until the last person retires to bed. The low level lamp is a practical addition to the traditional central hanging light or track light system. A person's eyes need to adjust to changes of light, and the hall lighting acts as a medium because it is the place where people step into from the dark outside, or come to when they leave the brightly-lit sitting-room.

The shape you choose for a central hanging lamp sheds light on your style. There are all the variations of the chandelier and cut glass school which suggest formality and grandeur; sleek steel or industrial style lamps dictate an atmosphere of efficiency and the Tiffany shade which has spawned many related shapes from painted glass shades to the silky fringed versions offer the warm look of tinted light plus a certain allure. Paper balloons are economical but soon look grubby and lanterns need to be chosen with care to avoid folksy fustiness.

Sculpture or a group of pictures can be highlighted by the judicious use of a track light or spotlights, but to avoid the feeling you are standing under a glaring surgical lamp strategic planning is needed with these downlighters.

A skylight offers a clear gaze at the stars but if you have windows by the door at ground level, and you are reluctant to exhibit the layout and contents of your hall to the world, then a mask needs to be devised. Inset panels of decorative or coloured glass, slatted blinds or shutters or curtains in a loosely woven material are some ways of covering windows that diffuse light and allow you to look out while obscuring the view of outsiders. A thick glass door in a wooden frame that leads from the hall into the main room introduces natural light and works well in a modern house or anywhere the existing doors are not worth keeping. Also, for those with a nervous disposition the glass door idea contributes to the occupant's peace of mind because you can see from one room to another very easily.

A looking-glass hung in the hall is a symbol of hospitality and the reflected images create an illusion of more space. Also, like a clothesbrush kept on the hall table, the mirror is usefully placed for last minute attention to personal appearance.

STEPPING OUT

The options for what you walk upon depend as much on your lifestyle as your budget. A pale carpet is much less fuss to maintain if you live in a flat and cross other indoor surfaces before reaching your own, than if the front door of your home opens onto the street. Wood surfaces which are scrubbed, polished or painted are long-lasting and easy to clean but check the floorboards for any creaky habits. Surfaces like marble, stone, concrete and quarry tiles are hard, cold and noisy and are feasible so long as the clatter of feet in the hall does not disrupt the peace in rooms used for study or sleep. A noise-muffling floor covering makes sense in areas through which people often pass. If you decide on a fabric covering, then it is better long-term value to go for good quality cord, in preference to impressive looking, but low quality carpet, even if the price is about the same for both. Cork tiling is soft and warm to the touch, and cuts down on the noise of echoing footsteps. It makes an appropriate choice if you want an air of informality in the

hall. The floor covering should be secured under doors with aluminium strips.

A stair carpet needs to be firmly fitted and it is wise to have this job done professionally if possible. Ensure that the treads are fitted with carpet grippers because these are better than nailing the fabric to the floor and easier to move when the carpet gets worn. Stair treads have a tough job withstanding a procession of feet while the risers get no wear, so install a sufficient length of carpet to allow the fabric on the risers to be shifted to cover the treads.

If your hall tends to look like a crammed garage with a parked pram and bicycles jostling for position, then a wallcovering that does not easily reveal the damage from assorted wheel

Far left: Creams and earth colours for the very countrified looking entrance hall in a Manchester town house. The warm, welcoming appearance of the space is accentuated by the curvilinear alcove and furniture. The oval picture-frame repeats the top curve of the recessed alcove at the foot of the staircase and the double arches carved in the doors of the dresser complement the carved sides of the charming painted washstand. Pink tones predominate in the needlework and cotton print cushions, and in the bunch of dried hydrangeas and basket of glazed porcelain cherries.

Left: Worth more than a passing glance: objects arranged on a ledge to lead the eye round the corner, minimizing the narrowness of the staircase.

Right: The oak staircase of a Victorian house in the Welsh countryside is carpeted in the same pink Wilton as the rest of the corridors and the main rooms. Harmonizing pinks for the wallpaper and blind lighten the sombre tones of the oak, and the ruched blind gracefully solves the problem of how to dress the unusual and deep-set window on the half landing. The glass in the back door is left free for the view of the extensive private grounds.

Below: To give the illusion of less lofty heights in this tall and narrow hall and landing area, the ceiling is painted in a dark colour to match the bitter chocolate carpeting on the stairs. The large mirror also helps to give an impression of width.

and handlebar scrapes, the snail trail of dirty hands and shoulder scuff marks, looks good for longer. A washable wallpaper in a bold print and a deep colour tone stays the course best.

Many halls, stairs and passages have little natural light and so a fairly light-toned paint or wallpaper can help to make the most of what there is. Suitably placed mirrors can also improve matters.

If your hallway and landings are gaunt and tall you can achieve the effect of a lowered ceilings by painting it in a dark colour, and if the mouldings are especially attractive then you can consider accentuating them in a different shade. If you like a yesteryear club style then you can affix a false wainscoting and also a picture rail painted in a different colour: the idea of hanging a picture by ribbons and rosette from the rail instead of picture hooks behind the frame makes a pretty finishing touch.

When you want more storage space consider how you can use the wedge-shaped space tucked under the stairs for a home office, workshop, telephone corner or even a spare bed. And lastly, be sure that your front door has sufficiently strong locks and the spare key is not tethered to the end of a string inside the letter-box.

BEAUTIFUL BEDROOMS

The way in which your bedroom is decorated is strongly indicative of your character. Sometimes, too, the way in which you adapt a certain look also offers a clue to another lifestyle which you would like to adopt, or at least dream about, instead of your own. The young girl who believes it would be fun to experience living a fairytale existence will enjoy the make-believe of her bedhead being transformed into the Sleeping Beauty setting she has seen in a storybook illustration, with muslin drapes fixed to an ivyleaf covered corona. Or if the bedroom of an efficient town flat becomes cluttered up with patchwork, quilting and sprigged cottons, it is possible that inside the urbane girl executive who sleeps there is an old-fashioned country milkmaid who is just longing to get out.

In an ideal setting, your bedroom is your private stronghold, somewhere that you can retreat to and pull up the drawbridge, lower the portcullis and simply pad about the place as you wish, a law unto yourself. It should be your refuge when you want to retire for any of several reasons, and your own secluded domain where you will first encounter the world again when you wake from a comfortable night of peaceful sleep.

In reality, of course, things are different, and your bedroom may not be quite as private, spacious and comfortable as you would wish for, and therefore it is a place where there is some room for improvement, even if there is not much more space for furniture. But more of this later, and for a moment back now to the traditional bedroom and its various functions.

RIGHT FROM THE BEGINNING

The bedroom is the place where you are tucked up at night when you are small, and where you are most likely to feel safe and secure. Much of a child's early memories are of the bedtime hours and the smell and look of the surroundings. This is the room that you share with other young children and if there is the joy later of having a room all of your own, then this room is going to be a bedroom. If you are lucky, and sufficiently encouraged to develop, with some guidance, your own ideas about decoration, then you will

be allowed as a teenager to make a pad where you can sort out your own personality, instead of feeling just one of the offspring hedged in with the old familiar nursery wallpaper.

A PRIVATE SANCTUM

Your bedroom is where you are based if you are ill or in a state of convalescence, and so you will feel more comfortable in a place that is soothing and restorative both in the colour scheme as well as in the touch of crisp sheets and warm blankets. And you are likely to find it greatly comforting if there is a bookshelf of favourite reading near you, a group of special photographs or pictures, and favourite objects even if that is one single mirror, coupled with a pervading atmosphere of quiet.

This is the room where a person should be able to feel quite at ease to carry on any of such diverse occupations as reading a book at

An exercise in using the same pattern and colours in two different ways. The same padded bedhead linked to a brass curtain pole, and bedside wall lights are used in each of the rooms.
Above: The co-ordinated look, with wallpaper, blinds, bedcover, bedhead and cushions all in the same pale print. A sharp contrast is provided by the dark wood of the bureau. The quilted bedcover with borders matching those on the wallpaper, flattering deep pink fitted carpet and ruched Austrian blinds are decidedly feminine.
Left: The Roman blind and neat pelmet combine with the creamy carpet and fitted bedspread to give a more tailored look than the room before.
Right: Details of the adjoining boudoir and the circular corner table.

bedtime, indulging in a private quarrel or taking the steps to call a truce, concentrating on revision for exams, experimenting with makeup, practising the clarinet, studying tropical fish in a small aquarium, sewing or making love. The bedroom is a place where you can be alone to stare in the mirror and compose your thoughts before some event that first requires a mental pep talk with yourself, and equally it is the room where you may hold court and gossip with friends while you and the family cat lounge on the bed and the coffee cups pile up on the bedside table. It is where you dress and undress, and usually where you store most of your clothes and where you arrange your appearance at some form of dressing table.

The bedroom is where you sleep alone with the cherished freedom to listen to the radio or read until the small hours if you are so inclined. If it is the lair you share with your partner, a room plan needs to be made with such care and dexterity as to cater for the needs and comforts of both people.

If the room is rented accommodation you share with a friend then it may be a revellers' crash-pad where you go for a short lie down before breakfast, and be the sort of place where the top of the wardrobe is silted up with suitcases and half a dozen coats cling to the single hook on the back of the door. Yet even if temporary the place will be all the more agreeable with some form of home decoration.

The bedroom is the background to plenty of ordinary human drama. This is the place where many of us are born and die and where loving relationships are made, consummated, broken and repaired. Here is the room in which we are at our most naked and delicate.

FIRST PRIORITY
So with all this activity in the bedroom, just what is the single most important quality that the place should have, and how best can one or more persons' needs be accommodated in the space? The first priority for most people and partnerships, except in a trap specifically fixed to jolly along the act of seduction, is to have a place that feels full of peace. The aim of the room is to create an atmosphere of serenity in visual, in spiritual and in practical terms.

PLAN YOUR DESIGN

So having taken a look at the room which more than any other in the house has the potential to speak for its occupants, it is rather odd to find that the bedroom often lags behind in the scheme of planning and decoration.

One answer is that because the bedroom is the private sanctuary or the children's dormitory it is located in a different part of the house from the main rooms and is seldom revealed to the public view, and therefore it often lacks the money and time spent on the overhaul that is given to the main rooms elsewhere. Sometimes there is a definite intention to make a beautiful bedroom but the funds are drained by the time the dry rot is discovered and dealt with, or the housewarming party has been given, or the deep freezer has been, after all, finally bought. Or, simply, everyone means well with initial plans and little samples of fabric stuck on the walls, but setting the kitchen to rights absorbs the energy allocated to decoration, and instead the occup-

ants get used to the bedroom as it is, and slowly adjust to the uncomfortable room, while they get on with the business of living. However, a more satisfactory way to run the home for long term comfort is to decide that the most vital purchase, taking absolutely top place on the shopping list, is a really comfortable bed. Sleep is a serious business and so as soon as possible after you move into the new place allow some hours, care and cash on the creation of the very personal room in which you rest, and from which you re-enter the mainstream.

And so, onto some ideas about the different styles of decoration. How you will interpret any of the rooms photographed here to fit into your own way of life entirely depends on you, and the finished result will be the mark of your own style. If you love looking at light seen through coloured glass then it will occur to you to keep Bristol glass scent bottles in a window alcove rather than arrayed on a dressing table, if you feel most at home in a setting that has overtones of a seraglio then you will be inclined

Here are three happy examples of master bed-rooms where the style of the past is given a fresh and colourful interpretation to bring the look right up to date. To satisfy the need for really good reading lamps the shades have plain, large, slightly conical shapes, and the velvets and damasks that would have been used in the past are replaced with harmonising cottons that are easier to handle. However, the very civilized atmosphere remains. In each case the focal point of the room is the bed.
Left: The steel and brass four poster bed is simply dressed with a gathered canopy and pillowcases of pristine white lace. The curtain pole and the background to the corner wall cabinet are both painted in navy blue and lighter tones of the blue are seen in the china animal ornaments on the corner shelf and in the pattern of the floor rug. The trunk and wood chest both serve as table surfaces and as useful storage for spare blankets.
Below left: Window detail shows the wooden shutters.
Right: This large double bed is made memorable with a bow-tied canopy and corona, and the co-ordinating bedspread is inset with a large central detail of patchwork. This bedroom suite is com-pleted with an adjoining dressing room also in the plum and sand colours and then onto a bathroom where the scheme is modified to sand and white patterned tiles and the same sand cotton pattern for a window seat and curtains. The pale fitted carpet is used throughout.
Below right: What a delicious invitation to have a light breakfast and a lazy morning tucked up in bed. When the covers are turned down the differing patterns of the quilt and lining and the plain sheets make an effective contrast. Each of these three rooms is a first floor front bedroom with fine side windows. This one has sills deep enough to use as shelves, on which to display a collection of cherished objects and a free-standing mirror.

to have a floor, level bed and infuse the decoration with cushions, shawls and low lighting, and if you really rather yearn to camp in a desert tent, then given the chance you will drape the ceiling of your room regardless of its proportions. All of this is to say that what really matters is not so much where the ideas and influences in doing up a place stem from, as how you feel in your interpretation of them.

THE PATTERN OF BEHAVIOUR

Although often neglected, the bedroom once decorated is the room which is re-done most often. It is likely that you will want to alter the style in here rather than embark on a complete redecoration of the kitchen or the drawing-room, and possibly this is because the time we spend in our bedroom is when we are in a state of relaxation and go through the stages of becoming familiar and then bored with the wallpaper. Or, like buying clothes, it is just the desire for change and a dislike of looking slightly outdated.

Simple quilting gives a warm, comfortable texture and looks very luxurious. All three layers are stitched together, you can use a number of traditional quilting patterns. An economical solution to the padding in the middle is an army blanket. Ideas for a bedroom include quilted café curtains, bathrobe and slippers, lining for wicker baskets to hold bits and pieces, and even chair covers.
Left: Ten different cotton fabrics are gathered up to co-ordinate the style of a Victorian bedroom. The bedspread is piped in yellow and quilted.
Below: The headboard is quilted in the same crisscross print, matching the bedspread and pillows.

A QUESTION OF STYLE

The different styles of bedroom which are shown in these pages are these: first, the town house room which is as well appointed as a luxurious modern hotel with good lighting, deep comfort and plenty of storage being the important keynotes. Then there is the fresh, innocent and very pretty cottage style which is fairly inexpensive and simple to assemble. There are certain basic ingredients for this style which are useful if the look is to be successfully achieved. These include a pretty bedhead whether made of padded material or wood or brass; lace, either used lavishly or to trim pillows, but it needs to be in evidence somewhere in the decoration; and walls either painted in a pale colour or papered in a small print with the simplest style of curtains in a plain material or a co-ordinating print with the paper. The furniture is usually pine and kept simple with the addition perhaps of a squashy comfortable armchair near the bedside. Patchwork, tapestry cushions, dried flowers

and grasses, gentle pictures and flower prints in light wood or fabric covered frames are the attractive props, and the floor is either carpeted in a plain colour or if the wooden floorboards are in good repair then they are scrubbed and polished, painted, stained or stencilled. Lighting for cottage bedrooms is often the romantic oil lamp converted for present day use, or a variation of the student's lamp with glass shade and brass base with the addition of a small reading lamp beside the pot of garden flowers on the bedside table. This style undoubtedly looks most effective in a small or moderately-sized bedroom.

LOOKS THAT LAST

The Victorian style of bedroom is also nostalgic of times past, but it is a look that evokes not so much the Kate Greenaway charm of the cottage style, but rather the prosperity, solid, leisurely comfort and ornate trappings with which the well off family surrounded themselves at the height of the British Empire. There

are specific props for this look which include a four-poster bed, or a bed with a fine looking brass bedstead, handsomely framed mirrors, and some good pieces of furniture probably in mahogany. The windows are dressed with ruched blinds and the curtains swagged, piped and draped in elaborate design. The wallpaper is often a motif of leaves, birds and flowers mingled together in a swirly convolution and there will be a daybed or large chest at the foot of the bed. While this style of decoration was originally geared to a look of opulence with all the attendant details like ivory hairbrushes, cut crystal bottles and small silver boxes all most beautifully finished, the atmosphere was a bit oppressive and mysterious in a velvety, rustling way. The interpretation given today to the style is lighter, easier to maintain and to live with.

Then there is the attic, garret and box-room space where the challenge lies in taking an awkward shaped room and turning it, with the help of pretty wallpapers, rag floor rugs and painted iron bedsteads into an attractive eyrie. If the attic window is set into the sloping ceiling then a blind or shirred curtain will be the easiest solution. Small upright windows need only the simplest of curtains, in spotted white muslin for example, with the addition of green velvet ribbons shaped into a bow for tiebacks. The attic bedroom style is really a romanticized idea of how the servants' upper floor sleeping quarters were designed. A pine washstand

Right: A chilly attic bedroom warms up with the dash of dacha peasant style: reds, lace, braids. Just as the padded bolero looks correct with the layered skirts and frills of gipsy costume, so too the padded bedspread here is in appropriate style.
Below: Make the most of your extra bits of space and fabric. Here, an alcove turns into a bookshelf, a quilted remnant into a runner.
Below right: Here quilting both covers the bed and is used as a luscious wallcovering. Stitching and the tidy cotton print echo the strict lines and natural tones of the bamboo bedside tables and the rattan headboard.

with flower pattern jug and bowl, old fashioned nightdress and candlesticks on the mantelpiece are complementary to the style: all similar to the country cottage bedroom but usually more spartan and a way of utilizing an otherwise dusty attic.

The English country house style of bedroom – another possibility – is at its best with well proportioned rooms and tall windows decorated with a flowery glazed chintz of a larger pattern than the small scale cottagey styles, painted furniture or fine period pieces, large beside lamps, plenty of books, and decoration in the muted colours and soft tones in keeping with the walled garden and lawns outside.

Above: Pretty print radiating from sunburst pleating under the bed canopy.
Above right: A voluptuous festoon blind.
Right: An exotic setting is dreamed up with deep blue walls, heavily swagged pelmet and canopy draped over the bed, and candlelight.
Opposite right above: Lace goes on a flight of the imagination to make a languid, sensual bedroom. It decorates the bed, the lamp, and the mantelpiece runner. Ruched blinds in velvet, and narrow mirror panels painted with bulrushes complete the fantasy.
Opposite right below: The effect of delicate lace is maximized when shown against this apricot wallpaper.

A ROOM FOR ALL SEASONS

The styles continue with the different sorts of rooms that make best sense for the age of childhood and adolescence: the child-proof, easy to maintain and safe nursery comes first. Then the bedroom for one or several children which can be shared with the new baby, and on to the teenager's own den. Also required by many households, whether the set-up is confined to a small space or a large house, is the dual purpose room, the place where two into one will go. This is, for instance, the study which can be transformed when necessary into the spare bedroom, or the luxury of a television room which allows the viewers to congregate in one place while the others can get

on with their conversation in peace elsewhere and which can easily be converted into a place to sleep for an overnight guest. A natural progression of this dual purpose style is the one-room living space which is needed when a room is let off as a bedsitter or when the household includes an elderly relative who benefits from a private room that can give a feeling of comfort and a sense of independence.

THE ILLUMINATION OF FANTASY

For the very individual and independent minded person there is the fantasy bedroom which makes a glorious foray into the realms of imaginative escapism. If this person has a partner, then with luck their fantasies will dovetail over the interior decoration. The fantasy room may be an eclectic mixture of colour and style or it can be done by taking a single favourite fabric and using it in extravagant quantity to satisfy a particular whim.

The last in this collection of styles is the tailored room which in concept borrows from the masculine dressing-room rather than the boudoir. Here the choice of wallpaper and fabrics is more likely to be a neat geometric print or a stripe than an abundance of chintzy florals, and the orderly designs can be outlined with contrasting borders in paper or paint. Instead of lace or flounces the cushions will be neatly piped or shaped into bolsters. The

valance and curtain pelmet will be as crisply cut as a well made suit and everything from the door furniture to the bedspread will be relieved of all unnecessary trim. This is the look that suggests an atmosphere of restraint, efficiency and a definite elegance where there is a place for everything, and the slippers are doubtless always put back in their place. In order to be certain that this more austere and masculine style does not feel drab or utilitarian special attention must be given to the hidden comforts. For example, if the occupant is a light sleeper then the curtains should be suitably lined to keep out the light; there will be a bedside telephone, good lighting inside the hanging cupboard and a carpet on the floor of the adjoining bathroom.

All the styles referred to here are examples of a clear reaction to the stark, shiny and functional look which has been proclaimed as fashionable and chic over the last decade. This attitude does not mean a rejection of glamour, for glamour and deliciously sensual surroundings have been happily in full swing since the days when Cleopatra set off downstream in her scented barge.

What it does mean though is a reassessment of the old values, looking at the styles that have stood the test of time comfortably and seeing how they can be adapted to work for interior decoration in the bedroom of the 1980s.

THE ROOM OF YOUR DREAMS

When you design your bedroom it is logical to first consider the amount, the shape and the location of the space that you have, and then go on to work out just how the area can be put to the best use for you.

Sometimes the first priority a person gives to the bedroom is what colour it is going to be, then there is a rush to decide on papers and fabrics before working out whether these can be accommodated comfortably in the room. For instance, when you have set your heart on a blue bedroom but the room in question faces north, then the result could be rather bleak unless the look of coolness and the feeling of chill is offset by or combined with another colour for visual warmth – or you could change your allocated space and give yourself a south facing room instead. Or if you particularly fancy a large scale flowery print but you are stuck with a small squat room where you both sleep and work, ponder whether such a print would appear both overblown and distracting in such a cramped space.

If you live in a town house you must decide whether you want to adopt the first floor room overlooking the street for your sleep. If you are easily disturbed by noise you might find it more restful to have a smaller room at the back which, with luck, overlooks a garden. If you run an office from your home then the ground and first floor rooms may be devoured by the work, cooking and dining areas, in which case

you are pushed to the upper regions of the house, if you have them, for the sleeping quarters. You may want to convert the attic space into bedrooms or invest in building an extension for a bedroom suite at the back of the house. If you have young children then it is only natural that you will all feel more secure if their room is within earshot of yours. Also, if there is only one bathroom in the house it needs to have the bedrooms situated as close as possible to it, to avoid extra walking from room to room.

EVOLVING EXTRA SPACE

If you decide to extend your home up under the eaves then invest in a professional survey before you embark on the project. Joists in the attic floor are not as sturdy as those on the lower floors and you want to avoid a guest on the loft level making an unheralded arrival through the ceiling and landing on top of your bed on the next floor down.

Few homes offer so much space that there are several spare bedrooms kept unused except for guests, and when there are rooms to spare, these often assume other roles such as utility room, a place for table tennis or a workshop. Yet if you need a bed for someone staying overnight, then space must be found. The possibilities include the kind of beds that shut away into the wall, convertible sofas and a combination of two single beds in a stacking arrangement. The latter is a device whereby

you pull out the bed from underneath to raise it to the height of the upper one and in this way form a double bed. There are other ingenious styles of beds, for example one that folds up to stack neatly under a shelf or one that is converted from a deep armchair.

Some beds can be stored away with their bedding in them but if not you must come up with a solution to the problem of storage for duvets, blankets and pillows. One of the most basic forms of disguise for the bedding, and one which is pretty primitive but nevertheless can look neat and attractive, is to have a large square of cloth with two sturdy loops on two opposite sides of the fabric. One side, with the edge of the fabric held out straight, has the loops attached to a couple of hooks and these are screwed with rawlplugs into the wall, possibly above the dais or divan. When the bedding is finished with, it can be tucked into the cloth which folds over and the remaining two loops slung over the hooks. The result is a trim parcel which is stored within comfortable reach and available to unwrap at a moments notice. Meanwhile the dais is left looking less like an inviting nest and more like a practical seating unit for the daytime.

Finally, if you have sufficient space and height on a landing or in the hall, could you build a gallery large enough to support a bed with a ladder or staircase approach?

Four bedrooms decorated with restraint. As a backdrop to the arrangement of the furniture in each of the rooms are wallpapers and fabrics in various sombre tones. All are planned for an air of calm and uncluttered ease.

Above left: The perfect spare bedroom: neat, compact and nothing too fussy: virtues that make the room agreeable for most guests, with nothing too frilly to maintain. The tailored blind and the desk make good use of space and plump cushions add comfort.

Left: Crisp, smart and urbane: the appearance of an elegant headboard is achieved with a panel of fabric inset below the narrow window sill, and a bolster cushion at the top of the bed. A bamboo blind filters the light and the businesslike and functional look is emphasized with an adjustable aluminium light by the bed.

Above: This bachelor room is decorated with a certain chic restraint. The fine carved wood and rattan bed is the same as the one in the room on the right; this photograph shows how the furniture can be used for an alternative scheme that quietly boasts a masculine appeal and an atmosphere perfect for peaceful study.

Right: The central position of the bed adds to the ease of bed-making in this oasis of dark green leafy print. The pine blanket chest is used to double as an extra table.

Four different bedrooms and a bathroom take part in an interesting colour and design exercise to show you the various interpretations of a line of daisies enclosed in borders of the same hue.

Right: This bedroom shows how you can pamper an ordinary built-in cupboard unit and turn it into something very special with inset borders cut from wallpaper. The floral design is carried through to the rug and the festoon blind is piped in moss green.

Below right: The pretty pink stripes of the wallpaper are here repeated on the tailored headboard and bedspread and picked up in the lines of the pleated lampshade.

Below: The well proportioned window of this first floor bathroom is dressed in total simplicity. The unlined curtains are threaded with two brass rods and can be easily untied for privacy.

PLAYING THE WHERE TO PUT GAME

Once the decision is taken about where to have the bedroom, then you must decide how to arrange the space. Does it feel like life on the ocean wave in your room because you have a huge bed which is like a ship lapped by a small surrounding sea of carpet? If so, or if you have a small room that serves to house masses of your books as well as clothes, then you will feel less constricted if the place is run on lines as ship-shape as possible.

Wall-fixed shelving instead of bedside tables, and spot lighting affixed to the wall instead of bedside lamps will simplify clutter. A wall-hung mirror with a shelf for hairbrush and make-up, and a simple curtain that pulls back or panel doors on a glide track instead of open-out doors to the fitted clothes cupboard will all save space. A blind instead of full curtains will also give an illusion of space. Decide whether you like to get yourself ready sitting down at a dressing-table or whether your habits dictate that a well-lit bathroom mirror is the place for doing hair and make-up. Or perhaps you prefer just a hand held mirror near the maximum light in which case all you need is a small surface for cosmetics and hairbrushes near the window. A small pine wash-stand could be ideal.

THE WORKING BEDROOM

If you are a keep-fit enthusiast or go in for yoga, enough space left on the bedroom floor unhampered by trailing wires and chair legs is helpful. Some form of a trolley easily summons the task to hand if you are the sort of person who is in the habit of working in bed: a white room with a white shelved unit on castors, with the telephone and pencils kept uppermost, makes a practical and starkly glamorous bedroom for the pillow-propped workaholic. Or camouflage the unit with stick-on fabric or paper and fix castors to a small bamboo table so that the object looks in place.

The idea is that the work-place-cum-bedroom should look integrated, rather than uncomfortably housing two separate functions. The keen dressmaker may want a bedroom sewing corner. Or you may decide to use the space under the window for a desk, and equally you may need a home office, but do insist that your room be a retreat where you can recharge from your heroic endeavours. If this is impossible, then another place to work must be found, perhaps a section of the sitting room.

Right: The blues of a cloudless English midsummer sky are chosen for a guest bedroom suite in the British Embassy in Washington. Seven different prints plus a solid colour cotton are integrated with the versatile stripe. This pattern makes a good choice for the fitted seat cover on both the upright chair and stool. In the looking-glass a reflection can be glimpsed of the curved headboard and bedspread which are in the identical print and vermicil quilting to the frilled mats on the mahogany dressing table.

Below: Finally, a summery bedroom in a château in northern France, where the varying tones of greens and yellow in the colour scheme extend naturally to views of the garden and the Picardy countryside beyond. Simple curtains grace the tall windows on either side of the Chippendale shaving table and the gilded picture frames enhance the happy atmosphere of warmth and sunlight. Leading off this bedroom is the bathroom in the opposite photograph. The style of the furniture and bedside lamp in the bedroom is continued, happily in keeping, with a Victorian glass and metal wall light and flower-painted black lacquer mirror over the wash-basin in this adjoining room.

Soothing variations on a blue and white colour scheme for two town house bedrooms, both of which have tall, finely-proportioned windows framed in deep pelmets, and an extravagant sweep of full, ruffled curtains.

Right: The simpler story of the two is told with a mini-geometric print fitted cotton bedcover, tailored pillow shams bound in blue, and a shirred valance to hide the legs of the bed. A plump button back armchair is upholstered in cornflower blue linen. The casual throwover bed-cover is in a random pattern patchwork, styled with patches of blue checks and stripes and occasional squares of red. The green glass lamp casts an intimate light.

Below: Layered, pleated and partnered in bamboo, this is an altogether more elaborate version. Twice as many cushions are piled high and the rug adds more colour and luxury. The setting is gently formalized with pieces of bamboo furniture and a pleated lampshade, and the contrasting materials of the valance are gathered about in generous layers.

When you have a long narrow room you may find that the space is a more agreeable shape if you place the bed across one of the shorter ends rather than aligning it with a longer side wall. If you have a spacious room in which to spread yourself, experiment with placing the bed at different angles. If there is a view outside that gives you pleasure and you like to lie in bed watching one tree in different seasons, and this takes priority over the glare you get from the light, then place your bed opposite the window. Or place the bed in the centre of the room like your private island.

WAKING UP TO COLOUR

When you choose the colour for your bedroom first assemble bits of the fabric, paper and floor covering and brush a stroke of paint onto a piece of board. Then do a simple test with your assembly board: put it in the room and study it by natural light and in electric light. Now work out a selection of tones of the colour which you might use to create light and shade. An entirely scarlet room can make a small space feel tiny but if this is what you crave then go ahead: really your bedroom is at least one place where you should be able to fulfil your dreams. As a very general guide the effect of different colours is this: blue is soothing and cool, green is restful and good for concentration; pinks are pretty, flattering, feminine; apricots and reds are warm and stimulating, and yellow is a happy, sunny colour but should be used with care in a bedroom as much of it reflected on your skin can make your complexion look poorly. White, creams and beige tones can be very chic and sumptuous.

Two double bedrooms in blue and white.
Right: In a spacious room where not every alcove is utilized for storage, a feature is made of this fireplace corner. The circular table is dressed in floor length skirts of a flower dotted fabric edged in blue. This niche makes a safe place for a precious collection of very elaborate china containers and a wicker sewing box.

Above: A close-up of more of the treasured group of ornaments in the room on the right. These are lined up on a chest of drawers which is placed on the opposite side to the corner table and mantelpiece. The perfectly laundered cloth is white linen with a crochet edge.

Below right: Neat borders meet the gaze in this snug master bedroom. They trim and tailor the bedding, run parallel with the skirting board and where the corners meet on the walls, and they also outline the floor rug.

Below: A detail of the bedroom in the photograph on the right, showing the borders more closely. Pink roll-up and zipper bags are tidy hold-alls for make-up and manicure kit.

Make the most of sloping ceilings instead of trying to ignore the irregular lines and beams. Under-the-eaves rooms possess eccentrically built corners and windows that enhance feelings of cosy privacy.

Above: This garret makes a fuss-free bachelor's bedroom, decorated with restraint in a smart navy blue and sand colour scheme. Honey emulsion paint appears to raise the ceiling, and the angular walls are papered in a trim stripe. The window is snappily clad with three roller blinds.

Right: Cinderella-sized bedroom disguises its awkward shape by covering the walls and ceiling in the same print. The tiny window is screened with curtains attached to casing rods.

Opposite left: with a natural pine ceiling combined with the poppy flower print and carnival stripe the total effect in this room is of a rustic log cabin filled with sunlight. The appearance of the window is broadened with curtains hung from a pole in front of the recess.

Opposite right: Two glimpses of a room where the slope forms an alcove for walk-in storage.

IN SUPPORT OF GOOD SLEEP

Buy the best bed that you can afford. You will spend about one third of your life in it and good sleep is vital to the priceless state of good health. Try to make your investment at a specialist bedding centre where you will get good advice on the mattress and bed base that suits you best.

Choosing the right bed to give you the correct degree of firmness and support for your back involves a very subjective judgement. A bed which is too soft or too hard can be the source of back complaints. If you are a couple buying a bed, do not feel embarrassed about both stretching out full length on the bed and bouncing about on several to find which is the most comfortable: the well trained salesperson is sympathetic to the customer who wants to be quite sure. Dispel any mystique about what you are lying on by getting the store's advice on which is the right mattress and bed base for you: there are at least three different kinds of sprung mattress, as well as the foam type, and several different kinds of bed base on a wood framework.

FLEXIBLE BEDS

If you are a couple, a zipped and linked double bed is worth noting as the bed is formed from two separate mattresses and this allows you to be restless without disturbing your partner. Storage beds give more space: divan beds are available with lift up divan bases and drawers at the end or the sides, but these extra compartments are happiest filled with items you do not need to rummage for very frequently.

Sitting up in bed is more comfortable with a headboard to lean against, and there are many styles to choose from. There are buttoned and padded fabric ones and shapes made from brass, metal, solid wood or a peacock fan of delicate cane. You can make the simplest headrest with a cotton lace covered pillow looped over a brass rod fixed to the wall behind your bed, but if you decide on a permanent fabric board, choose one which can be sponged easily. Testers and four-poster beds tend to look most appropriate in spacious rooms, as do elaborate canopies. You can buy assembly-kit wooden four-poster beds now with or without matching drapes, and while you save up for the fabric you want in the long term, your four-poster clad with full curtains of plain calico is disarmingly pretty.

Is there enough privacy in your bedroom? When you decide on the curtains, consider whether you need some sort of screen as well. If your window overlooks your own rolling acres, you can probably dispense with a blind or voile curtain, otherwise you will need some form of translucent cover to ensure privacy. While on this subject of screening your room from the outside world, make sure you have window bolts that you can lock at night, so the windows are open the small amount you want but immovable.

The British have a puritan attitude towards the well-heated bedroom that might tempt one to loll around in a state of languid undress on top of the bed, and the national preference has usually been for an unheated room in which disrobing was an act to be done at top speed, before a pyjama clad nosedive under blankets. There is also an indigenous custom about windows flung open at night even in winter. However, some fresh air is a good idea, as is some form of heating. Any electric and gas heaters should be switched off at night as they are a fire hazard and if you enjoy the luxury of an open fire in the bedroom, romantic as it looks, please extinguish the fire before retiring.

Your bedroom floors may be bare wood in which case a rug by the bed is a warming thought, but you may decide to give your room the all wool luxurious carpet which is too costly for a big downstairs area. Certainly this makes a welcoming and very pleasant sensation for bare feet as one pads along to an adjoining bathroom.

Left: When you live in an apartment block but nurture a longing to live in the country, or when you work in a modern environment, all functional chrome and glass, but daydream about a life down there on the farm, then you long for a gentle bedroom to return to, a room that will greet you with a nostalgic charm, conjured up by innocent-looking cottons and airy freshness.

The casual, pretty look of the room is quite easy to achieve with inexpensive materials and careful work. The canopy of the modern campaign four-poster is made of lace. Look underneath the graceful fold and you notice the pleasing effect the fabric has of diffusing the light in much the same way as do branches of green leaves when observed from below.

Glass jars with tapered wire frames form the basic homemade lamps which are then skirted with handkerchief lampshades, the simplest of styles to make. The broderie anglaise trim is also on the circular cushions.

The rocking chair is overhauled with paint and decorated with children's transfers, and the elaborate junk shop mirror and dressing table you see reflected in the glass are given coats of shiny white gloss.

Rustic wainscoting is produced by sheets of panelled wood or board carefully nailed to the wall. The chair-rail moulding at the top of the wainscoting comes from lengths of wood with enough width to form the surrounding shelf. Windows are outlined in moulding, though you could add shutters to fold open, or glide to and fro on a cupboard track.

A good spot for reading is on the porch seat which is hung over by the window for the maximum amount of daylight. This swing chair is secured into the ceiling joists and is suspended by the four chains fixed to the arm-rests. And up above are hanging baskets filled with pots of fresh flowers. Alternatively, you could suspend a rod between lengths of cord like an old-fashioned wooden clothes pulley and hang bunches of dried flowers. The floor is painted white with green lines forming large windowpane checks.

Some more ideas for ways to create this type of look are as follows: The lighting choice could be a pair of oil lamps with transfers of the same flowers as on the chair stuck on to the glass shades. Or you could stencil a pattern on to the chair and lampshades, and on to plain painted walls. Or try covering the walls with fabric and using the same or contrasting materials for the wood slatted canopy. A rag rug plaited in cottons of the same colour is a warming thought if you like a cosy surface to step out on from the bed.

Another way to cover the curved frame top could be with a fringed chenille velvet rug caught at the four poster corner poles with thick tasselled ties. Or two bead curtains laid across the top would lend a gipsy air.

Two very differently decorated dual purpose rooms, each an example of a room where the bed has been placed on a platform and natural textures maximize the feeling of space.
Left: The whitewashed open brickwork walls combine with bare beams and a beige fitted carpet to create an atmosphere of restful, rustic calm. The rug-covered bed placed across the window with a carpeted step offers a choice of comfortable seating areas and simultaneously makes the position of the bed unobtrusive. A slatted blind can be pulled down over the window and a second one unrolls as a room divider or a screen to shut off the sleeping area. Diffused light from the slats makes the space more visually interesting, and there are ample storage drawers under the platform.
Right: A friendly bolthole for a student or au pair. This interpretation of garret life is brought up to date with the visually cosy effect of pine-lined walls and floor, and the bed turns into an easily-tidied seating area for daytime. The worktop sensibly placed as near as possible to the window is very straightforward to make: a slab of fabric-covered board is placed on two wooden supports that blend inconspicuously with the rest of the woodwork. Wooden units for storage can easily be retrieved from under the bed, and the high ceiling and window frame are painted in a bright deep blue to increase the snug log cabin-cum-sauna effect. The wall shelves are covered in the same fabric as the desk and the foam mattress is tailored with a fitted cover in plain blue repp. The result is an altogether successful exercise in simplification with the rise and fall coolie lamps to provide an adjustable light and a lace curtain to diffuse daylight.

Ideally, one room living means minimal decoration, space that is absolutely functional and an environment in which the occupant feels at ease. The reality for many people is different. One room often means the isolation of a bedsit with restricted surroundings and other people's cumbersome or wobbly furniture with loose covers in unsuitable fabrics like a soon grubby damask of distracting flowery chintz. Yet whatever size of room you live in, whether studio, loft or bedsitting room, the major issue which confronts every occupant is how to organize the space.

Here then are the basic points that you will need to deal with whether your life is spent in a room of your own or if you are sharing it.

BE A MASTER OF SIMPLIFICATION
Adaptability is the room's single most important quality. This is to say that you need to make the room work for you, by having the layout of the space as flexible as possible so that the room can, as it were, expand to accommodate

a group of people if you are inviting friends to a meal. Then you want the layout to adapt to your activities when you are working at home with books, files and typewriter spread about, or enjoying spare time with sewing machine, or paints. If you can adapt to the space yourself and pare your possessions down to the essentials, then there is more room for mobility.

Let us suppose your space is not completely furnished for keeps by a landlady, and so you can use your own furniture – in which case your choice of flexible and adaptable furniture can be worked out from some of these ideas.

Multi-purpose lightweight furniture includes bamboo or brightly coloured metal chairs which can be folded flat and hung on hooks when not in action and deck or directors' chairs which neatly stack flat. Tables can extend to twice their width, or fold flat with flap-down sides, and there is always the folding butler's tray. You can buy brightly coloured folding desks with chairs to match. Garden furniture looks light and airy in slatted wood

and a folding garden table is made that adjusts to different heights – so you can have one height for serving a meal on and then lower your sights to make a bedside table.

Aim for objects that serve a dual purpose. A pine chest can store equipment such as typewriter and materials if you work from home, so there is no sign that you toil where you sleep. The chest also works as a table surface, seat, headboard to the bed or footboard. A blind or a screen doubles as room divider and hooklined surface from which to hang belongings. A plank placed on two ladder rungs offers basic shelving, and you can hang or place things on the rungs.

Consider a rise to new levels. If it is at all possible you might build a platform, gallery or dais for your sleeping area. If you buy a new lamp make it a flexible anglepoise or a clamp lamp. Lastly, a word about colour. Natural colour tones and textures are more liveable with than traditional bedroom pastels, if you are spending day and night in the same room.

Imagine that a young girl's bedroom is being redecorated to celebrate becoming a teenager. Here are two quite different rooms to show how the same colour scheme and co-ordinating prints can be used in contrasting ways with the idea extended to a matching bathroom, when her primary choice is a jolly, straightforward red.
Below: The sofa of nursery days is revitalized with loose covers which are easily whisked off for washing. Wallpaper is pasted onto an old scratched coffee table and glass is cut to fit the top. The unlined curtains have a pelmet made from hardboard trimmed with scallop edge and painted white, and the seaside canopy effect softens the harsh lines of the windows.

Below right: The opposite corner of the same room. A bright patchwork quilt combines all the patterns in the red scheme while stripes on the valance and pillow shams relay the fresh leaf green from the strawberry motif wallpaper. The padded bedhead, bed and table are all dressed in a manner that is frankly girlish and feminine.
Right: A cottagey bedroom with a vaulted ceiling, latticed windows and a carpet of old brown cord. An informal style is used to make the most of the room's individual atmosphere. Ceiling and woodwork are left white and the walls painted red which makes a bold and uncomplicated setting for the private picture gallery. This complete array looks all the more arresting because of the

thoughtful way in which the composition has been arranged. All the space is put to good use. The child-sized wooden chest of drawers grows up with a coat of scarlet paint and the central light has a lampshade in fabric to match the scheme. The valance and curtain headings are gathered into an informal style and with the continental quilt for bedding add up to a look that is easy to keep looking tidy.
Opposite below: And so through to the luxury of a really pretty teenage bathroom, a happy progression from the years of shared nursery bath times! The window has a shirred curtain and the accessory fitments are lollipop red acrylic. The decoration is spot on with either bedroom scheme.

then fine, the bed can be left just so, otherwise a disguise is called for to give the place an agreeable daytime appearance. A steady bedside table and stable reading lamp, properly placed so that the light falls on the book when the person is in his favourite reading position is conducive to relaxation. A light with articulated stem and shade is a good investment. One budget solution to the table problem is an upturned tea-chest: first erase splintery edges with glass paper, then stain or spray-paint a good colour and add two coats of varnish. Another possible alternative is to paint or otherwise re-cover an old school trunk. While discussing ways to adapt low cost and utilitarian containers, why not convert the humble wood fruit box from the greengrocer's?

ROOMS FOR WORK AND PLAY
A strong work-top of enough height to tuck knees under, and an upright chair with support in the correct place for the person's back is one intelligent way to encourage study. A mimsy, fragile desk with spindly legs is off-putting.

While young children require the basics of a place to sleep, a surface to sit up at and the floor for playtime, teenagers benefit from some seating they can sprawl about on, that is easy to clean and not too precious. Unit seating is ideal. An oval hanging basket seat is fun, and big floor cushions are fine if they can be stored off the floor, to reduce the amount of cleaning necessary. Dense foam slabs covered with

A room to grow up in which young people can call their own is one of the most reassuring send-offs into adulthood. For it is vital that an adolescent be given as much scope as possible in which to develop the different aspects of his or her personality. This, of course, applies to the practical everyday side of life as well as to the emotional and inner life.

The right room for a teenager is one which feels friendly and is clean and young-looking. Decoration should both stimulate the senses and contribute towards an overall atmosphere of well-being. The most appropriate place is one that consolidates the occupant's feelings of belonging and sense of identity. It also needs to feel unconstricting and free.

There are definite priorities to consider when planning how best to organize the space, whether it be next door to parents in a tiny flat or over in the rambling west wing. These are as follows: flexibility, privacy, relaxation, sleep, storage, light and safety. The most important of these is flexibility, both in the choice and maintenance of the furnishings and the other paraphernalia in the room. Sometimes the space needs to enclose, and at other times be left uncluttered with the maximum light.

Healthy teenagers enjoy a place where they can make music, have friends to stay overnight, sulk, daydream, stamp about and let off steam as well as snooze or study. If lucky enough to have a bedroom with adjoining sitting area

fabric are inexpensive and adaptable, and fold-away lightweight metal chairs come in good colours and clean cut design. The latter are practical when a group of friends are over, say, to gather round and play cards. Afterwards the chairs can be hung flat on a wallhook or stacked into a recess.

If space permits a second work surface is a real bonus, where projects like a collage can be left carefree for days with work in progress. Simplify the early childhood collections. The once cherished gang of miniature animal ornaments become babyish and stultifying. Instead a pinboard with boxed supply of map pins is an instant filing system and an efficient way to keep pace with the interests of its owner.

Soundproof the room: foam ceiling tiles and extra floor rugs are basic sound mufflers. See that stereo speakers are placed against an outside wall. Ensure that privacy is respected.

Do as much as you can to encourage the occupant to take pride in the room and its contents. If there's a bookshelf, books are better taken care of. If there's a mirror and somewhere for brushes, then interest in appearance is sooner cultivated. If a laundry basket is to hand, then sorting dirty clothes is easier. Every teenager needs to be harried from time to time about belongings. So anticipate ways to make the room easier to organize. The less people are nagged, the more they enjoy staying around.

THE YOUNG IDEA

When a child feels at home in his or her room, the place feels cosy but properly aired, secure, safe and clean. Interesting items to look at develop mental growth, stimulating colours and shapes aid the vital process of discovery, while things that sound and smell friendly will one day form an important part in the backlog of good childhood memories. Contentment is induced with the tick-tock of an old clock, the fresh whiff of non-carbolic soap, the knowledge that there is a night-light glow nearby to guide a small person safely from bed to lavatory in the dark, and that during a rest after lunch the pattern of the curtains diffuses the sunlight in an interesting way. These are some of the unpretentious, simple ways in which a youngster's room can be thought out.

In parenthood most of us need self discipline to break off whatever we are doing to help a child with a new interest when the moment of discovery arises. Take a first urge to knit. To rear a hobby you must join in, and having got the wools and needles, you must decide where

best to keep them in the room, so they are on hand and the interest sustained for all parties. This way a project has a place and is not put into some forgotten hideyhole.

A child who grows up in a place where his surroundings are a constant help in developing his individual interests, has self-confidence. And young children respond to surroundings that are structured to be a·help to the parents in their supervision. This means a room where there is a basic orderliness in the planning, however many times parental intentions fall apart, and where the place is run without a litany of scowling severity. Instead, encourage the child from early on to join in and put the objects back in their place. To prevent adults falling into the trap of always tidying up themselves, as it is easier and quicker than getting the child to do it, the surroundings need to be geared to making the business of housetraining youngsters as easy as possible. Simplicity is the key to this grand design.

All this sounds super but how does the busy and often tired mother achieve such goals? For

Left: Improvisation is the key to this blue bedroom designed on a scale that is in keeping with the lofty rooms of a first floor Paris apartment. The old school desk has been repainted to match the brass and iron bedstead, and a decorative screen hides the washbasin and clothes chest.

Below left: Swan about on pink coat hooks. More birds flank the circular washbasin mirror. You can make a similar plant box with a painted bicycle basket.

Right: A children's bedroom and playroom. The deep recessed areas on either side of the mantelpiece have been made into louvre-doored cupboards with a rail for hanging clothes in one cupboard and shelves full of toys, books and nursery paraphernalia tucked into the other. There is more storage space under the blue cotton covered window seat and underneath the sturdy wooden bunk beds, and up at one end of the bunk frame are more shelves for various sizes of books, plus boxed games. The oblong table is at a sensible height for very small children and with the green chair and banquette forms a comfortable storybook reading corner. Two lovely ideas for a baby's cradle are the wood slatted cot with a detachable quilted lining and the two-handled Moses basket lined and covered with sprigged green and white cottons.

Below: Two more views of the royal blue and apple green room which show how much fun you can have with an unusual colour scheme. A sheepskin rug is the cosy base for cot and castle.

young children are naturally messy, noisy and trusting. Your first aim is to tailor their room to allow for these characteristics. But, if you are forever plumping up cushions and restraining the hilarious fray of a pillow-fight, if you miss out on vital rest in order to line every drawer meticulously, then think again. Curb your zeal. It is wise to share and enjoy the fleeting time of childhood which is most infinitely precious to parent and child.

Arrange the room so that it is easy to care for and it is comfortable for everyone in the family. The easy chair to flop into by the lamp makes the bedtime story and a pre-lights out discussion about the day simply second nature.

PRACTICAL CONSIDERATIONS

So, down to decoration basics. Firstly, the heating. Control central heating radiators so that they do not become scorchingly hot; put any additional heaters high on the wall, well above a child's reach; do not use portable heaters with frayed wires or elements exposed. If a child is ill or convalescing, then dream up ways that make the stay in bed less boring. A tray with two unfolding supports acts as a bed table and keeps painting materials or food from slithering about; a hot water bottle is all the more comforting to snuggle up to if the cover has an interesting design, perhaps padded and appliquéd to resemble a tabby cat.

Costly floor-covering like thick pile carpet is extravagant. Whatever you walk on needs to be able to take punishment from spilt liquids and squishy substances. Time spent padding about on all fours is much more fun when piecing together a jig-saw than scrubbing stains. Coir matting or sisal is scratchy to bare young feet and plasticine becomes irretrievably embedded. Ensure bare wood floors are splinter free. One good solution is cork tiles that are warm to look at and touch, easy to clean and go well with warming extras like rag floor rugs. Leads sewn on corners underneath rugs or some form of rubber underlay between mat and floor will prevent slipping.

You may modify a desk from your own childhood or have a toy cupboard passed on from a friend but if you buy new furniture then

The baby's room is one you can really have fun decorating, and where, if you feel like it, you can go ahead and break the rules of traditional colour schemes. Apricot and green, both in the most gentle and refreshing tones, are ideal for a room that is decorated before the baby is born.

Right: View of the layout of the nursery. The table and upright chair by the window double as a convenient writing desk plus nappy changing area with the addition of a thin mattress covered in a washable plasticized green and white fabric.

Below: The white iron cot has a detachable, padded draught-proof screen that matches the floor mat and fabric playbricks in the main picture.

Opposite above: Built-in cupboards match the door and walls to create a calm, unified look. The scalloped edges of the handkerchief lampshades are accentuated with stitching in moss green and the high chair has a detachable, padded lining.

Opposite below left: The wall-tidy in fabric to match the wallpaper makes a convenient mobile store for nappy change items. You could also make it with a waterproof lining. The layette basket has a pretty ruffled lining and makes a good container for sewing, toys or baby's bottles.

Opposite below right: Close-up of the mattress and a beautifully dressed Moses basket. The zig-zag edged blind balances the lavish treatment of frills on the curtains.

try to resist the Lilliputian miniature pieces. Items on a dinky scale soon become outgrown and join other encumbrances in the attic. If there is money around for specifically child-like furniture then it is better put towards an antique rocking horse, a Wendy House or, if you have a garden, then a seesaw or a robust climbing frame.

If you buy bunk beds then check that the ladder is firmly fixed, that there is adequate lighting on the lower bunk and while the family is young that the older child has the responsibility of sleeping on the higher level.

For stowing belongings these ideas may spark imagination. Try making a clothes cupboard with the front designed to look like a

house — windows cut into the hardboard doors and glazed with cellophane, the roof and exterior details simulated with paint. Soft toys that are currently out of favour can be put into a plant hanging basket: secured to a ceiling hook by cords the effect is of a toys' balloon outing! Baskets hung on cuphooks from a shelf make extra at-a-glance storage for small items that easily get left around like socks, badges and hair ribbons. This is simpler, too, for the very young than the endless opening and shutting of cupboard doors and drawers.

PLAY SAFE

Finally, a few words about the need for safety precautions. Make certain that any heavy free-

standing pieces of furniture are firm on their feet and will withstand toppling in a game of hide and seek. Horizontal safety bars are as inviting as the branches of a climbing tree, so install vertical bars on windows. An electric kettle for brewing tea is too easy to trip over if it is left at floor level and should be placed firmly out of reach if on a tabletop. It is better kept on a tea-making surface in the passage. The theatre star dressing room style with a row of unshaded lightbulbs is glamorous and coveted by some young girls but beware of non-fire resistant objects like a hairbrush getting too near the naked light. Install a small fire extinguisher near to the children's area and be sure everyone knows how to use it.

BATHROOMS FOR ALL BUDGETS

EARLY BATHTIMES

Once upon a time the bathroom was a neglected place where the bath stood on four ornate feet like a portly stationary animal, with plumbing that was as ugly and complex as a ship's boiler room, and pipes and plug-holes that were apt to send forth curious gurgling sounds. It was in here that wet feet skidded on the polished linoleum, and draughts whistled under the door while dust entrenched itself in the crevices of the frosted glass window.

Although the bathroom is the last room to have joined our households, it was for long very low on comfort, planned without much sense of space and deprived of storage room. There are exceptions, of course, but for most people, the bathroom of all our yesterdays was a chilly, pipe-rattling affair. However, the bathroom can recall a decorative past if we leave aside the use of the space, and look at the details of interesting porcelain-topped tap fittings, gorgeously coloured and imaginative tile designs, enamel or porcelain-lidded soap dishes and then the family favourites of the bleached wood slatted bath mat and bath rack.

The wooden box stool with the cork-covered lid is just about the only piece of bathroom furniture from recent decades which is worth keeping for posterity. The flimsy wood clothes horse was useful, but easily toppled over and the wood clothes dryer lowered from the ceiling on a pulley was more often found in a laundry or utility room –

though these racks for drying laundry are now to be seen hung up in present day kitchens, as part of the revival of the commonsense household items from times past.

Bath, wash basin and lavatory fittings have known days when they were splendidly designed in great style even if they were installed in an isolated splendour without a built-in cupboard or a shower cabinet for company. There were, for example, the Italian marble suites in country houses and old, established, well appointed hotels, or the Victorian embellishments on fittings of cast iron and porcelain. Anyone who has looked down a Victorian loo and seen the china bowl painted with a riot of blue roses will recall such decorative depths forever!

COME CLEAN NOW

Technology today has now evolved for us the possibility of installing an efficient bathroom where water may quietly flush, towels soon dry and where man-made fibre carpets replace the cold lino or the carpets made of natural fibre like wool, which do rot in due course.

Now you can choose from a vast selection of baths and basins, showers and bidets, and there is choice in colour and style, plus a tempting array as well of accessory fitments such as towel holders, fitted cabinets and mirrors.

All of this sounds rousing for the new homemaker with decorative schemes afoot, but alas, most structural alterations and new

Opposite above: A border of green glazed tiles happily brings together the deep wall panels of white tiles and the area of wallpaper. The window sill is fitted with a length of marble. The lacquered mirror and a curtain made from a width of scallop bordered cream lace add charm to the country cloakroom.

Opposite below: A coach house conversion. This awkwardly-shaped attic room is made into a bathroom of decided character with the curious wall shapes in the far end cleverly streamlined by the use of a small print wallpaper. The deeply recessed window is left plain for maximum light and also because the room is not overlooked. A simple bath mat is made of cotton in the same design as the wallpaper reversing to thick towelling. The all-the-way-round tiling splashback is built with a deep shelf to hold bottles and plants and the glossy tiles give the feeling of more light in an otherwise rather dark room.

Above left: The warm, luxurious effect of dark wood in a bathroom combines with the femininity of pie-frill edged cotton curtains and a flowery wallpaper. You could also achieve a pleasant wood effect by boxing in the bath in tongue and groove pine, but remember to leave a panel which can be removed to reach the plumbing. The marble washbasin tones with the pale carpet.

Above: Two views of an efficient bathroom leading into dressing-room unit with a simple blind over the window by the bath and a shirred curtain for the window in the adjoining space. The units are neatly edged with wood and all the splashbacks are easy-to-clean white tiles.

Right: The under basin storage in this unusual bathroom is simply and smartly done with a built-in cupboard painted in glossy chocolate brown and the inset panels covered in the same scarlet pattern as the rest of the room. The deep brown wood panelling, modern bathroom fitments and the bolster at the head of the bath suggest a luxurious and richly warm place to linger in the suds. The thick pile carpet and suede on the chairs add a sensual touch.

Below: The wall hung cabinets and under basin storage cupboards are emphasized with inset panels of the same design as the walls and the piped ruched blind. Sealed cork tiles add to the rustic scene for the splashback, bath surround and floor under the trellis pattern rug. The wicker box is used to house towels, and doubles as a table beside a cosy chair, and the bath slots elegantly into the curved alcove. The blue of the ceiling is softly echoed in the towels, spotted curtain fabric and wallpaper, and in cushions, porcelain ornaments and the floor rug.

plumbing, and most of the new bathroom appliances, are very expensive. Even so, there are ways of cheering up the drab surroundings of an unsatisfactory existing bathroom, and making the place more congenial to be in, which do not present you with a steep bill. The room which everyone in the household visits with such frequency deserves to look good.

First then, to locate your bathroom. Ideally, the room needs to be near the bedrooms to cope with morning and bed-time rush-hour traffic. This does not take into account the more obviously comfortable household where there are several bathrooms, or at any rate a washbasin for each of the bedrooms. If your house is already plumbed when you move in, then your decision about where the bathroom should be will be affected by the location of the water supply and the waste pipes. In a two-storey house, the normal and most economical arrangement of pipes would mean that the bathroom is immediately above the kitchen. Regulations dictate that the rooms where you eat or you cook must not have a lavatory immediately leading off them, and so if you plan to install a new lavatory then make sure that it opens on to a properly ventilated passage or landing area.

DOUBLE LIFE BATHROOMS

If your bathroom is already installed and it is well off for space, but the room looks dull, then investigate the possible ways that will turn it into a place which serves more purposes. These are some of the roles you could give it.

First, the bathroom-cum-dressing-room. See if you can accommodate your dressing-table in the space, whether it is one of the long-skirted kidney-shaped variety with a three panel looking-glass, a professional work surface with laminated top, or a freestanding mirror placed

on a chest of drawers. And even a table top made from a shelf that folds down flat against the wall when not in use, is better than no dressing-table surface at all.

IDEAS TO SOAK UP

If there is an alcove or a recess deep enough to use as a hanging space for clothes, screen the area with a blind, or simple, full curtains secured with rings on to a painted wooden pole instead of swing-out doors. You could make the curtain for the recess in one material, make up café curtains or festoon blinds for the window in the same fabric and then sew welted square cushions in a plain colour, or a co-ordinating print, for a bath-side wicker arm-chair. You can spray the chair with a paint to harmonize with your overall colour scheme, paint the curtain pole and rings a different tone of the colour and choose the soaps, bath essence and all the bits and pieces for use in this room in shades of the same basic colour, or two colours that work well together like pink and green. If you are already well equipped with plain white towels and do not plan to buy new ones, then you could bind the shorter edges of the towels in a fabric to tie in with your scheme and use the same binding to tailor a plain terry towelling bathrobe. For the dressing-table or worktop seat you can use an upright kitchen chair in wood and either paint it the same colour as the wicker or the curtain pole, or strip the chair and polish it with plenty of

beeswax. A pretty addition would be a tab cover made in towelling or the same fabric as your curtains or blinds and also piped around the edges.

The bathroom can sometimes join forces with a desk, telephone and bookshelves, to form a warm work and study area, if there is nowhere else in the house to use as a work-room retreat. Or you could lodge one of those stationary exercise bicycles here and fit a full-length mirror to give you your own workout gymnasium space, given of course that you can clear enough floor space for exercises, and preferably with the addition of a floor rug for comfort.

As well as a sitting, writing, dressing-room

Above: A second bathroom in a tiny artisan's cottage in London is decidedly chic. Good use of minimal space is shown in the design of this small room without much natural light. A well-lit mirror over the washbasin is surrounded on three sides with a wall of cupboards to store all cosmetics and bathroom items. A glimpse of the open shelving system and further cupboards on the opposite wall is reflected in the mirror. The woodwork is painted a toning beige.
Left: The trim corner of a bathroom enlivened with a green and white colour scheme shows bamboo towel holders, and the bath neatly boxed in but with a door to reach the pipes.

or exercise area, you can give a bathroom of just about any dimensions the indoor garden treatment and this is a good facelift for an ugly room. Provided that there is enough light and some form of heating, then there are several plants which will flourish, such as the Swiss cheese plant, cape primrose, tradescantia and jasmine and the lovely lilac and purple African violets. If you are a reluctant gardener whose houseplants usually get forgotten and dry out in despair then you will find the routine of feeding, watering and generally pampering indoor plants much easier to attend to, if the healthy fern you have invested in is hanging in its basket right at your eyeball level when you come to clean your teeth.

The indoor conservatory look is fun to add to, and improvise with, in any bathroom: train an ivy to trail round the mirror or circumnavigate some nasty pipework, and if you have an ugly case of mouldy patches on the wall you can cover a multitude of sins with an attractively arranged group of potted plants or greenery growing in wall baskets.

There are now so many products to use and to adorn the bathroom with compared with the early days of little storage. There is a veritable inventory to be listed from the hairdryers, hair and nail brushes, hair accessories, shampoos, cosmetics and all manner of personal toiletries, bath cleaning stuffs and bulk buys such as soap, cotton wool and lavatory paper. All these can be stocked in the amply fitted bathroom. Then there needs to be space for a lock-up cabinet to store medicines out of reach of young inquisitive children, though this could well be kept out on the landing. Space may need to be found for scales and an electric toothbrush unit. As well as any under basin storage and any cupboards you can fit in, you need somewhere to hang and fold towels, clothes and items like bath hat and bathmat. If possible have a heated towel-rail, otherwise a heater over the door is useful with a pull cord switch to operate it. And one detail: when you want to save money and already have a couple of pretty china containers, then use them for storing the lavatory paper roll and the lavatory brush instead of buying new plastic items.

Much bathroom space is in constant use within arm's reach of the bath and the basin, but what about wall space above eye level and the ceiling? You may have spare space above the lavatory seat and cistern to use cunningly for storage, or a slatted wood ceiling grid for storing towels or upon which to hang clothes for drying. Are there any spare wooden ledges which could take a row of cup or coat hooks? If you have any extra wall space, you can make a most original picture gallery by grouping a collection of framed montages of old photographs, or holiday snaps or theatre programmes, or any other collection of images you like, instead of putting a cherished painting into the room which could become damaged with condensation. On the other hand, if you do have the right layout, quite one of the most pleasant images to look at in a bathroom is simply provided by having a window which is in a position so that you can lounge in the bath while looking at the view – and a porthole shaped window would be an attractive idea with a decoration around the bath of large seashells.

SPLASH OUT ON STYLE

If you prefer to have the textures of old furniture in your bathroom but at a reasonable cost, then set to work on adapting and modifying lesser priced antique shop and flea market finds. For example, the contrasting surfaces of shiny smooth and cool ceramic tiles with the

Far left and centre left: A bathroom that very successfully combines antique furniture with gleaming modern tiles. The tallboy is used for a stylish linen cupboard and white curtains, towels and ceiling offset the woodwork and wallpaper. The mirror over the handbasin is set into a gilded picture frame.
Left and below: Two views of a blue and white bathroom full of femininity in styling. In contrast to a fast-paced day this room suggests a time of leisurely hours spent amid girlish clutter. The antique corner cupboard is painted white, and the Austrian blinds edged with deep frills in white cotton contrast with the formality of stripes.

warm, worn feel of a restored pine cupboard is an agreeable tactile mixture; and the door of a hefty old mahogany wardrobe with mirror panel front makes a handsome alternative to a new mirror fitment.

FROM SHOWERS TO SPLASHBACKS

If you remodel an existing bathroom or plan one from scratch, then it is easier to work out where to put the fitments if you draw up a plan on graph paper first. You may want to find extra space for a bidet, or if you decide on having a shower cabinet as well, then see if there is somewhere else in the home that you can install one. Is there any good spot where you can combine space with the nearness of the drains and water supplies, such as under the stairs or in a corner of a utility room? A shower unit is an altogether extremely practical idea for many households because it combines both economy and hygiene. The cubicle only takes up one square yard of floor space and uses on average only one fifth of the water required for a bath, and you are running clean water continually over your body rather than simply steeping yourself in a bath full of water.

Ceramic or cork tiles make practical floor-coverings as alternatives to fibre carpets. If you use wallpaper then it is a wise move to affix sheets of perspex over the paper around the bath and basin areas to make easy to maintain splashbacks. You can buy baths built for one or for two people and in addition to the usual shape you can now purchase round, oval or corner shaped ones to fit neatly into place. Cast iron with the glossy finish of enamel fused onto metal is the traditional material that baths are made of, but you can also buy baths in pressed steel which are less expensive, lighter and so easier to move about. There are also baths in plastic and acrylic; the latter can be moulded into different shapes and colours but is very vulnerable to nail polish, cigarette burns and paint stripper. A bath should be sloped at one end to support the body comfortably and there should be indented and lowered sides to make the bath easier to get in and out of. Grab rails are useful for safety, and so is a rubber mat which can be placed in the bottom of the bath for young children.

DECORATIVE EXTRAS

THE FINISHING TOUCHES

Up to now in this book we have looked at some of the various ways in which you can decorate the inside of your home. You could say we have stripped back to the bones of your place to see how they are formed, because we have examined how best to build up good ideas in your house or flat according to the structure of its shell. And we have discussed some of the numerous colour themes of contrast and harmony which you can, if you like, put into action to suit your needs, your style of life and your budget.

Above all, we have chosen ideas here that will help to act as a catalyst for your own when you reflect your personality with an individual style of interior decoration. So now we allow some time to get down to the last but all-important aspect of doing up a place: the final detail. This means taking a perfectly ordinary well-made object, lavishing that extra care upon it, and producing something very special and significant for you. You could make the cushions for your sofa really special — any oddments of the fabric you have left over after making curtains, loose covers, blinds, table-cloths and so on for the room can be put together into a marvellous patchwork or imaginative appliqué pictures. Or, again, think of a utilitarian tin kettle discarded because the lid is lost or the spout is rusty. Jazz it up with a shiny coat of gloss or enamel, say in a lacquer

red, and then draw or stencil a simple flower motif on the spout or handle. Colour your design using any paint you may have left over from other jobs, or use the tiny tins sold for painting models. Fill the pot with fresh flowers, and by means of your thoughtful finishing touch you have turned the banished old friend into a completely different kettle of fish.

You may live in a country cottage with low ceilings, coconut matting covered floors and unusually shaped rooms, or a narrow 19th century terraced house with half-landings and two rooms knocked into one on the ground floor, plus the legacy of a rather poky basement. You may live in a modern house, well proportioned but without any particularly large rooms. Or perhaps your way of life is dictated by the responsibilities of an altogether earlier, classical house on a larger scale. Or maybe you have made your home in a converted outbuilding like a stable or barn. If any of these sounds like your home base in some way, then our aim is to help you with ideas that respect the architecture and the environment in which you live.

Alternatively, you may live in a minimal space, perhaps in a cramped bedsitting-room, a boxy-shaped converted flat or a daunting tower block, so you may want to try to make the building more tolerable by creating within your four walls, a retreat or an oasis of fantasy. If this Follow the Yellow Brick Road outlook is rather like your attitude, then there are ideas in this book that are fun and escapist, but at

Far left: Reverse it. The professional look in warm apricot and white graced by an arrangement of objects and a glass box of pot-pourri. The curtains and lampshade are neatly complemented by the double layer of tablecloths in reverse print, apricot on white, and the painted borders behind.

Left: Filter it. Pretty as a painted window, the ever-shifting and translucent effects of light when seen through glass are well shown in this simple display. The Naples yellow painted walls and white edged window emphasize the illusion of a sunlit space.

Below: Line it. Admiring glances towards the display in the glass-fronted cabinet are held longer by a light and attractive backdrop.

Bottom: Border it. A snappy way to paper a dark corner of very basic shelving and give it a contrasting edge to turn it into a light and integral part of the sitting room.

Right: Panel it. Apple green paint and co-ordinating prints are used to create an impressive panelled effect in the lofty ceilinged dining room of an apartment in Paris. Next to the massive fireplace, a circular table makes a sideboard in the round where the final course of fresh fruit is kept ready.

the same time quite possible to achieve.

If you have a roller blind that covers an ugly stairwell view in a tiny city kitchenette, or the door to the toy cupboard in a children's playroom, why not use the bright coloured over-the-hills-and-far-away image of the Over the Rainbow fable? You could paint the winding yellow brick road onto the blind so that the image is of a magic landscape seen through the window, or you could paint the picture on to a toychest, or stitch it in felt on to a curtain that screens off clothes instead of a wardrobe. You could even have the rainbow or turreted castle on the horizon of your picture!

THE PERSONAL TOUCH

So, before going on to the second section in this book, which deals with the practicalities of how to make the items for your home, let us take a look at the finishing touches, the absorbing subject of the decorative extras that put the undeniable stamp of the individual and his or her personality, on a place. This applies whether it is an office setting that has a pleasant orderly atmosphere conducive to serious work, or the front hall of the flat in which a busy family lives. Look up at office block windows and you often see one which is decked about with houseplants. You can be sure some person has decorated their own small space effectively as a leafy rear guard action to drab uniformity. If they have been allowed a pinboard, too, then the chances are that it has been attractively covered with the extra touches of pictures and objects as well as the office memos. In one office, however, a career girl determined to make an area well and truly her own patch has edged her metal office desk-lamp with white broderie anglaise, which seems like a desperate bid against filing cabinet functionalism. Even so, it is the personal touch: the act of someone who wants to make surroundings more agreeable. And it does illustrate the point that you should believe in yourself enough to go ahead and fix your possessions just the way you want to, provided it is not with a total disregard for the comfort and feelings of others.

Left: Cover it, if you have a dark corner table with ill-matched lampshade and oddments, a smart solution is to take a distinctive print and bring together all the items with it. Here the panels of wallpaper with borders emphasise the distinctive lines and corners of the room.

Below: Shelve it. Make use of all available storage space – this humble wall shelf is ideal for books.

Right: Stencil it. The colour scheme here is the timelessly fresh pink and green with sapphire blue bows added. With an old towel rail repainted the transformation of a dull flush door is complete.

Below right: Decorate it. Stencilled furniture such as this provides a highly decorative and colourful change from the normal plain pine pieces and spartan look of recent years.

Far right: Patch it. Titivate an austere high backed wooden seat to make a soft seat of very pretty appearance to put against a bedroom wall or at the side of an upstairs landing. The seat back makes a good place to display the patchwork bedcover in midsummer or to show off all the year round if the cover is an extra one. The leafy wallpaper and moss green colour scheme are all followed through in the china lamp base.

FIRST IMPRESSIONS

The first thing you see in anyone's place is the front hallway as you enter. Here, again, the final details contribute to making the place look and feel both well-run and welcoming.

A felt-covered board criss-crossed with some ribbon and framed in wood makes a practical notice-board near the front door. It is a functional, thoughtful idea, and a stylish way, too, of showing at a glance all the school timetables and notes about activities that a family need.

If you do not have exactly the right piece of furniture, then getting a different item to double up and do the job is another masterly finishing touch. Take the same family hall, for example. If there are no coat racks or chests of drawers for storing away items of outdoor clothing, but there are oddments of garden furniture, then improvise with these. A wire jardinière which looks well in the garden or bay window holding plants, also doubles as an

ingenious glove, hat and scarf holder, and with its slim rectangular shape, looks at home in a narrow hall. Another idea is to key visual images to the appropriate activity area, and to display them accordingly. Take the character of Squirrel Nutkin from the famous Beatrix Potter stories: there is a marvellous picture of this animal high-stepping with delightful exuberance. A framed print of this image is fun placed at eye level by the hook for the garden door keys. So is the framed image of the Tailor of Gloucester mouse sitting on a cotton reel reading the newspaper, if the picture is pinned next to the place where the sewing box is kept. The picture is likely to bring a quiet smile to anyone who is rummaging for a needle, to replace in haste a lost shirt button.

Finishing touches are fun, and when they make a happy surprise or add amusingly to an idea that is basic commonsense — such as one of those net jar covers weighted at the edges with blue glass beads to put over a blue and white

china pot filled with sticky jam — then they give an extra dimension to the owner's setting in the way that a hand-sewn hem does to a dress.

DETAILS TO DELIGHT

The simplest ideas, such as fresh leaves or flowers in a jar in the bathroom, or filling the air near your pillow with scent when they are placed on the bedside table, are more than compensation for somewhere untidy or in need of a dust.

Extras like sweet-smelling soap in the spare bathroom and a supply of basic comforts such as toothpaste and tissues in the cabinet or a pretty tin filled with fresh crisp digestive biscuits by the bed are considerations that put your guests quickly and naturally at their ease. These are the touches that kindle life into a place that can otherwise be a trifle impersonal, and in a household where there is already the evidence of a purposeful life going on, like well thumbed music books at the piano and much-

worn gardening gloves hanging by the secateurs, then it is the injection of these decorative extras that makes a place rare and very special indeed.

You could argue that finishing touches, well executed, are simply an expression of good manners. A family and their friends feel more at peace and able to get on with the business of living in a place where time has been invested in a large amount of intelligent attention to detail. And, of course, putting other people at their ease when they are on your own home ground, is partly what good manners are about.

Attention to detail need not always be out there on show ready to receive compliments. The finishing touch can also be subtly hidden. For example, try the old idea of covering your cushions in an inexpensive and humble fabric, like smart cotton striped mattress ticking or the linen that is used for glasscloths, but invest in deep comfort by filling the insides with softest down instead of foam.

The decorative additional plus is usually done at the end of the main list of jobs but this is not to say that the finishing touch is the same as an afterthought. The extra detail is more likely to be an idea that has been germinated or carefully thought about beforehand.

LAST BUT NOT LEAST

Think out all the detailing first if you can, but only attend to these extras after the big tasks like glazing, making good and building are done. Engage your brain and energies first for the top priorities. Then, once the major part of the worksheet is nearing completion, decide how much time you will give the finishing touches. If you are making a patchwork quilt, then you can spin out the last details for ever, on the basis that doing up a home is like the creation of a garden, never completely finished, and, therefore, giving lasting pleasure!

If you are already coping with a family and perhaps a demanding job too, with little help around the place, then you may decide on a schedule of pottering along with the needle-work chair cover you are making, as one of a set of eight for the dining table, between the lagging of the boiler and the sewing on of nametapes. Or, you may enter into the fray while minding small children and paint a frieze in the nursery in between the constant apron string pulling of youngsters.

Far left above: Tile it. A good matching pattern for when you build a bath splash-back, with a partnering pair of curtains. The result is a glamorous way to hide any ugly taps or shower attachments from the beholder on the other side of the bathroom.
Far left below: Seat it. Make a feature of a tall narrow window with a cascading Austrian blind, tailored window seat and an array of cushions.
Left above. Curve it. What a satisfactory line the bottom of this blind makes with the fine sweep of the edge piped in navy. The string pull has a neat acorn end. The brisk, tailored look is entirely suitable for a busy, efficient kitchen and the windowsill serves as an interesting display place to

balance visually the plain white work top and steel draining board.
Below left: Ruche it. That sparky daisy print again, now growing up the cupboard walls to make inset borders and another flamboyantly curvaceous blind. The contours of the ruching are accentuated by a narrowly piped edge of dark moss green.
Below: Match it. When you want a peaceful all-in-one look, dress the windows with the simplest of curtains to match the wallpaper and line them in white or a pale colour to allow the light to filter through prettily. Make a screen of potted plants when you have an ugly radiator and the heat is turned off.

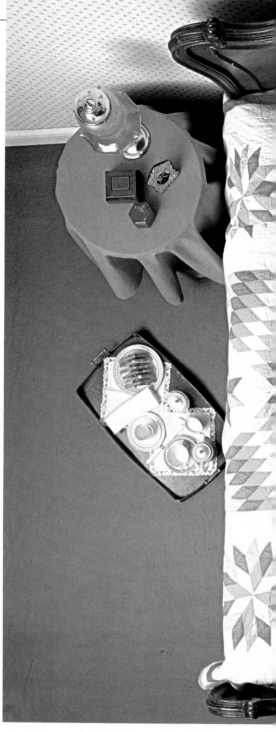

Or you may have a place you want to make perfect, and become obsessive for detail. And remember one small word of warning: dogged obsessiveness is often the result of physical fatigue when you begin to get ground down by the home decorations. Like one imaginative person who became disenchanted with pushing roller-loads of emulsion around the house. So she decided to revolt against the monotony of life at the top of the ladder, and descend a few rungs to sample life at the bottom, glamorizing the network of hot water pipes that channelled their way round at the less energetic working level of the skirting boards. The best way to enhance them, she decided in a fit of decorator's zeal, would be to turn the

long round pipes into brightly coloured and patterned snakes, and turn some more pipes up in the bathroom into branches of trees complete with leaves and birds' nests. Consequently there is a snaky look in the kitchen corner and an arboretum up above the linen cupboard, with much midnight oil assiduously spent in the process of turning radiator taps into flowerheads. Yet, to this day a vast amount of the general paintwork in the rest of the house remains incomplete. Charming, but rather erratic. So, guard against the risk of definitely extra-curricular refinements preventing you from getting the main jobs finished. Keep the extras in perspective. Once embarked on, the finishing touches can be most

absorbing and satisfying to do; in fact one bonus of the finishing touch is that it is as much a therapy to do as it is a delight for the person who discovers the result.

FLIGHTS OF FANCY
The ways in which you inject these special elements can be anything from the style in which you choose to re-net and line the silk curtains of an antique four-poster bed, to the paper you choose for lining a chest of drawers.

Paintwork, of course, lends itself to all sorts of interesting extra touches and so do the arts of stencilling and patchwork. Application of borders may round off an ordinary space into somewhere more formal and impressive look-

Opposite above: Dress it. A window seat gives a cosy look to a room, or any window recess where there is enough space. This one, in a tiny dressing-room-cum-bathroom, has front curtains with a deep frill and tassel tiebacks in the same beige. The seat is made comfortable with a tailored squab and a group of scatter cushions. The window is veiled with fine net and the warm, natural tones are continued in the bathroom accessories.

Opposite below: Appliqué it. Leftovers are used to make the most individual cushion cover pictures, the appliqué on the left a landscape, and on the right a jolly couple. Both cushions reverse to different coloured cotton prints and are edged in yet another pattern; a total mix which is bound, like patchwork, to go together with any plain or contrasting print of similar scale and material. The strategic placing of the mirror appears to double the size of the room.

Left: Quilt it. Patchwork looks completely at home in a bedroom, and goes naturally with old-fashioned oil lamps, lace, carved wood, bric-à-brac and small allover patterns of sprigs and flowers. Vibrant, soft colours radiate from this mid-nineteenth century American quilt in the Star of Bethlehem design.

Below: Skirt it. Co-ordinating daisy fabrics for a classic kidney shaped dressing table.

CREATING CHARACTER

Borders mark out territory whether applied to interior decoration, dress or utensils. They work as margins, and within these lines there is a contained space. So the overall effect of a straight border is to formalize. Hence, just as the effect of a young person sporting a navy and white sailor suit is immediately one of restraint and elegance in fresh Sunday best, so one's first impression of a room with borders on the walls or the furnishings, or both, is one of neat regimentation and clean line. Borders create a tailored look, and lift or subdue tones. They can produce the authorative, rather severe atmosphere of a men's club. Try this out in a study or den decorated in dark colours.

ing. And home-sewn accessories can give enormous lasting pleasure, just as the greetings card which is painstakingly made by a child is naturally more cherished than one which has been bought at the expense of previous pocket money.

One aspect of the finishing touch is that it stamps a place with the quality of ownership. These statements of ownership can be made with great style, though spoken in a soft voice. You might plant jasmine or a strong smelling climber rose so that the branches curl up to the bedroom window and fill the evening air inside with their fragrance. Another example is the person who put loose covers and curtains made from yards of calico into a formal dining room, while saving for a costly gold coin spotted silk. To dress up the calico to look brilliant by night, she then painted on splodges of gold straight from the bottle. Or try making curtains with the hems left a few inches longer than ceiling to floor so that they fall in a theatrical sweep and so complement an elaborate pelmet. The finishing touch is the bringing together of a good idea and a successful way of carrying it out.

So, onto some suggestions. You may be bursting with ideas for how to finish off a room or renovate a piece of furniture. However, you might also like to have some more ideas that after you have brooded on them may help to product the perfect answer.

Borders can create a look of efficiency and hygiene when combined with tiles in a bathroom or kitchen, and of graphic interest visually when used for floor coverings. The effect of borders when combined with cream and brown tones is chic and serene, and in blue and white combinations are restful and summery. Rather like the artful gilding of cosmetics on a face, borders pull together space. They also act as frontier lines, so if you prefer the ambience of neutrals and maximum space, then leave borders out of your scheme.

Borders can co-ordinate all the furnishings in a room, and add prominence to a design feature. An oak leaf cornice around a ceiling, say, is very decorative when picked out in autumnal colours of green and ochre paint and then a stencilled border used to repeat the pattern round the fireplace. Use a braid border in a bedroom and repeat the fabric round the edges on a monogrammed towelling bathrobe. Pick up the colour theme of a dining room or eating area with table linen piped, bound or bordered in the same or a contrasting shade. Bor-

ders used to emphasize walls and woodwork can be elegant: one example of understatement in design is the application of three almost imperceptibly different tones of grey for the borders in an off-white painted room.

Fabric offers multitudinous ideas for the extra personal touches from making a rag rug to covering a collection of motheaten recipe books.

Stencilling is a lovely way to tell the same story again and again. Stencil your floors, walls, and even materials, and you produce a unique effect which is as much part of yourself as your own mural or piece of dressmaking. The craft is satisfying to pursue, but it requires some finicky preparation, and can be physically tiring to carry out if you are dealing with large, tall surfaces. Stencilling has evolved since earliest times but was developed in the United States from around 1775. Then travelling stencillers such as Jo Eaton were responsible for introducing the trend to the homesteads of the early settlers. Furniture, containers, walls and floors were covered with the bold designs. The pineapple, a symbol of hospitality, is a favourite from those days. The craft fell from favour when the Industrial Revolution produced wallpapers within the price range of the masses, but now stencilling is enjoying a revival. And, as a way of putting a finishing touch, the craft has never lost, when well done, a very friendly style. Flooring needs several coats of varnish after stencilling, but it still looks good when it eventually becomes worn. You can stencil flowers over an ugly corner and you can get up to all sorts of visual jokes like a flock of stencilled ducks flapping along a wall where a slope of three flying ducks, would, to many beholders, look awful. You can stencil a dark blue ceiling with silver stars for an attic bedroom under the eaves or nursery.

Curtains can be elaborate with ruffles or shirred on rods. They can be used to emphasize a window's shape or to screen both doors and windows at once. They can cover half the window in the café curtain style. Or, as added protection against draughts, a thick padded curtain can be hung over a door.

Above left: Crowd it. Too precious for daily use or insufficient pieces for a matched gathering at the table, plates are grouped all around the redundant chimney-piece. A lone china dog guards the bottleneck of glass jars and ornaments and a necklace is put on a broad-chested brown jug.

Left: Lace it. Starched white, crisp and clean old linen pillowcases and tablecloths, aptly laced with frills, inset panels and hand-drawn threads, are as much in line with the times past bedroom revival as eyelet embroidery peignoirs and Victorian cotton knickerbockers. If you do not possess a cloth like the one here, then use a second pillowcase. The ethereal snowflake look of lace is most effective when put over a coloured backcloth.

Above: Display it. Borrow an idea from the shelves of a tiny corner shop where you see thrifty use of space, and show off your wares. Utensils that are only in occasional use are hung in precise style on the right of the picture, and items in current use on the left. The oven glove and pot-holder are secured to the flue with magnets, keeping them easily to hand.

Left: Frame it. Dark green paint and handsome deep frames to the paintings suggest the quiet calm of a clubroom or library in this skilful arrangement. Glass containers follow the line of the lampshade.
Below: Hang it. A lively way to show the snaps. The striped walls are an unusual backcloth to a black and white private picture gallery.
Bottom: Mix it. Here a group of receptacles in a wide range of textures meet on the round table; your collection can start with just one linking theme.
Right: Collect it. A last look at the round table and its permutations of dress: here, a chenille rug. Everything in its place: a witty touch is the monkeys all set for a ride in the dish hung from the ceiling. All the occupants of this antique shop line up to bid you au revoir.

Blinds offer infinite scope for finishing touches. Austrian blinds are back as an established current fashion. They can be extravagantly feminine in style and combine well with lace, beads, frills or pleating to create a feeling of yesteryear magnificence. However, like frilly petticoats, they should be used with subtlety and discretion.

It is sensible and also fun to put a good deal of effort into the decoration of your surroundings, but it is sad to become a slave to perfection. This also makes one a bore. Home decoration needs to be dovetailed in just the right amount and to balance with the overall interesting business of getting on with living. As one great woman designer is reputed to have said, 'We should not allow ourselves to make our homes into our prisons'.

Rather, then, our homes are the places where we are free, and our strongholds from which we go out into the world. Without our own comfortable arrangements of the domestic interiors, a home can be a place of neglect and chilling indifference. The house that is well loved and decorated by someone with an attentive eye for little details and the finishing touches, is a good place to return to. A home which is looked after with an individual touch is a place that has one of the most important qualities for a happy life. And a home that abounds with such love is a place with true spirit.

With a lick of paint and a few metres of fabric a bare Edwardian conservatory becomes a pretty dining room for lazy summer meals. As well as saving you money, doing your own decorating and soft furnishing will give your home an individual, personal look it might otherwise lack.

DECORATING
AND SOFT FURNISHING

Bring up the subject of do-it-yourself, and there's little doubt it will divide any company present into those who take to it like ducks to water, and those who wish they had never heard of it. (They are still recoiling from the memory of that fatal day they dropped oil paint on a brand new carpet.)

Even so, absolutely nobody could deny that if you can do almost anything yourself around the home these days, it can save a small fortune, and is almost the only economical way of putting together an entirely individual look. And that must be exciting. What worries lots of people is just how far their do-it-yourself abilities will stretch, if in fact they possess any at all. Since not even professionals take degree courses to qualify as wallpaperers or curtain makers, it's safe to assume these skills are simply acquired through practice, and potentially they are within everybody's reach. You just have to decide to have a go, and follow the instructions patiently.

This section of the book is designed to encourage anyone still dubious about their ability to paint a room or make a cushion cover, by setting out the instructions very simply, and backing them up with lots of visual explanations. There are instructions on how to make most of the ideas illustrated in the first section of this book, although the more elaborate pelmets and bed canopies have been deliberately omitted and would be better made by a professional.

The terms printed in brackets are for American readers. And for readers on both sides of the Atlantic, all metric measurements are followed by imperial measurements in brackets.

In the chapter on curtains American readers will find the different curtain headings difficult to recognise, because they are not widely available in the USA. In these cases, when headings are referred to, simply follow the manufacturer's instructions for the heading you wish to use. But the methods given for estimating fabric quantities and making up the curtain still apply.

For those with relatively little experience of do-it-yourself, it is worth taking a few general tips from the old timers. They set great store by a working discipline which includes having the right tools for the job and keeping them in good working order. Trying to cut delicate scalloped curves with long straight scissors is asking for trouble. Finding the glue pot has dried up, because the last person who used it left the top off, is bound to dampen your enthusiasm. So, before starting any job around the house, check you have everything you need, lay your tools out neatly on the floor, and put them back in the same position each time you finish using them.

There is no doubt that having to tidy away an unfinished job at the end of each day (when you are feeling at your most tired) is a chore most people could do without. If you can set aside a permanent room to use for sewing, woodwork etc., it will encourage creativity. Storing tools and materials in special cubby holes not accessible to the rest of the family is the best way to remain organised. After all, who but a saint still feels eager to put up a shelf or picture hook after wasting half an hour tracking down a hammer which wretched Johnny hid in the sand pit?

Refusing to work in a hurry is as important as refusing to work in a muddle. Attempting to make a loose cover for a sofa in one afternoon flat, is about as silly as trying to build Rome in a day. So turn a deaf ear to plaintive whines like "Mom, will it be next Christmas before you finish wallpapering my room?" Overstretching yourself by overestimating what can be reasonably achieved in a day will only make you feel tired and cross, and that is when you are most likely to fall off a ladder.

Finally looking at the increasing figures of people involved in do-it-yourself activities, it is obvious that most of us, once we embark on home decorating, really find it absorbing and very enjoyable. So for readers still wavering on the side line, the chances of success are weighted in your favour. Working out one's own combinations of colours and pattern, and thinking of ways to make inexpensive furniture look pretty, appeals to the nest building instincts in most of us. And irresistably, at the end of the day, the room you create will contain exactly what you want and have an individual stamp to it, which is something money cannot easily buy.

DECORATING

Painting walls, ceilings and woodwork

The golden rule for successful painting, irrespective of what you are intending to paint, is to prepare your surfaces really carefully. Unless you wash the old paintwork thoroughly first, you may find your new paint simply will not stick. In the same way, you cannot paint successfully over distemper or peeling walls. So take your time and prepare well before you start. With care you will then achieve professional-looking results.

WALLS AND CEILINGS

A new paint colour is one of the easiest and least expensive ways to give a room new life. With new drip-proof paints and rollers, painting is easier than ever before and preparation by far the hardest part of the job.

Preparation

First spread plastic sheeting or brown paper over the floor. Remember that paint can seep through newspapers or dust sheets, so they are second best. Next prepare walls and ceilings by washing down with a sponge, warm water, and if they are particularly grimy, sugar soap or detergent. Then rinse to remove the sugar soap or detergent. Scrape away peeling paint with a scraper or sandpaper. Fill defects with a filler, and when dry, sandpaper gently. Any walls previously painted with gloss paint must be sandpapered to provide a key (rough surface) for the new paint to adhere to.

How to work

Try to paint each wall and ceiling in a single operation, otherwise you will find that an ugly join will appear between two painted areas, even if you only stop for a short break.

Start by painting the ceiling, then the woodwork (see page 99) and finally the walls. Work away from

the window into the room, so that you can see what you're doing. Remove lampshades from central lights (for their protection, and also to give you an unobstructed view of the surfaces to be painted). Rig up a working platform (Fig 1) using two trestles or household steps with a plank wedged safely between. Be warned, this is safer than standing on chairs which easily tip over.

Rollers. Professional decorators are apt to look down upon rollers, but they are ideal for applying paint quickly in large areas — either using gloss paint or emulsion (flat). However, they do cause splashes. Generally a long pile roller is suitable for textured surfaces, a short pile for smooth. They are particularly good for ceilings, where speed can save an aching arm.

To paint a ceiling with a roller, first paint a narrow margin around the edges and corners of the room using a 2.5cm (1in) wide paint brush (Fig 2).

Next apply diagonal strokes of the roller working in alternate directions (Fig 3).
Finally work straight strokes towards the window (Fig 4).

Brushes. Make sure you always use a brush at least 10cm (4in) wide, and work in good long strokes of about 30cm (12in), beginning at the wall opposite the window and working towards it (Fig 5).
The edges of the ceiling need special care, and you may find a small paint pad useful, as it enables

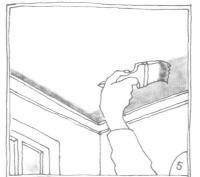

you to apply paint evenly and accurately (there are no bristles to fray out at the edges, causing uneven lines). If you are applying emulsion (latex or water-based) paint on walls, you should work from the top, across the room, in bands of about 30cm (12in) deep (Fig 6). This way you will be able to smooth over any drips.

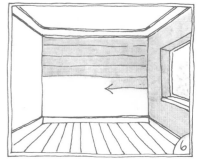

Painting with oil based or alkyd paint requires more concentration and care. If you are painting a ceiling, brush three parallel strokes in one direction, leaving a gap of about 2.5cm (1in) between them, and then paint across them (Fig 7), without reloading your brush.

If you are painting a wall with oil based or alkyd paint, start at the top right-hand corner of the wall, if you are right-handed, the top left if you are left-handed. Use the method of application described above, painting in 60cm (24in) squares all the way down the wall. Then return to the top and repeat, until you have worked all the way across the wall (Fig 8).

WOODWORK

Painting woodwork – windows, doors and furniture, is not difficult, but as you should use gloss paint as opposed to emulsion (flat) for the best practical results – be warned: it's harder work than painting walls and ceilings.

Preparing wooden windows

Again, thorough preparation is all-important. First, wash them well with warm water and soap or detergent. If you are going to use an oil based or alkyd paint, rub the surface with sand- or glass-paper to form a key (rough surface) for the new paint to grip. Remove flaking areas with sandpaper or stripping knife. Any very thickly overpainted mouldings should really be stripped to reveal the original shape of the wood. Defective paintwork must be stripped too. Various brands of paint-stripper are available: the best are those which can rake off all the old coats of paint at once, and do not burn the skin if there is any accidental contact.

Use a moulding shave hook to strip the mouldings and a flat blade stripping knife for flat surfaces. Wash the frames and leave to dry before filling cracks with wood filler. When set, sand thoroughly and prime bare wood ready for undercoat and a final top coat.

Preparing metal windows

Take great care to protect your eyes (goggles are best but even sun glasses will help) as you will need to tackle rusty window frames with a wire brush. Sand them down, and treat rusty areas with a rust killer. Prime bare metal with metal primer before repainting. Sandpaper painted window frames to provide a key (rough surface) for new paint.

Painting casement windows

Begin by painting the sections of the window which can be opened (in some casement windows, some parts are fixed) so that you have plenty of time to let the paint dry – otherwise you may have to leave the windows open on a cold night. To avoid getting paint on the window pane, cover the glass with masking tape, and remove when dry. Make sure it really is dry; if not the paint may peel away with the tape. Alternatively you can get a 'cutting-in' paint brush with bristles shaped to give an angled edge specially made for window frames.

The professional order of what to paint is worth following as it is based on common sense (Fig 1).

For instance, the window sill is the last to be painted as it is the most vulnerable to accidental touches and likely to be leant on as you work, and the inside of the frame is the first to be painted, because it is the first you want to dry, and the least vulnerable.

Sash windows

Prepare in the same way described above. To paint, lower the top frame and raise the bottom to enable you to paint the middle rail, and then follow the procedure given for casement windows.

Doors

Doors and door frames should be prepared in the same way as windows. Again there is a sensible and well tried order of painting (Fig 2).

Unless you can see a door from

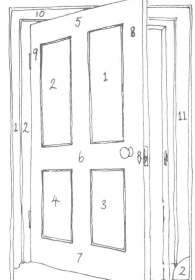

above, there is no need to paint the top of it, or the top of the frame, but if you have to do so, be sure it is clean before you start any painting at all. Specks of dust can ruin wet paintwork. Paint the hinges with great care as you can cause sticking or clog the screw holes. Remove door handles and key latches before you begin.

Furniture

The same rules apply to painting furniture as to door and windows. Wash down the woodwork and sandpaper carefully. Remove handles before you begin. For extra smooth results, sandpaper between coats, using a very fine texture.

Finally, it is very easy for other people or members of the family inadvertently to smudge wet paint, rendering all your hard work less professional looking, simply because they forget that the paint is wet. So it really is worth a visual reminder – just a piece of cardboard, with 'Wet Paint' written on it.

Wallpapering

First prepare your walls. Hanging new paper over old is never satisfactory so, strictly speaking, you should remove old papers. Then sandpaper your walls to give them a smooth finish, fill holes and cracks with filler, and sand again. Paint on a coat of size to prevent the wall from absorbing the paste when applied. This is particularly important on newly plastered walls. Leave them for six months if at all possible to dry out before applying wallpaper.

MATERIALS

You'll need wallpaper, paste and a brush for applying it (unless you are using a ready pasted wall-paper), a brush or sponge to smooth it with, a pair of scissors, a plumb-line, a long flat smooth table top (or ideally a wallpapering table, which is made specially narrow) and an overall or old skirt with large pockets in which to put scissors and other tools. This saves endless hopping up and down ladders. For ceilings, you will also need two stepladders, a wooden plank at least 25cm (9in) wide, a straight ruler about 1m (1yd) long, string, a pencil or chalk and a long cardboard tube about the width of your wallpaper. For papering walls you will need a step ladder, or a sturdy chair with a wooden seat will do. Two people working together makes wallpapering much easier.

CEILINGS

If you are intending to paper the ceiling, this should be done before the walls. As a general rule, the paper should run parallel with the main windows so that the joins are not highlighted, but since most paper is sold in 10m (33ft) rolls, and the average room is between 3m (11ft) and 4.2m (14ft) long you may find this hopelessly un-economic. You may only get two lengths from each roll, leaving you with lots of waste. However, a lot depends on the rest of the room, and if you are using the same paper on the walls. A professional

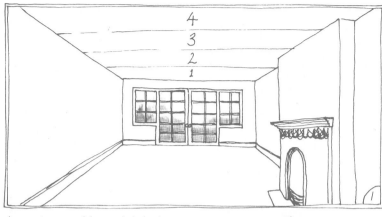

decorator would certainly insist on this method, and would also start from the window and work inwards (Fig 1).

Begin by measuring the width of your paper, and take away 12mm ($\frac{1}{2}$in) to allow you an overlap at the wall angle. Set up your plank between two stepladders or trestles, parallel with the window. Mark the width of your wallpaper on the ceiling at both ends of your plank. Pin a piece of string between these marks, and pencil some marks along the string to guide you (Fig 2).

Measure the length of the room and cut the number of paper lengths required. Match the pattern on the floor, before you cut (Fig 3). Add a good 5cm (2in) to each end of each length, to cater for bumpy top edges to the walls, which may not be apparent now, but may well be found later.

Paste the first length and fold over about 30cm (12in) of one end. Then make a second fold of about 60cm (24in) and turn back the first fold (Fig 4).

Continue to fold the pasted paper

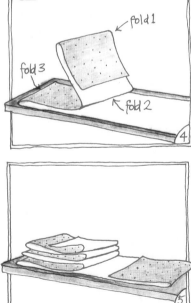

into a pile. Turn in the last 30cm (12in) towards the pile (Fig 5). You will find that this neat folding makes the paper easier to handle. Lay the pile of paper over your cardboard tube or a spare roll of wallpaper, holding the folds firmly between fingers and thumb. Starting in a corner, peel back the last

fold and press it to the ceiling, making sure the outside edge butts along the chalk line (Fig 6). As you walk along the plank, release folds of paper and smooth the paper

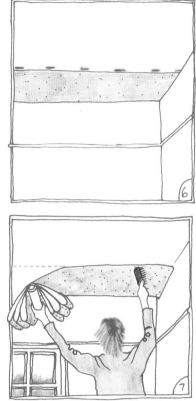

onto the ceiling with your brush (Fig 7). Make sure that you keep the folded paper close to the ceiling.

Score the paper with the blunt side of your scissors at the beginning and end of the paper length pressing into the angle (Fig 8). Pull back the paper, and cut along the score mark made by your scissors, but leave an extra 6mm ($\frac{1}{4}$in) to paste back onto the

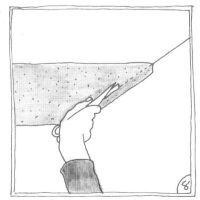

wall. You will find that this ensures a smoothly papered corner between the ceiling and walls – otherwise you can leave tiny gaps. When hanging each length of paper, make sure it butts up to the previous one.

When you come to a ceiling rose (light fixture), switch off the mains, undo the cover of the fixture, release the screws holding the flex and remove the

lampholder and flex. Temporarily screw back the cover loosely and turn on the electricity if necessary. Push the tip of your scissors through the paper at the centre of the bulge. Cut along the paper in the direction you are laying it, about 5cm (2in) on either side of the initial slit, and then make a second cut across the centre to form a cross (Fig 9).

Smooth the paper against the ceiling, pressing it around the edge of the ceiling rose. Make any necessary extra cuts, pull back the surplus flaps of paper, score the crease with the blunt edge of your scissors as before and trim along the crease line (Fig 10).

WALLS

Always start at one side of the main window in a room, work round the room, and then return to the other side of the window. Hold a plumb-line from the top corner of the window frame to see if the frame is exactly vertical; if not you will need to draw a guide line. To do this, measure the width of your paper, subtract 6mm ($\frac{1}{4}$in) and mark that distance in pencil from the edge of the frame onto the wall. Hang your plumb-line just slightly to one side of your mark and draw a straight line through the mark following the line of the plumb.

Cut the paper following the instructions given for papering ceilings. Paste the first length and fold both ends in, one end about half as far as the other (Fig 1). Carry the paper over your arm and hang your first length against the window frame. Hold the pasted side against the wall, keeping the outer edge parallel with the plumb mark, and flip up the top, smaller fold. Press against the ceiling and smooth down, then unfold the lower end of the length and smooth down the wall (Fig 2). Smooth out the paper with a brush getting rid of the bubbles

and score along the ceiling angle with your scissors. Peel back the paper from the ceiling line and cut along the score line as before. Then, with your brush, press the paper into the angle between window frame and wall and score down the overlap (Fig 3). Peel the paper gently back from the frame, and cut from the bottom upwards along the indented line made with

your scissors. Score along the bottom of the paper, peel back and cut as for the top.

Wallpapering a corner

You should not try to paper around a corner, as nine times out of ten the angle is neither vertical nor a right angle, and you will probably find that the paper buckles once you have turned the corner. So measure the distance from the edge of the last piece you have pasted up to the corner at the top, middle and bottom (Fig 4) and add 12mm ($\frac{1}{2}$in) to the widest measurement.

Cut your paper so that only 12mm ($\frac{1}{2}$in) extends around the corner and paste in position. Then cover the overlap with the first length on the next wall.

Windows and doors

When you come to papering around a protruding window ledge or shelf, employ the same principle as that used to fit the paper around a light fitting. Cut the paper to allow for the protrusion and score along the angle. Trim surplus paper to fit.

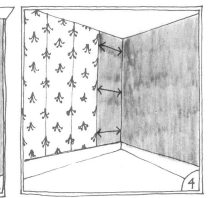

Around the corner of a door or window, cut diagonally from the corner, about 6mm ($\frac{1}{4}$in) beyond the edge of the door or window frame (Fig 5).

Then press the paper against the wall and smooth into the angle with your smoothing brush (Fig 6). With the blunt edge of your scissors score along the angle around the door frame, peel paper back gently and cut along the crease made with your scissors.

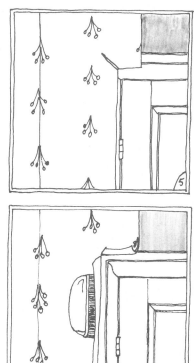

Light switches

To paper around a light switch, first switch off the electricity at the mains (main switch), and then

unscrew the switch plate creating a narrow gap between it and the wall. Some types, particularly in the United States, can be unscrewed entirely, which of course makes the job much easier. Position the pasted paper over the switch and cut the paper into the corners of the plate diagonally (Fig 7). Score the edges with the blunt edge of your scissors. Cut the paper 6mm ($\frac{1}{4}$in) in from your crease line (Fig 8) and then ease the extra 6mm ($\frac{1}{4}$in) into the gap behind the switch plate.

Smooth the paper around the light switch, and sponge off any excess paste. When the paper is dry, screw back the plate and turn on the electricity.

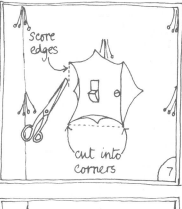

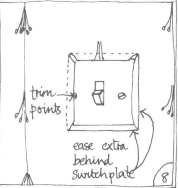

Removing bubbles

You may find it difficult to get rid of all the bubbles of air under your wallpaper. You can remedy this by carefully peeling away the piece from the wall and sponging some extra water on to the patches which are not adhering. If when your paper has dried you still find some offensive bubbles remain, here are two useful remedies. Either you can inject

extra paste into the middle of the bubble, let it soak in, and flatten with your smoothing brush. Or you can make vertical and horizontal cuts through the centre of the bubble with a Stanley (utility) knife (Fig 9). Pull back the corners and apply a good dollop of extra paste. Let the paste soak into the paper, and then flatten the area with a roller or smoothing brush. Peeling edges can be given extra paste too.

APPLYING BORDERS

Decide first how and where you want your border. As many houses have skirting (base) boards and ceilings which are not always even and horizontal, it may be wise to set your border a few inches above the skirting (base) board, and a few inches below the ceiling. Or you may want to run a border below a dado or picture rail. These are usually straight.

The way to establish a perfectly horizontal line for a border is by using a straight edge in the form of a wooden batten, which you can pin lightly onto the wall. Check that it is horizontal with a spirit

level, and then mark a straight pencil line along the wall which you can use as a guide line for your wallpaper border.

You should mitre the border at the corners. For instance, if you are putting a border round a door frame, paste it in place, leaving a good 15cm (6in) unpasted overlap at the corner (Fig 1). Draw a diagonal line with a ruler and sharp pencil across the dotted line marked. Cut along this line and paste the loose ends in position (Fig 2).

Tiling walls

The secret of successful tiling is careful planning and a dry, level surface. Mark a long batten with tile lengths and use this to work out how the tiles will be arranged around worksurfaces, windows, or other fittings. You should try to end up with equal-sized tiles in corners and either side of a window and full size tiles over sinks and work surfaces and on the edge of window recesses.

As skirting (base) boards are seldom exactly horizontal, the professional's tip is to fix a wooden batten along the bottom of the wall, its top one tile's depth above the lowest point of the skirting board, to support the first row of tiles and make sure all subsequent rows are straight. So begin by finding the correct horizontal line for your batten using a spirit level (Fig 1). Nail the batten in place with masonry nails, avoiding pipes or wires.

When tiling a plain wall, you should work out the rows so that equal-sized tiles will be left at either end of the wall. To do this,

you start in the centre. Measure the length of the batten and divide in two to find the centre point of the wall. Mark this with a vertical line using a plumb-line (Fig 2).

If you end up with narrow gaps at either end, move the centre tile to one side and rework the line to leave a larger space at either end. Apply your tile adhesive to the wall above the batten using a notched spreader (Fig 3).

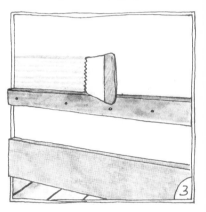

Manufacturers often supply one of these with the can of adhesive, and they are vital. You will need a waterproof adhesive if you are tiling around baths, basins or kitchen sinks. If your walls are particularly uneven, be liberal with the adhesive. A thickness of 3mm ($\frac{1}{8}$in) is normal. Cover one row at a time.

To cut a tile at the end of a row,

place one complete tile over the one you have just laid. Then place another complete tile on top of it to span the gap between it and the wall. Score the surface of the middle tile, using the edge of the top tile as a guideline (Fig 4). Then lay the tile, glazed side up, on top of a matchstick, with the match set directly under the score line. Push both sides down firmly, so that the tile snaps along the line (Fig 5). Press the cut tile in place.

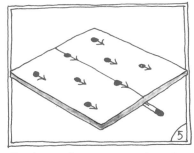

Cutting a tile on a curve is not as easy. First mark the shape to be cut on the face of the tile, and then score the tile with the tile cutter, going over the curved line several times. Then, with pincers, break away the tile bit by bit (Fig 6) until you have achieved the right shape. Smooth away any jagged edges with pumice stone or a file.

Continue row by row up the wall until you reach the ceiling. Leave until the adhesive has dried, usually about 14 hours later, then remove the batten and complete the bottom row, cutting as necessary.

You should finish by grouting the gaps between the tiles with a white filler. Make up the grouting cement following instructions on the packet, and then apply it, remembering to wear rubber gloves. You can use either a sponge or a small palette knife. Clean up the tiles when you have finished and when it has started to dry smooth it off with a rounded implement, such as a thick pencil, to give a neat finish.

Floorcoverings

Floors can be covered in a variety of ways: vinyl, cork or ceramic tiles, hardboard, parquet tiles, sheet vinyl, or of course carpet. Sanding and sealing your floor boards, if they are in reasonably good condition, can look very attractive, and if you are planning to move on soon you can invest in rugs to move with you. Your final choice will depend partly on your budget, partly on the function of the room.

LAYING FLOOR TILES

First prepare your surface. A cement floor may be uneven, and it will certainly need cleaning. To smooth out the bumps you can buy a special filler which you simply mix with water and apply with a trowel. The mixture will automatically smooth itself out, finding its own level. To prepare wooden floor boards for vinyl or cork tiles, first cover them with hardboard. (See how under 'Laying Hardboard' below.) Ceramic tiles should only be laid onto a concrete screed, as they need a really firm foundation. The 'give' in wooden floor boards, even when covered with hardboard, will only crack them up in time.

Planning the layout

The walls of a room almost never make exact right angles with each other. This means that you should always lay floor tiles of all kinds working from the centre of the room outwards. To find the centre point of the room, measure the two shorter facing walls, and mark their centre points X and Y (Fig 1). Draw a line between X and Y and mark the centre of this line M. Measure points A and B 90cm (3ft) either side of M. Then make up a piece of string 135cm (4ft 6in) long with one end tied to a piece of chalk and the other to a drawing pin. Pin the drawing pin into point A and draw two arcs, one on each side of the line. Do the same with the pin at point B. They cross at points C and D (Fig 2).

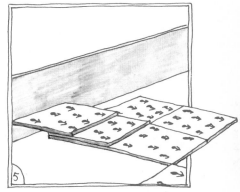

Next mark a line between C and D, and continue this on to the two longer walls (Fig 3). You will now have divided the room into four equal parts. You may need a second pair of hands to help you, and while this may seem to be a great deal of unnecessary trouble, it's the only accurate way to plan the layout of your tiles.

Laying vinyl or cork tiles

You should lay your tiles in the

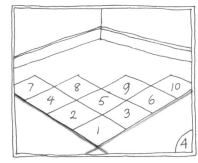

sequence indicated in Fig 4, spreading the adhesive first with a notched spreader.

Continue laying your tiles in this way until you reach the walls. To cut a tile to fill a narrow gap next to the wall, place one complete tile on top of the one you have just laid (Fig 5). Then place another

complete tile on top of it, to span the gap between it and the wall. Score the surface of the middle tile, using the edge of the top tile as a guideline. Cut along the score line (see 'Tiling Walls' Fig 5). Once all the tiles have been laid, do not walk across them until the adhesive has had time to dry.

Laying ceramic tiles

Mark the floor as described above, to plan the layout. Lay your tiles

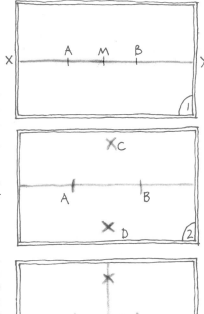

out dry along the centre line before sticking them down. If there is a gap at either end move the centre tile over to allow room for two cut tiles of equal size at either end. If this is necessary, mark the position of each tile with a pencil before you stick the first one down. Lay the tiles in the same way as for ceramic wall tiles.

LAYING A HARDBOARD FLOOR

First of all, prepare your floor surface. Begin by punching nails to sink them below the surface (Fig 1). Sweep the floor and check whether you need to replace any of the floor boards.

Most hardboard is sold in

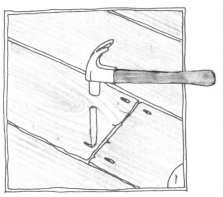

2.4 × 1.2m (8 × 4ft) sheets, but if you can, order it in 1.2m (4ft) squares or cut the sheets in half yourself. First find the centre point of the room (see 'Floor Tiles'). Then find the centre of the square of hardboard, by marking the diagonals with a pencil and ruler (Fig 2).

If you are going to cover the hardboard with tiles, lay it rough side up, if not, smooth side up. Place the centre of the hardboard

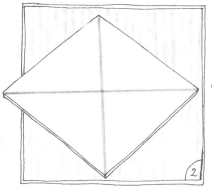

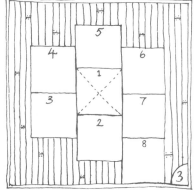

on top of the centre point of the room and then lay the remaining squares around the first board, working clockwise, and staggering the joins (Fig 3).

To fix the boards, use 2.5cm (1in) nails and hammer around the edges 12mm ($\frac{1}{2}$in) in, leaving a gap of 10cm (4in) between each nail. Then hammer in rows of nails about 15cm (6in) apart, leaving a gap of 15cm (6in) between each nail. Work from the centre out.

To cut the edge strips to fit the skirting (base) board (which may of course not be straight), lay a piece of hardboard on top of the boards already nailed in place, making sure it is sitting squarely

and parallel with the nailed boards but just touching the skirting (base) board (Fig 4).

To mark the shape of the skirting (base) board, hold a pencil against a small wooden block wider than the maximum gap between the hardboard and the skirting (base) board (about 5cm 2in square should do) and push the block and the pencil along the skirting (base) board (Fig 5).

Cut along your pencil line, and

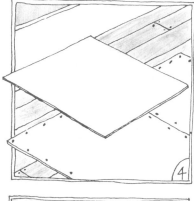

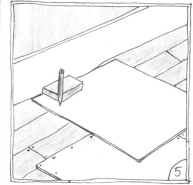

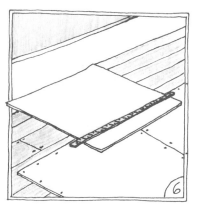

then push the board into place, against the skirting (base) board. Next mark on your loose board the position of the edge of the adjacent nailed boards (Fig 6).

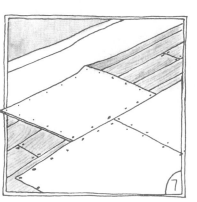

Draw a pencil line joining them, using a straight edge.

Cut the board along your ruled line and nail it in place (Fig 7).

To cut hardboard pieces to fit around any awkward shapes such as door frames or bay windows, make a paper pattern and use it to cut out the appropriate shape of hardboard.

LAYING PARQUET FLOOR TILES

First lay a hardboard sub floor (see above) and then follow the instructions given for laying floor tiles, but when you reach the edge of the walls, leave a 12mm ($\frac{1}{2}$in) gap to allow for expansion. To span this gap, nail a 2.5cm (1in) thick quadrant (quarter round) moulding to the skirting (base) board (Fig 1).

Once you have laid the floor, sand away any bumps which may have occurred where the tiles join, and then apply a suitable seal. If you want a shiny finish, then you may need to apply several coats. Allow each coat to dry thoroughly before applying the next.

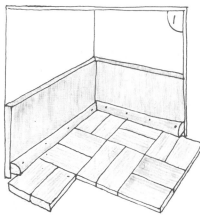

LAYING SHEET VINYL

This is one of the easiest floorings to lay, although handling extra wide rolls can be tricky. For really professional results, it is worth making the effort to avoid centre seams if you possibly can.

Firstly, unroll your flooring and spread it out over the floor. Let the edges curl up over the skirting (base) board by 2.5cm (1in) and if you have any seams, overlap these by 2.5cm (1in) making sure that the pattern matches (Fig 1). Leave the flooring to settle for a couple of days before fitting it exactly. To cut accurately around obstacles like a chimney, make a paper pattern and transfer markings to the sheet vinyl.

To make a seam in unpatterned

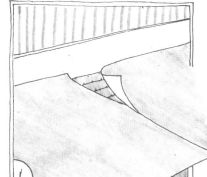

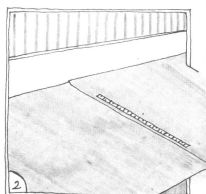

vinyl, lay a steel ruler or straight piece of wood to line up with the centre of your 2.5cm (1in) overlap (Fig 2). Then, using a Stanley (utility) knife, cut through both layers of vinyl. The pieces will then fit exactly, even if the cutting line is a little uneven. Patterned vinyl must be butt jointed accurately or overlapped by a complete pattern width.

Peel away the strip you have cut off the top layer, fold back the top layer for a few inches and then remove the cut off strip from the layer below it (Fig 3).

Fold back both pieces of vinyl at the seams and apply adhesive to the sub floor. Stick vinyl down firmly, weighted with piles of books or any suitable heavy weight, for 12 hours or so.

Trim the sheet against the skirting (base) board with your knife. Draw the knife along the angle between the floor and skirting (base) board, slowly and firmly, pressing into the angle (Fig 4).

Fold back the edges of the vinyl

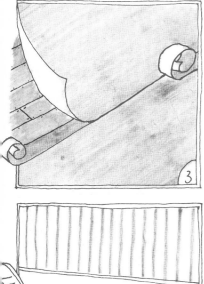

and apply adhesive to the floor as before. To cut the vinyl at corners (Fig 5), you should press the sheet into the corner and then clip the 2.5cm (1in) overlap as shown. Make two clips for an internal corner, meeting at the corner point, and one clip for an external corner.

LAYING CARPET
Latex backed carpets
These are obviously the easiest to lay for the amateur. Unlike carpets with a woven back, they do not need to be stretched, or gripped at the edges. Follow the instructions given for laying sheet vinyl (see page 104) but you will not of course need to overlap joins. Simply fit them together with adhesive carpet tape which is made specially for the purpose. Alternatively you can use a 2.5cm

(1in) wide woven tape. Apply your latex carpet adhesive to the underside edges of the carpet and to the tape. Then press the edges firmly onto the tape, making sure they are butted closely together (Fig 1).

Hessian (jute) backed carpet
To cope successfully, you need to hire or borrow a 'knee kicker' which stretches the carpet over gripper pins nailed all the way around the edge of the room. It is a tool used by professional carpet layers, and most do it yourself hire (rental) shops stock them.

Begin by covering your bare floor boards with grey felt carpet lining paper. You can staple this in place. Next fix carpet gripper strips around the edge of the room,

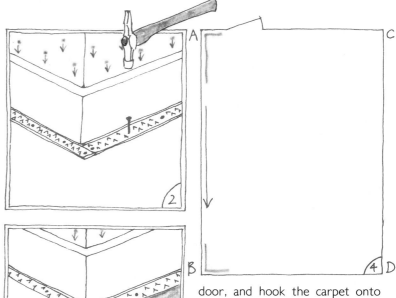

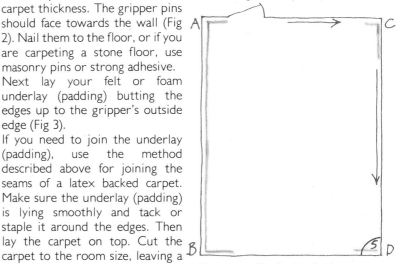

leaving a narrow channel between each strip and the wall, half the carpet thickness. The gripper pins should face towards the wall (Fig 2). Nail them to the floor, or if you are carpeting a stone floor, use masonry pins or strong adhesive.

Next lay your felt or foam underlay (padding) butting the edges up to the gripper's outside edge (Fig 3).

If you need to join the underlay (padding), use the method described above for joining the seams of a latex backed carpet. Make sure the underlay (padding) is lying smoothly and tack or staple it around the edges. Then lay the carpet on top. Cut the carpet to the room size, leaving a 7.5cm (3in) margin if there is carpet to spare, as the carpet should first be fixed to the grippers and then cut exactly to size. But if you only just have the right amount of carpet and no more, it does not matter. You will have less to play with if the walls happen to be out of line, but you can usually mask any gaps with extra stretching.

Start in one corner (A in Fig 4), preferably the one nearest the

door, and hook the carpet onto the gripper pins for about 30cm (12in) on either side of the corner. Then stretch the carpet by hand and hook it into corner B in the same way.

Go back to the first corner and hook the carpet onto the gripper strip all the way along the wall between AB. Then work from A stretching the carpet by hand into

C corner. Finally hook the carpet into D corner – again stretching by hand (Fig 5).

At this point you need to stretch the carpet with the knee kicker. To use it, you press down the pronged end into the carpet, and bang the padded end with your knee, stretching the carpet until you are able to hook it onto the gripper pins (Fig 6).

Work across the room stretching the whole carpet towards wall

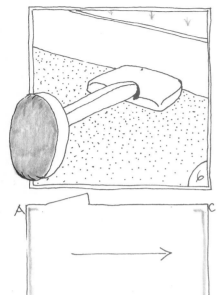

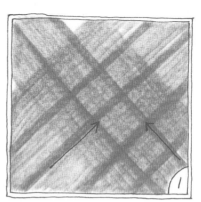

Covering walls with fabric

other fixtures, work carefully, cutting a little at a time (Fig 8).

Next, using a bolster chisel (or flat trowel, or even a narrow piece of wood) push the raw edge of the carpet down into the channel between the gripper and the wall. You may find it helps to use a hammer as well to get the carpet properly wedged (Fig 9). Finish off the raw edge at the doorway with a metal edging strip cut to size, which you simply nail in place.

row by about 7.5cm (3in), and if necessary repeat the process in the opposite diagonal direction (Fig 1).

Change to a medium or fine abrasive paper and sand the floor again, but this time moving in the same direction as the floor boards. Overlap each row in the same way, and cover the area twice in opposite directions. Along the edges next to the skirting (base) board, you will need to use the small sander or power drill, and any awkward corners such as around the door frames may need to be sandpapered by hand.

Finish off with a thorough vacuum clean before sponging down. Then leave to dry and apply your floor seal. You will need several coats; leave each one to dry thoroughly before applying the next.

One of the easiest ways to apply fabric to walls is to buy a professional decorator's system which has been adapted to suit a do it yourself market. Most of these systems contain plastic or metal battens designed to screw vertically onto the wall, and which incorporate some kind of grip edge into which the selvedges of the material are slotted.

A far cheaper alternative is of course to make your own frame using 2.5cm (1in) square timber battens, cut to the height of your room. These are screwed vertically to the walls, the fabric tacked in place and the seams covered with braid.

First make a sketch of your room, drawing up the measurements of one wall at a time. Include features like doors, windows or fireplaces. Measure the distance from the top of the skirting (base) board to just below the ceiling, to give you the height of your vertical battens, then draw them in position, remembering that separate areas, such as above a door or above and below a window, need separate frames (Fig 1). Measure the distance between the vertical battens to work out the length of the horizontal battens you will need in order to frame individual sections of the walls.

Next, cut your vertical battens to size and screw them in place. Cut the horizontal battens to fit in

CD, and hook it all the way along. Finally hook it on to the two remaining walls, AC and BD (Fig 7). At this stage the edges will be folded up against the skirting (base) board. Even if your carpet is a very close fit, you should still have worked up a bit of surplus, which should now be cut away. Using a sharp Stanley (utility) knife, cut away this surplus, leaving enough to tuck into the gap behind the gripper strip. About 6mm ($\frac{1}{4}$in) should be enough. Around door frames or

SANDING A FLOOR

The simplest way to sand a floor is by hiring a large sanding machine for the main floor areas. To get into the edges and awkward areas of the floor inaccessible to the large sanding machine, you will need a smaller rotary sanding machine or an electric power drill with a sanding attachment to which you fix an abrasive disc.

First make sure that all the floor boards are firmly fixed. Check that all the nail heads are punched in or you could damage the sanding machine.

Sanding is a messy operation, so be warned. Apart from wearing your oldest clothes, you will find that a scarf tied loosely over the nose and mouth helps prevent your breathing in fine wood dust. Seal the room with plastic sheeting from the outside, to stop dust coating the rest of your house.

Begin with a heavy weight abrasive paper on the machine, start at one corner of the room and work diagonally across it. To re-sand the same line, you should pull the machine backwards without tilting it. Overlap each sanding

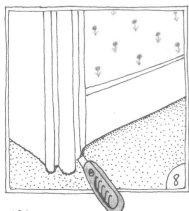

between the verticals and butt them above the skirting (base) board and below the ceiling. Screw them in place.

Next, taking each wall at a time, work out how many widths of fabric you will need to join together to cover each wall. Remember to add 12mm ($\frac{1}{2}$in) on each side of the side hems and a 12mm ($\frac{1}{2}$in) allowance for each seam. Match patterns carefully and if your pattern has a large central motif, it is important to place this in the centre of the wall, joining fabric pieces at each side, so that the seams balance.

Cut the appropriate lengths of fabric, adding 5cm (2in) to the measurement from the top of the skirting (base) board to the ceiling. This will allow you a 2.5cm (1in) hem along the top and bottom edges. With right sides facing, stitch the fabric lengths together in the right order.

Cut away the selvedges and press seams open. Then turn in 2.5cm (1in) to the wrong side along the top and bottom edges, and stitch in place, as near to the outside edge as possible. Next turn in a 12mm ($\frac{1}{2}$in) hem along the side edges which will butt into the corners of the room. When you have stitched together all the pieces needed to cover one wall, tack the fabric to the batten at the top left-hand corner of the wall, using 12mm ($\frac{1}{2}$in) upholstery tacks. Stretch it across the top batten, leaving a distance of about 7.5cm (3in) between each tack.

Then stretch the fabric lengthways, and tack it along the bottom horizontal battens above the skirting (base) board. Finally stretch the fabric widthways, and tack the outside edges to the vertical battens. You can if you prefer use an industrial staple gun to secure the fabric, but if you want to remove it for cleaning at a later date, upholstery tacks are easier to remove, and will not damage the fabric as much as staples. Once the room is complete, you should cover your rows of tacks with upholstery braid, using a light clear glue.

Tenting a ceiling

First, with a pencil and straight edge draw a continuous line around the walls of the room, level with the top of the door or the window, depending on which is higher (Fig 1).

Measure the length of the line on each wall and cut battens of 2.5cm (1in) square timber to fit all the way around the wall, butting the bottom edge of the batten onto your pencil line. Measure the distance from the centre of the ceiling to the corner bottom edge of the battens (A to B in Fig 2).

Cut out a paper pattern, a large

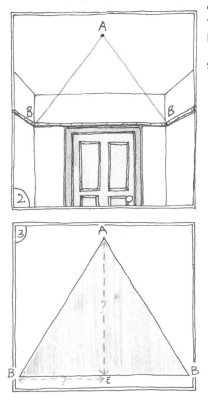

triangle with two equal sides measuring the same as from A to B plus 5cm (2in) and the other side as long as from B to B in Fig 2. Fold the pattern in half, along the dotted line A to E in Fig 3 and measure the distance from A to E and B to E. Cut along your dotted and folded line.

Cut out a rectangular piece of paper measuring A to E long and B to E wide. Sellotape (tape) this piece in between the two triangles, butting A to E lines together (Fig 4).

Using your paper pattern as a

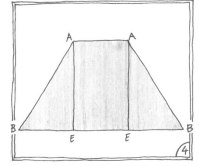

guide, cut and sew together your fabric to make up four shapes like the one in Fig 4, one for each side of your four-sided pyramid. If the room is not perfectly square, check the measurements of your walls, and adjust the size of fabric pieces appropriately.

With right sides facing, machine stitch the four sides of the pyramid

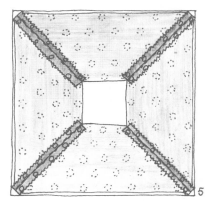

together (Fig 5). Press seams open. Turn in a 6mm ($\frac{1}{4}$in) fold around the inside edge, and then a second 12mm ($\frac{1}{2}$in) fold. Pin, tack (baste) and stitch, to make a casing all the way round. Leave a small gap in the stitching, and thread string through. Run two lines of gathering along each of the four outside edges, the first 12mm ($\frac{1}{2}$in) in from the raw edge, and the second line 6mm ($\frac{1}{4}$in) in. Draw up the gathering threads until they match the width of the batten onto which they will be fixed. Next make up a continuous fabric pelmet (valance) with a zig-zag or scalloped edge (see page 153) to fit all the way around the room. It should be the same length as the sum total of all four battens.

To join the gathered outside edges of the tent to this pelmet (valance), first mark the position of each wall length on the pelmet

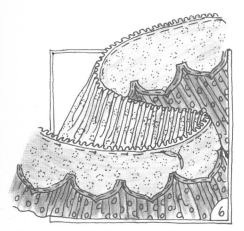

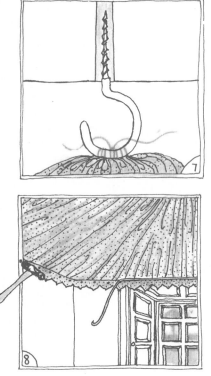

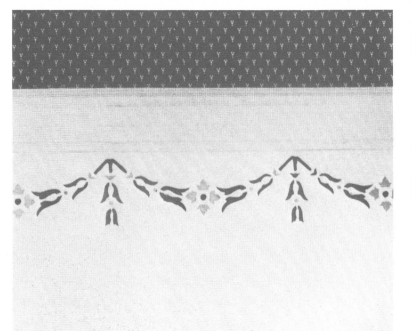

Stencils

Stencils can be applied to all kinds of surfaces: walls, furniture and even fabric blinds (shades) can all look very decorative and original. It is always a good idea to test your stencil first on paper, to work out the right colours, and how much pattern you want to apply to the room or furniture you intend to decorate.

TO MAKE YOUR OWN STENCIL

Work out your design first on a piece of paper (or make a tracing of a suitable shape). Transfer the design onto thin cardboard, then cut out the shapes very carefully using a sharp scalpel or knife. Simple shapes work best and the cut-outs need to be divided by a small but not too narrow space between each, so that different colours do not run into each other.

STENCILLING ON WALLS

First place your stencil on the wall and tape it firmly in position. Then you can either draw around the stencil shapes using a hard pencil, remove the stencil and paint the shapes by hand, or you can spray paint. The first method takes longer, but is easier to master and makes it easier to apply different shades of one colour. The second method can be messy, so you must mask the area of wall around the stencil. Following the instructions on the aerosol can, hold it about 15cm (6in) or more away from your stencil and apply a light spray. Do not overpaint: all too

(valance). Then with right sides facing, and raw edges lined up, pin, tack (baste) and stitch the gathered outside edges of your tent to the pelmet (valance) top (Fig 6). Drill and plug a hole at the centre point of your ceiling and screw a good strong hook to it (first ensuring there is a ceiling joist above to carry the weight). Then draw up the string threaded through the casing of the tent, and tie it to the hook (Fig 7).

Tack the pelmet (valance) to the battens screwed around the edge of the room with 6mm ($\frac{1}{4}$in) upholstery tacks along the top edge of the pelmet (valance) (Fig 8). Finally, lightly glue braid over the line of tacks to conceal them.

easily the paint can begin to run. If necessary spray on a second coat, but apply each coat like very gentle rain, sparsely and evenly. Leave the paint to dry before removing your stencil.

To apply more than one colour, mask with shiny brown paper or cardboard all areas not to be painted with that colour. For example if you were applying the stencil shown in Fig 1, you would need to mask the leaves, stems, flower petals, and centres, before applying the colour intended for the flower pot.

You would then mask the petals, flower centres and flower pot while applying the colour intended for the leaves and stems and so on.

Depending on how experienced you are (or become) it is also possible to shade individual areas of a stencil using an aerosol can. Practise first on paper, to see what different colours look like next to each other.

STENCILLING ON SOFTWOOD

The wood must be carefully sanded first, and untreated. One of the easiest ways to colour the stencil is to use felt tipped pens, but you should first test your pens on a spare piece of wood. You may find some pens run and others do not, so experiment first. Apply the stencil as described above, firmly taping it to the area to be decorated. Once you've coloured it, leave to dry, and then remove the stencil. Seal with a clear varnish. Leave to dry, sand the surface, and apply a second coat. For an extra shiny finish, leave to dry, sand again and apply a third coat.

STENCILLING ON FABRIC OR HOLLAND BLINDS (SHADES)

This can be done with felt pens, as described above, but to be strictly practical (if you want to be able to sponge your blinds, or wash the fabric), you need to pencil the outline of the stencil and then paint in the colours with fabric paints such as those made by Dylon or Rowney. To fix the colours, wait for them to dry and then very carefully iron, placing a scrap of lightweight material between the iron and the stencilled area of fabric. (Read the fabric dye manufacturer's instructions and stick to them. Some may need a longer exposure to heat than others.)

WINDOW DRESSING

Making your own window coverings is one of the biggest money savers there is for home sewers. It is also one of the easiest home sewing projects for beginners to kick off with. On the U.K. market there is a good range of different heading tapes to choose from. In the U.S. curtain tapes work on a different system and the standard gathering tape referred to in the following section is not available, so American readers should follow manufacturer's instructions for the curtain headings.

Curtains

Curtain (drape) styles should vary to reflect the style of your room. For example, half length curtains with frilled edges, will look cottagey. So consider the options carefully.

Choosing the style

As well as creating a certain 'look', curtains can also produce optical illusions, so that the dimensions of the window, even the room, can seem to be altered, as these examples show.

To make a window look wider: extend the track (rod) beyond the frame (Fig 1). Because this means

the curtains need not overlap the window when they are pulled back, an extra advantage is that the maximum light is let in.

To make a window look taller: position the track (rod) some distance above the top of the frame, perhaps about 20cm (8in), to fake extra height (Fig 2). By covering the space between the top of the window and the track with a

pelmet (valance), the illusion is maintained even when the curtains are drawn back (Fig 3).

To disguise architectural irregularities: treat different shapes and sizes of window and even doors in the same way (Fig 4). If necessary,

have an entire wall covered with fabric when the curtains are drawn across.

To reduce the height of a window: reduce the window area with a shaped pelmet (Fig 5) or a draped valance (Fig 6). This always looks elegant and the deeper and more ornate the pelmet or valance, the grander the effect.

To reduce the width of a window: use tie-backs and join the curtains at the top (Fig 7).

To make a small, high window look larger: improve the proportions by mounting café curtains on a track (rod) or pole which is

wider than the window (Fig 8). You could also hang café curtains from the sill to cover the wall below.

To maximize the light from a dormer window: use a right-angled, U-shaped track (rod) so that the curtains can be kept clear of the window when they are drawn back (Fig 9).

To enhance a beautiful window: ensure that the curtains do not obscure it. If you are lucky enough to have a window which is archi-

tecturally pleasing, emphasize its unusual shape. Over an arched window, for instance, use a curved pelmet or valance (Fig 10) or, for a simpler treatment, use a rod or pole which is wide enough to clear the curtains from the window during the day.

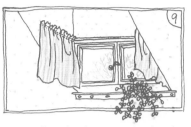

To set the style of the decor: remember that, as a general rule, full-length curtains look elegant and often rather formal (Fig 11). Sill-length curtains, on the other hand, will look more informal (Fig 12).

Choosing the heading

The curtain's heading will be determined by the effect you want to achieve and by your budget. Some headings require more fabric than others. Standard gathering tape requires a fullness one-and-a-half times the track (rod) width. Pencil pleats take two-and-a-quarter times the width and pinch pleats two-and-a-half times (Fig 13).

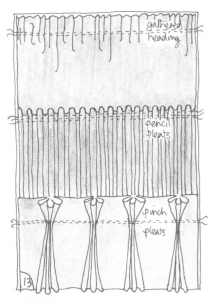

Measuring up

First measure the finished length of the curtains (Fig 14) and add 22cm (8½in) for hems and heading. This allows 15cm (6in) for a double 7.5cm (3in) lower hem and 7cm (2½in) for a standard gathered heading. Next, measure the width of the *rod* (not the window) and add 5cm (2in) for each side hem and a further 15cm (6in) if the curtains are to overlap at the centre. Multiply this measurement by the fullness dictated by the style of heading (see Choosing the heading). Divide this total width by the width of the chosen fabric –

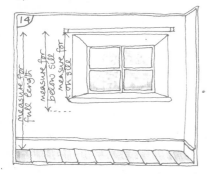

usually 122cm (48in) – and round up to the nearest full number to find how many widths of fabric the curtains will take.

Finally, multiply the curtain length and turnings by the number of widths to find the amount of fabric to buy. If the fabric is not pre-shrunk, allow about 2.5cm (1in) per metre (yard) extra. If the fabric has a pattern repeat, allow extra for matching, i.e. the depth of one pattern repeat for each width.

Cutting out the fabric

Lay the fabric flat on a clean floor or on a large table if there is one big enough. It is important to cut straight across the fabric at right angles to the selvedge, otherwise the curtains will not hang straight. Make one end straight either by drawing a thread which runs across the weave and cutting along this pulled thread or by using a set square or a square edge of cardboard to mark a straight line with a pencil and a straight edge.

Measure the length of the first width down each selvedge and mark with pins. Fold the fabric along the pin line and cut along the fold.

If the fabric has a large pattern,

plan the length so that the *hemline* (i.e. 15cm [6in] up from the cutting line) comes below a complete pattern rather than cutting one in half. A half pattern is not nearly so obvious at the top of the curtain where it is absorbed in the heading (Fig 15). Cut the number of widths required in the same way, making sure that on a patterned fabric each length starts at the same point of the pattern repeat. To cut a half width, first fold the

cut length in half lengthways and then cut along the fold.

On fabric which has a high sheen or a pile such as velvet, mark the top of each length so that all the fabric will hang in the same direction when the curtain is made up. With these fabrics, the way the light catches them can make a noticeable difference to the shade. With a pile fabric particularly, you first decide which way you prefer it to hang – when the pile runs upwards it makes the fabric look darker and richer, but it also collects the dust more quickly.

UNLINED CURTAINS

Unless curtains are sheer, they will hang better when lined. However, there can be occasions when unlined is preferable and the technique for making them is basic to making any curtain.

Matching patterns where necessary (see page 150), begin by joining the widths and any half widths using a flat seam (see page 149) with a 12mm (½in) allowance. Trim off the selvedges as these will pucker the seams because the weave is tighter than on the main body of the fabric. Alternatively, make notches along the selvedge at 15cm (6in) intervals or so. Press the seam open.

Turn in and press 5cm (2in) on each side edge. Make a double 2.5cm (1in) hem, pin, tack (baste) to within 6.5cm (2½in) of the top edge and 15cm (6in) of the lower edge. Turn up and press 15cm (6in) along the lower edge.

Press in the mitre at each corner (see page 151) then turn in and press the raw edge to make the double 7.5cm (3in) hem.

The side turnings (hems) can be machine stitched but, for a more professional finish, hand stitch them using a loose slip stitch (Fig 1). Stitch the mitre then stitch the hem using either the same loose slip stitch or herringbone stitch (Fig 2).

To weight the curtains, before stitching the hem and mitres either insert a polyester weighted tape through the hem and stitch in place or sew lead buttons into the corners (Fig 3).

Turn down and press 6.5cm (2½in) along the top of the curtain. Make a line of tacking 4cm (1½in) down from the foldline.

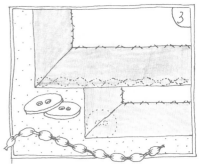

Standard gathering tape

Cut the tape to the width of the curtain plus 5cm (2in) for turnings. Pull out about 2.5cm (1in) of the cords at each end of the tape. Knot the cords together on the wrong side at one end of the tape and knot them loosely together on the right side at the other end. Position the right-side knot at the outer edge of the curtain, i.e. *not* the edge where the two curtains will meet. Turning under 2.5cm (1in) at each end, pin and tack the tape to the wrong side of the curtain with the top edge along the line of tacking. Next tack the ends and lower edge in place. Machine stitch the tape, working both top and bottom edges in the same direction. Draw up the cord from the loosely-knotted end to fit the track (rod) and space the gathers evenly. Knot the cords to hold them in position then tie the long ends in a bow.

Pencil pleat and pinch pleat tapes

These are applied in the same way as the standard tape except that they are positioned almost at the

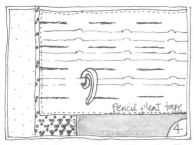

top of the curtain (Fig 4). To arrange pinch pleats symmetrically, gather the tape before attaching it to the curtain and mark the positions of the pleats with a pencil. Do not place a pleat on the outer edges where instead there should be a single hook. Where curtains overlap at the

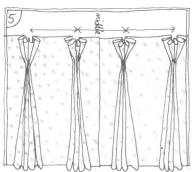

centre, position the pleats so that their spacing will be even across the two curtains when closed (Fig 5). Once the pleats are marked, smooth out the tape again to apply it to the curtain.

LINED CURTAINS

Unless curtains are specifically intended to filter light and create a semi-sheer effect, it is best to line them. This will protect the main fabric from outside dirt and from rotting and fading in strong sunlight and also give better insulation. The curtains will also hang much better.

Loose lining

This is one of the quickest and easiest methods of lining curtains. First work out what your curtain should measure when made up. The lining should be cut out to this size. The curtain, unmade up, should be 12cm (5in) wider and 22.5cm (9in) longer than the lining.

Join the widths of the curtain fabric and then of the lining fabric. Place the lining on top of the curtain, right sides facing, the top of the lining 7.5cm (3in) below the top of the main fabric and with side edges matching. Pin the side edges together and machine stitch 12mm ($\frac{1}{2}$in) from the edge, from the top of the lining to 15cm (6in) from the bottom of the lining (Fig 1). Remove selvedges or notch seam allowance.

Turn up and press 5cm (2in) to the wrong side along the lower edge of the lining and make a double 2.5cm (1in) hem. Machine stitch. Turn up and press 15cm (6in) to the wrong side of the main fabric, press in the mitres and tack a double 6.5cm (3in) hem, thus making the lining 5cm (2in) shorter than the curtain (Fig 2). Turn lining and fabric right sides out, matching centres so that there is a

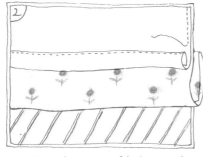

border of curtain fabric on the wrong side (Fig 3). Slip stitch (see page 148) the remaining side edges of the lining to the curtain. Stitch the mitre (see page 151) and hem (see Unlined Curtains) of the curtain and remove tacking threads.

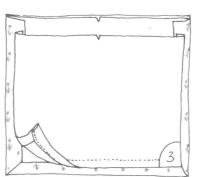

Turn down and press 7.5cm (3in) along the top of the curtain and press in the mitres. Tack in place over the lining. Pin and tack the heading tape in place then complete as given for unlined curtains. Trim away excess curtain fabric at the top edge after tacking in place over the lining if standard gathering tape is to be used, so that the raw edge will be hidden under the tape.

Locked-in lining

This is the method most often favoured by the professionals because it gives the best hang of all. As with loose lined curtains, the curtain fabric should measure 12cm (5in) wider, and 22.5cm (9in) longer than the finished flat curtain. The lining should be 4cm ($1\frac{1}{2}$in) smaller all the way round.

Join the widths of the curtain fabric and then of the lining in the usual way.

On the curtain fabric, turn in and press 6.5cm ($2\frac{1}{2}$in) down each side edge and 15cm (6in) along the lower edge. Press in the mitres (see page 151). Loosely slip stitch the side turnings, stitch the mitres and either slip stitch or herringbone the hem (see Unlined curtains).

Lay the curtain fabric face down on a large, clean surface. Using tailor's chalk and a long ruler draw vertical lines every 30cm (12in), or 39cm (15in) on a very wide curtain.

With wrong sides facing, place the lining on top of the curtain fabric, positioning it 2cm ($\frac{3}{4}$in) below the top edge.

Fold back one side of the lining lengthways to reveal the first chalk line. Beginning 18cm (7in)

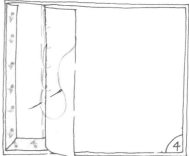

down from the top of the curtain, lock stitch the lining to the curtain (see page 148) (Fig 4) making large, loose stitches about 10–13cm (4–5in) apart. Continue down to the top of the curtain hem.

Smooth the lining out again and fold back the other side to correspond with the next chalk line and lock stitch as before (Fig 5). Continue in this way until the lining is stitched in place at each chalk line.

Turn in and press 2cm ($\frac{3}{4}$in) along

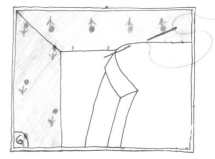

each side edge of the lining and 4cm ($1\frac{1}{2}$in) along the lower edge. Slip stitch the lining in place along these three edges.

Turn in and press 7.5cm (3in) at the top of the curtain and 7cm ($2\frac{3}{4}$in) at the top of the lining, both to their respective wrong sides. Mitre all corners. Slip stitch in place (Fig 6) and apply the heading tape as before.

Interlining

This is the ultimate luxurious finish for curtains. The special fabric, known as bump or domette – a fleecy flannel – gives them a lush thickness and is very effective as insulation against the cold.

To join the widths, overlap the edges and make two parallel lines of machine stitching as shown in Fig 7. Make up the widths to measure the same as the curtain fabric without any additions for side turnings or hems.

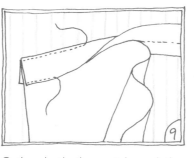

Lay the interlining on the wrong side of the curtain fabric, positioning it 7.5cm (3in) from the top edge and 6.5cm (2½in) from each side (Fig 8). Lock stitch the interlining to the curtain fabric in the same way as for locked-in lining.

Turn the side edges of the curtain over the interlining and press. Turn up and press the lower hem along the edge of the interlining, pressing in the mitres at each corner (see page 151). Loosely stitch the side edges and hem as given for unlined curtains, slip stitching the mitres.

Apply the lining to the interlining as given for a locked-in lining.

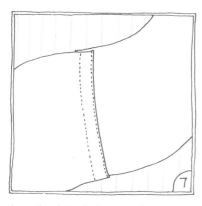

Thermal linings are available either foam-backed (in the US only) or of milium. These are attached to the curtains in the same way as a normal lining and eliminate the need for interlining.

Detachable lining

This makes a useful protective cover to the back of a curtain and some, like milium linings, provide effective heat insulation. It is easily removed for frequent cleaning which is particularly necessary in a dirty city. It will not, however, improve the hang of the curtain.

Make up both the curtain and the lining as given for unlined curtains. The curtains will be finished off with the chosen heading tape as usual but the lining requires a special tape for detachable linings. The top edge of the lining slips between the two layers of the tape (Fig 9) and is machine stitched in place. The top edge of the lining does not require any turning. Measure the finished depth from the base of the heading tape.

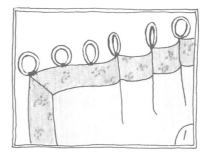

Gather both the curtain and the lining to the required width. Insert the hooks through the buttonholes at the top of the lining tape and then through the heading tape pockets before turning them round to their correct hanging position. In the USA a special snap tape is available.

CURTAINS WITHOUT HEADING TAPE

For all the tailored sophistication you can achieve with ready-made tapes, the old-fashioned methods of headings without tapes still have a simplicity and prettiness which make them worth considering. They may also fit in better with your chosen style of decoration.

Sewn-on rings

Perhaps the simplest method is the brass or wooden curtain ring sewn directly to the top of the curtain (Fig 1).

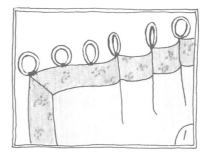

Make a proper turned-in hem at the top of the curtain where the raw edge of a single turning would normally be covered by the heading tape. Sew the rings firmly to the top edge, leaving gaps of about 10cm (4in) between each one. Slide the rings onto a wooden pole or metal rod.

Clip-on rings

Several curtain accessory firms now make simple clip-on attachments as an alternative to the curtain ring. These operate rather like bulldog clips and are attached to the bottom of the ring which then slips onto a rod as before.

Finish off the top of the curtain as for sewn-on rings and attach the clips every 10cm (4in) (Fig 2).

Cased heading

This is an ideal method for net curtains or any curtain which does not need to be drawn open and closed. It does, however, limit the fullness of the fabric; one-and-a-half times the width of the track (rod) is about the maximum unless the fabric is very sheer. The curtain could, of course, be held open with tie-backs and closed by releasing the ties, as shown in Fig 3,

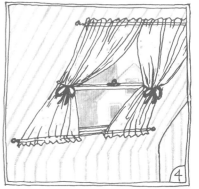

or on an attic window where the curtain is attached at both top and bottom, as in Fig 4. The casing runs across the top of the curtain, through which you slot a wooden pole, metal rod or spring wire (Fig 5). The edge of the fabric forms a ruffle.

Join the fabric widths as for unlined curtains, making the side

turnings and lower hem in the usual way.

Turn in and press 10cm (4in) along the top of the curtain. Make a 5cm (2in) double hem and machine stitch close to the lower edge. Stitch a second line parallel to the first at a distance of about 2.5cm (1in) (Fig 6).

To hang the curtain, slot the rod or wire between these two lines of stitching. If you wish to use a thicker

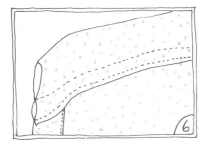

rod, allow extra fabric to make a wide enough casing and to keep the ruffle in proportion.

Scalloped heading

This is a slightly more decorative form of the sewn-on ring heading. There are many versions, one of which is a plain one, topping a flat café curtain (Fig 7), in which the width of the curtain matches that of the rod or pole.

Make up the curtain as given for unlined curtains, making the side turnings but leaving the top and bottom edges unfinished. Allow only 6mm ($\frac{1}{4}$in) extra at the top of the curtain for turnings.

Work out how many scallops will fit across the width of the curtain.

As a general guide, a good width to make each scallop is about 8cm (3in) allowing a space of about 2cm ($\frac{3}{4}$in) between each one. The amount of fabric left over is divided equally between the end

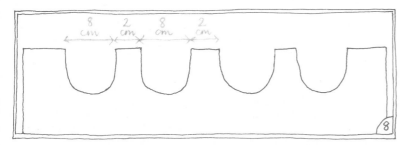

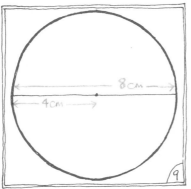

spaces (Fig 8).

Make a template of the finished scallop in cardboard by drawing a circle, using compasses, with a radius of 4cm (1$\frac{1}{2}$in) (Fig 9). Using a ruler, pencil in the diameter horizontally. Then, using a set square or improvising with a book, a bread board, or any other right angle, draw a rectangle with the diameter forming the base and the sides measuring 6.5cm (2$\frac{1}{2}$in) (Fig 10). Cut out the templates as shown in Fig 11.

Mark the scallops on the wrong side of the fabric with either a pencil or tailor's chalk, leaving 2cm ($\frac{3}{4}$in) spaces between and an equal amount of fabric at either end.

Cut a 15cm (6in) strip of curtain fabric 12mm ($\frac{1}{2}$in) wider than the

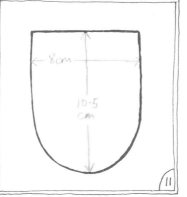

curtain to make a facing. Turn in 6mm ($\frac{1}{4}$in) on each short end, press and tack. Tack the facing, right sides together, to the top of the curtain. Turn up 6mm ($\frac{1}{4}$in) along the lower edge of the facing, press and tack.

With the wrong side of the curtain fabric facing, tack through both thicknesses along the outline of the scallops, making a straight line between the scallops 6mm ($\frac{1}{4}$in) from the edge. Machine stitch along the tacking line. Cut out the scallops 6mm ($\frac{1}{4}$in) from the stitching, clipping into curves and trimming away corners (see page 149). Turn right sides out and press. Slip stitch the side and lower edges of the facing in place. Sew a ring to the centre of each space between the scallops (Fig 12). Wooden rings often come with screw-in metal loops but these can easily be removed and the hole placed near the fabric where it will be less likely to show.

Slot the pole (rod) through the rings and hang the curtain to check the length of the hem. Pin and tack the hem and slip stitch in place. Press.

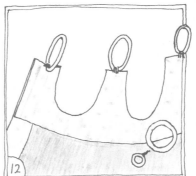

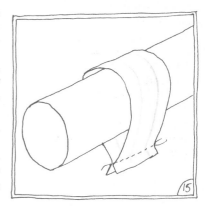

Tab heading

This method is suitable only for fixed curtains and is particularly good for café curtains, being easier to make than the scalloped heading. It is also useful for attaching wall hangings, back rest cushions or headboards to a pole or rod (Figs 13 and 14).

To find the length of the tab, measure the circumference of the pole, add at least 5cm (2in) for ease and another 2.5cm (1in) for seam allowances (Fig 15). As a general guide the width of each completed tab should be about 7.5cm (2–3 in). Place the end tabs about 2.5cm (1in) from the edges of the curtain, with the others spaced evenly between at about 10cm (4in) intervals. However, a lot depends on the width of the rod or pole and the weight of the fabric. Wider tabs spaced further apart or narrower tabs placed closer together may be in better proportion.

Make up the curtain, leaving top and bottom edges unfinished. Allow only 12mm ($\frac{1}{2}$in) extra at the top of the curtain for turnings. Decide on the number of tabs as for scalloped headings. Using either matching or contrasting fabric, cut strips of the required length and twice the width plus 2.5cm (1in) for seaming. With right sides together, fold each strip in half lengthways and make a 12mm ($\frac{1}{4}$in) seam down the long edge, leaving the ends open. Turn right sides out and refold so that the seam is at the centre back of the strip and press (Fig 16).

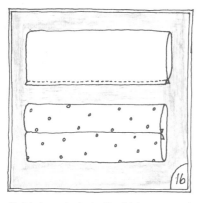

Fold the tabs in half widthways and pin at the correct spacing to the right side of the curtain, matching raw edges. Tack in place, 12mm ($\frac{1}{2}$in) from the edge. Cut an 8cm (3in) strip of fabric 12mm ($\frac{1}{2}$in) wider than the curtain to make a facing. Turn in 6mm ($\frac{1}{4}$in) on each short end, press and tack. Tack the facing, right sides together, to the top of the curtain. Turn up 6mm ($\frac{1}{4}$in) along the lower edge of the facing, press and tack (Fig 17). Tack and stitch along the top, 12mm ($\frac{1}{2}$in) from the edge, through all thicknesses. Turn right sides out and press.

Slip stitch (see page 148) the side and lower edges of the facing in place. Slot the pole (rod) through

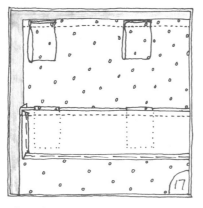

the tabs and hang the curtain to check the length of the hem. Pin and tack the hem and slip stitch in place. Press.

Shower curtains

These are very easy to make and if made in the pretty PVC (vinyl-coated fabric) prints available can look very original.

Because PVC (vinyl-coated fabric) does not fray, you only need to use single hems. Turn down the top edge once and make a line of eyelet holes with a special hole punch and eyelet setter available at most haberdashery (notion) departments. Special shower curtain rings are also available and these are rather like huge key rings which slot through the eyelets (Fig 18).

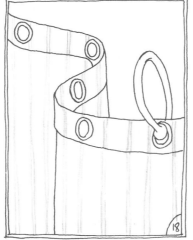

Close stitching will perforate PVC and will eventually cause it to tear so it is best to keep stitching to a minimum. Use large stitches and place a little oil on the tip of a very sharp needle to help per-

forate the PVC. Also, a light dusting of talcum powder between the layers helps prevent the fabric from sticking together. Alternatively, avoid stitching entirely by using a good plastic adhesive. Instead of tacking thread or pins, use Sellotape (Scotch tape), insulating tape or paper clips.

The finished length of the curtain will be from the lower edge of the shower rail to the floor; add 2.5cm (1in) for the hem and 5cm (2in) for the top turning. The finished width will be the length of the rail × 1$\frac{1}{2}$ for fullness; add on 2.5cm (1in) for each side turning.

Join the widths with a French seam (see page 149). Turn in and stitch the side edges and lower hem, mitring the corners (see page 151). Turn down the top of the curtain and secure it with Sellotape whilst making the line of eyelets, positioning them about 15cm (6in) apart. Insert the rings.

Another possibility is to make an ordinary fabric shower curtain, and use a clear plastic (vinyl) liner underneath, hanging from the same rings. This would be made in the same way as an opaque PVC (vinyl) curtain.

TIE-BACKS

Tie-backs add visual interest and prettiness to most curtains. On the practical side they hold back bulky curtains, letting more light into the room. From tall windows to tiny cottage-sized ones, tie-backs drape the curtains into soft, curvy folds. They are particularly useful for holding open fixed curtains or holding decorative drapes round a four-poster or behind a bed in place.

Choosing the style

The simplest treatment is to make a plain tie-back in a material matching that of the curtains. For a crisp, tailored effect, bind the edges in a contrasting fabric — this can be either a simple contrast of colour or a plain fabric tie-back edged with a floral pattern or vice-versa. For an ultra-feminine touch you can edge a tie-back with frills or decorate with a bow. For a

rather grand effect, scallop the lower edge of the tie-back (Figs 1–4).

Measuring up

To find the finished length of the tie-back, hold a tape measure round the curtain, creating the draped effect you want to achieve. At the same time, position the wall bracket, allowing about 2cm ($\frac{3}{4}$in) beyond the ends of the tie-back for the rings and hook. Mark the spot by holding the bracket in place and either making a pencil mark through each screw hole or drawing round the outline of the bracket as shown in Fig 5 before screwing it to the wall.

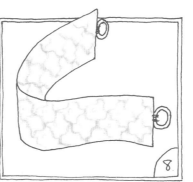

the opening and press. Sew a small brass ring to the middle of each end as shown in Fig 8.

Shaped tie-back

This requires a paper pattern. It is at this stage that you can experiment with different shapes, cutting them out and pinning them round the curtain until you achieve the effect you want.

Cut a rectangular piece of brown paper slightly longer than the required length of the tie-back and about 23cm (9in) deep. Fold it in half widthways. Draw out the design of the tie-back.

Cut two pieces of fabric to the same dimensions as the paper. Fold both pieces and the pattern in half widthways and pin the pattern on one piece of the fabric, folded edges together (Fig 9). Cut out the

cut a strip of brown paper 61cm (24in) long and 18cm (7in) wide. Fold the paper in half widthways and draw on it the shape on the chart (Fig 10). Cut out round the pencil line.

Cut two pieces of fabric each 23cm (9in) wide and 125cm (49in) long. Fold both pieces in half widthways. Pin the folded pattern to one piece of fabric, folded edges together (Fig 11) and cut out, adding a 12mm (½in) seam allowance all round. Cut the second piece of fabric in the same way.

Make up the bow pieces in the same way as the straight tie-back but using a lightweight Vilene (non-woven interfacing) instead of a stiff buckram. Instead of leaving an opening on one of the long edges, leave both short ends open. If, when the bow is made up, it is found to be too long the fabric can be turned wrong sides out again and a piece taken out of the centre where the seam will not show and the shaped ends remain unaltered. Tie the bow and pin it lightly to the tie-back. If the result is satisfactory, turn in 12mm (½in) at the ends and slip stitch them together. Stitch the bow in the centre at the back to the centre of the tie-back to finish off.

Straight tie-back

For each tie-back cut two strips of fabric measuring the required length plus 2.5cm (1in) for seam allowances by 12.5cm (5in) wide.

Cut an interfacing of either buckram or heavy Vilene (non-woven interfacing) measuring the exact finished length by 10cm (4in) wide. Pin the interfacing to the wrong side of one piece of the fabric, placing it centrally so that there is a 12mm (½in) allowance all round. Hem (catch) stitch (see page 148) the interfacing to the fabric (Fig 6). Pin the right side of the second piece of fabric against the right side of the interfaced piece. Tack in place then machine stitch all round 12mm (½in) from the edge, leaving a 10cm (4in) opening on one of the long edges (Fig 7). Trim the corners then turn right sides out. Slip stitch (see page 148)

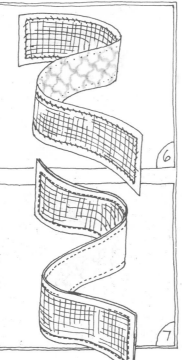

fabric, allowing a 12mm (½in) seam allowance all round. Cut out the second piece in the same way.

Make up the tie-back as given for the straight version, remembering to trim corners and notch curves (see page 149).

Bow tie-back

Make a straight tie-back in the usual way.

To make a pattern for the bow,

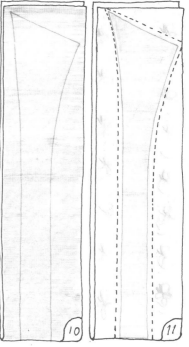

Pelmets and valances

Generally speaking, in the UK a pelmet is a smooth stretch of fabric and a valance is gathered. In the US both types are known as valances. They are used to cover the top of a curtain, either to hide the track (rod) or to create a certain decorative effect. They can also be used to disguise the proportions of the window (see page 109).

Choosing the style

Different shapes are synonymous with different styles. For example, smocked or ruffled valances will create a countrified look whereas a straight or pleated pelmet (valance) goes with a tailored, classic style. More ornate shapes, whether flat or draped, create a much grander effect.

The depth and shape of a pelmet (valance) will depend on the size and shape of the window and the character of the room. But, as a very rough guide, the average depth is 15–30cm (6–12in). Bear in mind that the pelmet (valance) should be positioned high enough to let the most possible light into the room, but still deep enough to cover the curtain track (rod) when viewed from below.

The simplest design is a straight box (Fig 1) which looks prettier and softer with a gathered or pleated ruffle as shown in Fig 2.

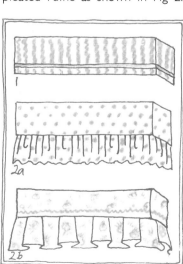

The severity of a straight box pelmet (valance) could, alternatively, be relieved by shaping the ends either in an angular step or with softly rounded corners as shown in Figs 3 and 4. Either

version can be bound at the edges or left plain.

Other classic shapes for flat pelmets (valances) include gentle curves meeting at a centre point (Fig 5), the simple arch with 'table

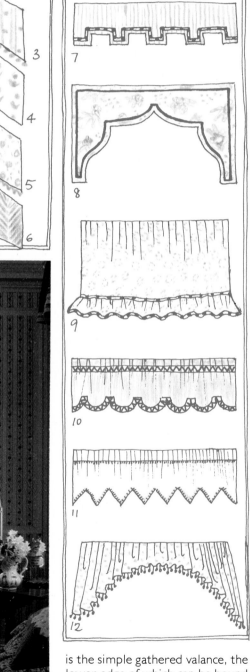

leg' ends (Fig 6) and the crenellated shape (Fig 7). For tall, elegant windows, the shaping can be continued down the sides giving a deep, ornate corner (Fig 8).

For a less formal, softer look, there is the simple gathered valance, the lower edge of which can be bound or ruffled or both (Fig 9). Variations of this come from shaping the lower edge, either in scallops as in Fig 10 or zig-zags, as in Fig 11. Alternatively, the overall

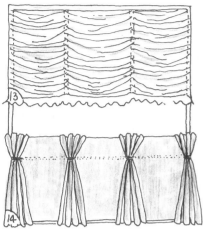

shape of the valance can frame the window (Fig 12).

For an extravagant, frilly, feminine room there is a valance which looks rather like a festoon blind, with or without a ruffle (Fig 13). Making a valance with curtain tape is one way of introducing further variations of style. Of course, the cost of the tape will make the job more expensive but it does make it a lot simpler. These would be made in the same way as lined or unlined curtains. One of the prettiest is the pinch-pleated valance (Fig 14).

Making the pelmet board

This is very like putting up a shelf. You will need a piece of 12mm ($\frac{1}{2}$in) plywood or hardboard which is the same width as the curtain track plus about 5cm (2in) – to give 2.5cm (1in) clearance on either side – and 10cm (4in) deep. Place it centrally over the window and fix it to the wall using angle irons (Fig 15). It should be at the height where you plan to have the top of the pelmet (valance). To fix

a board into the window recess, screw the angle irons to the top of the reveal (Fig 16). The board is cut to the exact width of the reveal and fixed at right angles to

it, across the front (Fig 17). It hangs vertically rather than sticking out like a shelf as it would over a window, flush with the rest of the wall.

Measuring up

Measure along the front and round the ends of the board unless it is fixed to the reveal, in which case measure only across the front. This gives the finished length of the pelmet or valance.

Fixing the pelmet or valance

The easiest method of attaching the pelmet or valance to the pelmet (valance) board is to tack it along the top edge using 12mm ($\frac{1}{2}$in) upholstery tacks and then to conceal the line of tacks with a braid glued in place with a suitable fabric glue.

Alternatively, glue one strip of Velcro to the edges of the board and stitch the other half to the back of the pelmet or valance and stick it to the board.

A third method, perhaps the neatest, is to sew small brass rings to the back of the pelmet or valance at each end along the top edge. Loop these round nails or screws fixed to the edge of the board so that the pelmet or valance is held tightly round the board (Fig 18).

FLAT PELMET (VALANCE)

Cut a strip of brown paper a little larger than the planned pelmet (valance). Fold it in half widthways and draw out the shape you want, marking the return, if there is one, with a dotted line (Fig 1). Cut out the pattern along the outline, unfold the paper and try it on the board for size and design.

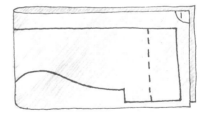

Cut the fabric as for tie-backs, adding 12mm ($\frac{1}{2}$in) all round for seam allowances. In the same way, cut one piece in lining fabric and one in interlining. Finally, cut out the shape in buckram or stiff non-woven interfacing but without seam allowances.

Lock stitch (see page 148) the interlining to the wrong side of the main fabric. Lay them flat and position the buckram or interfacing centrally over the interlining. Tack in place all round the edge. Clip into the seam allowances on the curves and then turn the fabric in over the buckram and tack in place (Fig 2).

Any fringe, pleating, ruffle or piping (cable) cord (see Basic Techniques) is added at this stage by stitching it to the stiffened fabric before the lining is added.

Turn in the 12mm ($\frac{1}{2}$in) seam allowance all round the lining, clipping where necessary. Press. Lay the lining on the pelmet (valance), wrong sides together, and slip stitch (see page 148) in place (Fig 3).

SIMPLE GATHERED VALANCE

Cut two pieces of fabric each twice the finished length and to the depth required, plus 12mm ($\frac{1}{2}$in) all round for seam allowances. An average valance would be about 23cm (9in) deep. For extra body, cut a piece of interlining to the same measurements.

Lay both pieces of fabric flat, right

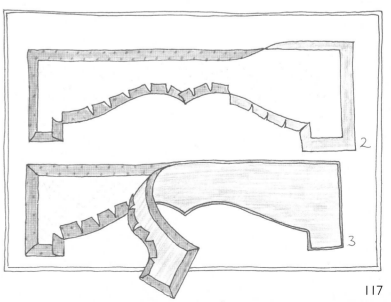

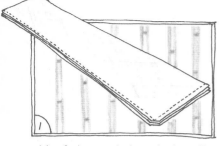

sides facing, and place the interlining, if any, on top. Machine stitch 12mm ($\frac{1}{2}$in) from the edge round three sides, leaving one long edge open as shown in Fig 1. Trim diagonally across corners. Turn right sides out and press.

Make a line of gathering 12mm ($\frac{1}{2}$in) from the top (open) edge through both thicknesses. Make a second line of gathering 3mm ($\frac{1}{8}$in) from the first, into the seam allowance. Cut a bias strip (see page 152) 2.5cm (1in) wide and the finished length of the valance plus 12mm ($\frac{1}{2}$in) for turnings. Apply the binding along the top of the valance, the edges along the lower line of gathering on either side of the valance.

GATHERED VALANCE WITH SHAPED EDGE

First decide on a width for each scallop or zig-zag; this must divide equally into the width of the valance. For example, on a 90cm (3ft) valance, 10cm (4in) scallops or zig-

zags would repeat exactly 18 times, as the fabric will be twice the finished width of the valance. Cut a paper pattern for the lower edge.

Cut the fabric, using the pattern, and make up as for the simple gathered valance, remembering to trim corners and clip curves (see page 149 and Figs 1 and 2).

ARCHED GATHERED VALANCE

Make a paper pattern as for a flat pelmet (valance) but making it twice the finished length.

Fold the pattern in half widthways. On the folded edge mark the depth of the valance at the centre of the window where it is shortest and on the opposite edge mark the depth at the outer edge where it is deepest. Draw a gentle curve evenly between the two points

(Fig 1). Obviously the dimensions will depend on the window and the effect you are trying to create but as a rough guide a steeply graded shape would have around 15cm (6in) at the shortest point and 46cm (18in) at the deepest. A gentler curve could be from 20cm (8in) to 30cm (12in).

Cut out the pattern and pleat it along the top edge to give a rough idea of how the completed valance will look. Hold it in place to make sure it is exactly as you want before cutting out the fabric.

Make up the valance as for the simple gathered version.

Blinds

Where windows have a work surface below, such as a desk, kitchen sink or work top and curtains would either block out too much light or simply get in the way, blinds are an obvious choice. For extra lushness, they combine well with fixed curtains, with or without tie-backs.

ROLLER BLINDS (SHADES)

The simplest form of blind (shade) is the roller blind (shade) which, when not in use, is rolled round a piece of wooden dowelling at the top of the window and which pulls down to hang flat against the window. The easiest way to make one is to use PVC (vinyl) or a special blind (shade) fabric such as holland, which is fairly stiff, does not fray and has a spongeable, fade-resistant finish. Alternatively, use an ordinary furnishing fabric and have it stiffened. There is a do-it-yourself stiffener available in either liquid or aerosol form; the fabric is either dipped in the liquid or sprayed or painted on both sides. Always test a sample piece of fabric first to see how well it responds. Remember, too, that many fabrics will shrink in the stiffening process so it is best to stiffen the fabric before cutting out.

For extra wide windows it may be necessary to join the fabric; it is best to put half the extra at either side to maintain a balance. There are two methods of doing this. One is to overlap the ready-stiffened fabric by about 12mm ($\frac{1}{2}$in) along the joining edges and glue them together. Alternatively, stitch the fabric in a flat seam (see page 149) and bond the seam allowances to the main fabric with iron-on adhesive hem webbing. As this must be done before stiffening, remember to allow for shrinkage. Stiffen a narrow strip taken from the full width to find exactly how much to allow.

Roller blind (shade) kits

These include a wooden roller with a square pin at one end, and a

round pin attached to a pin cap. This is hammered onto the other end once the roller has been cut to size (Fig 1). You can of course use the roller from an old blind (shade), cutting to size if necessary. With some kits the tacking line for the fabric edge is marked on the roller. If it is not, draw the line yourself, making sure it is positioned at right angle to the ends of the roller. An extra pair of hands or a vice will help to steady the roller. Also included in the kit are two brackets (Fig 2). These are for fixing the roller in place, either

to the side or face of the window frame, inside or outside the recess. One bracket has a slot for the square pin and this operates the spring winding mechanism, the other has a hole for the round pin. It is usual to position the square pin on the left of the window. This means that the fabric goes up behind the roller, leaving the rolled-up fabric on view along the top of the blind (shade). However, where a furnishing fabric which is not reversible has been used, this would mean that the wrong side would be on display on the roller. The alternative is to position the square pin on the right and have the fabric hang from the front of the roller.

Also included in most kits will be a stretcher batten to slot through a casing at or near the bottom of the blind (shade) and a cord holder and cord which screws onto the batten. The lower end of the cord

Above: Simple fabric roller blinds on a plain window.

is attached either to an acorn or a ring pull for lowering and raising the blind (shade).

Measuring up

For accurate measuring, use a wooden folding ruler or a metal tape, both of which give a more accurate measurement than a fabric tape.

Measure the length of the window and add 30cm (12in) to allow for a batten casing and enough fabric to cover the roller when the blind (shade) is down. For a blind to hang inside the window recess, measure from one side to the other and subtract the space required for the brackets. This gives the size for the roller kit and also for the fabric width. If you want the blind (shade) to hang outside the window frame or recess, allow 2.5cm (1in) extra on each side and 5cm (2in) above the window to prevent light showing around the edges.

It is unlikely that there will be a roller kit to fit the exact measurement you need. If not, buy the next size up and first mount the brackets in position on the wall or window frame to find the correct length for the roller before cutting it to size.

Cutting out the fabric

To ensure that the blind (shade) hangs correctly and rolls up easily, the fabric must be cut straight using a T-square (or something around the house with a perfect right angle). Use the wooden batten to draw straight edges.

Once the fabric has been stiffened it is unlikely to fray so it can be cut to the exact measurements of the roller. However, if you are not happy about having raw edges, particularly if there are already joins in the fabric, turn in a narrow hem on each side edge and bond it with adhesive hem webbing before stiffening the fabric, allowing for shrinkage.

Making up the blind (shade)

Once the fabric has been cut out or made up to the correct size, and unless there is to be a decorative edging, the batten is secured in place along the bottom of the blind (shade). This can be done either by glueing or by stitching a casing.

To glue the batten, lay the fabric wrong side up, spread glue on one side of the batten and position it along the bottom edge of the blind (shade). Spread glue on the second side of the batten (Fig 3), fold the batten over and weight it until the glue dries (Fig 4).

To stitch a casing, turn up a single

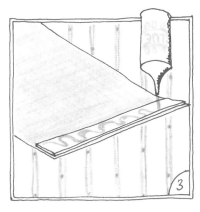

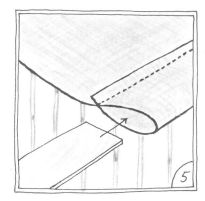

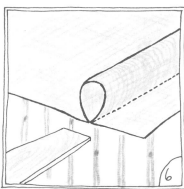

fold on the wrong side of the fabric and stitch close to the edge, making sure the casing is wide enough to take the batten (Fig 5). If there is to be a decorative shaped edge, make a tuck as

shown in Fig 6, about 7.5–15cm (3–6in) from the edge. If the fabric has an obvious pattern repeat which would look better continuing uninterrupted into the edging, stitch an extra strip of fabric across the back to form the casing.

To attach the blind (shade) to the roller, tack the top edge to the line marked along the length of the roller, securing it first with Sellotape (Scotch tape) (Fig 7). Use 6mm ($\frac{1}{4}$in) tacks – sometimes sup-

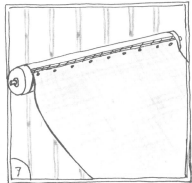

plied with the kit – spaced about 5cm (2in) apart. If the square pin is to the left of the blind (shade) and the roller is to be visible, tack the fabric on wrong side up. If the square pin is to the right and the roller to be hidden, tack the fabric on with right side up.

Screw the cord holder to the centre of the batten at the back of the blind (shade).

Decorative edgings

The simplest way of making a decorative edging to a roller blind (shade) is to sew a fringe or ribbon along the edge, below the batten. Alternatively, the edge can be shaped and trimmed with fringing, lace, a ruffle or a bias strip, either bought or home made (see Basic Techniques). There are various examples shown in Fig 8.

To attach a fringe or ribbon to a straight edge, lay the blind (shade) with the wrong side up and tape the trim in place – stiffened fabric is not easy to pin. Stitch through both tape and fabric and then tear away the tape.

For a shaped edge, first make a paper pattern by cutting a strip of brown paper to the same width

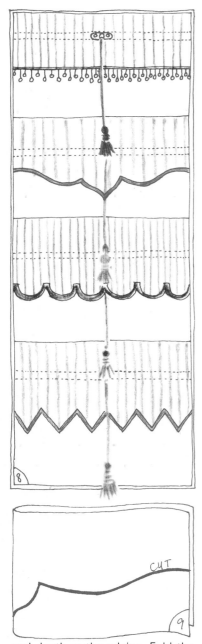

ROMAN BLINDS (SHADES)

These are among the most popular of blinds (shades) which can be made from non-stiffened fabric. They have a tailored, elegant appearance and draw up into horizontal folds.

Measuring up

You will need enough fabric and lining to cover the window with an extra 2.5cm (1in) added to the width for side turnings (hems) and 15cm (6in) to the length for top and bottom hems; small brass or plastic rings which are sewn to the back of the blind (shade) in vertical rows at about 15cm (6in) intervals, the rows being about 30cm (12in) apart horizontally (Fig 1); binding to sew to the back of the blind (shade) in vertical rows behind the rings (in the US tape is available which already has the rings sewn on); enough nylon cord to thread through each vertical row of rings, each length being twice the length of the blind (shade) plus the distance from the top of that row to the right-hand edge of the blind (shade) (Fig 1); one screw eye for each vertical row of rings plus an extra one to take all the cords together; a piece of wood 2.5cm

Below: A tailored Roman blind.

and depth as the edging. Fold the paper in half widthways, draw the shape (Fig 9) and cut out. Open out the pattern and tape it to the wrong side of the edging. Pencil round the shape and cut neatly along the pencil line (Fig 10).

To make a pattern for a zig-zag or scalloped edge, first decide on the width of each point or scallop. Fold the paper to this measurement as many times as it divides into the total width and draw the shape on the top layer as shown in Fig 11. Cut out the shape through all thicknesses then open out the

pattern, tape it to the edging and pencil round it on the edging. Cut out neatly along the pencil line.

If you decide to add an edging made out of non-stiffened fabric, you should cut a facing. Machine stitch it to the lower edge along the shape, clip curves and trim corners (see page 149), turn right sides out and slip stitch (see page 148) the side turnings in place. By adding extra depth to the facing you can then stitch two parallel lines through the double thickness to make a casing for the batten, opening up one side edge between the lines to insert it.

Add any binding or ruffle (see Basic Techniques), fringe or lace by taping it in place and stitching.

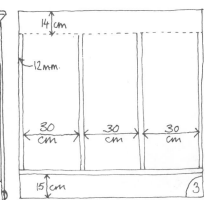

(1in) thick, 5cm (2in) deep and cut to the same width as the blind (shade); angle irons to fix this wood above the window unless it is to hang from the reveal in which case the board can be fixed direct; a narrow wooden batten to weight the bottom edge; and, finally, a cleat to which to secure the cords when the blind (shade) is raised (Fig 2).

Making up the blind (shade)

Cut out the fabric and the lining to the same size, i.e. the finished width plus seam allowances, the finished length plus 15cm (6in). Place them right sides together,

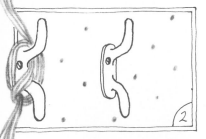

pin, tack (baste) and stitch 12mm (½in) from side and lower edges. Trim corners, turn right sides out and press.

Lay the blind (shade) flat, lining uppermost. With a pencil and straight edge (or the wooden batten) mark two parallel lines across the blind for the batten casing, the first 15cm (6in) from the lower edge and the second far enough above it to allow for the batten (Fig 3). Next mark double vertical lines for the position of the tapes, placing the first and last tapes 12mm (½in) from the edges and the others spaced evenly between no more than 30cm (12in)

apart. These lines run from the top of the batten to 14cm (5½in) from the edges at the top (Fig 3). With the raw ends turned under at top and bottom, tack (baste) the tape in place between the double lines and machine stitch along both edges of the tape through all thicknesses – fabric, lining and tape. Slip stitch (see page 148) the turned-under ends in place.

Turn in the top edges of the blind (shade) 12mm (½in) and slip stitch together. Sew the rings to the tapes by hand, spacing them evenly at about 15cm (6in) intervals and keeping them level horizontally.

Machine stitch along the batten lines, unpick one side edge between the lines to slot in the batten then slip stitch closed again. Fix the screw eyes to the underside of the wooden heading board, positioning one directly above each of the vertical rows of rings, the extra large ring to the right-hand end of the board.

Using 12mm (½in) upholstery tacks, tack the top of the blind (shade) over the top of the board (Fig 4).

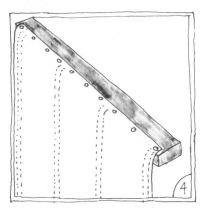

Cut the cords, one length for each vertical row of rings as described in 'Measuring up'. Lay the blind (shade) flat, lining side uppermost. Knot each cord to the bottom ring of its particular row, pass it through each ring to the top and then through the screw eye and across the top through the other screw eyes to the side one (Fig 5). When all the cords are through the side screw eye, knot them together about 2.5cm (2in) from that screw in an overhand knot (Fig 6), then, keeping them level, knot them together again on a level with the bottom of the blind (shade). Trim the ends.

Fix the heading board in place either above the window with the angle irons or directly to the reveal. Screw the cleat to the wall near the bottom of the window.

As the blind (shade) is drawn up the fabric will fall forward into folds across the front (Fig 7). Keep

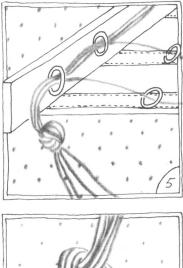

the blind drawn up for a day or two to fix the pleats.

FESTOON OR AUSTRIAN BLINDS (SHADES)

These work on the same principle as Roman blinds (shades) except that they are usually unlined, have

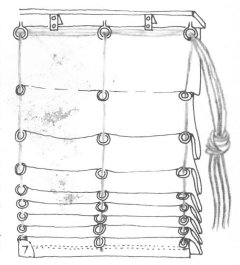

a gathered or pleated heading and have no wooden batten bracing the lower edge. When drawn up they fall into soft swags, usually ending in a ruffle.

Measuring up

You will need enough fabric for double the width of the window plus 5cm (2in) for side turnings, 4cm (1½in) longer than the window but deducting the depth of the ruffle if you plan to have one; small brass or plastic rings which are sewn to the back of the blind (shade) in vertical rows at about 20cm (8in) intervals, the distance between the rows is about twice the width of the finished swag (Fig 1); binding to sew to the back of the blind (shade) in vertical rows behind the rings (in the US tape is available which already has the rings sewn on); enough nylon cord to thread

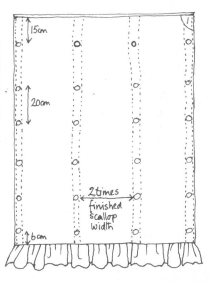

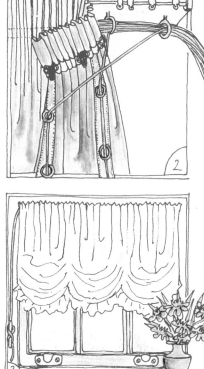

(shade) to the curtain track (rod) (Fig 2) using conventional hooks. Alternatively, you could use U-shaped staples fixed into the heading board to hold the curtain hooks. Fix the heading board and the cleat in place as for Roman blinds (shades).

As the blind (shade) is drawn up the fabric gathers into swags as shown in Fig 3.

Above: Festoon blinds soften the lines of a window.

through each vertical row of rings, each length being twice the length of the blind (shade) plus the distance from the top of that row to the right-hand edge of the blind (shade); one screw eye for each vertical row of rings plus one big enough to take all the cords together; curtain heading tape the width of the fabric when laid flat; curtain track (rod) the width of the blind (shade); a piece of wood 2.5cm (1in) thick, 5cm (2in) deep and cut to the same width as the blind (shade); angle irons to fix this wood above the window unless it is to hang from the reveal in which case the board can be fixed direct; a cleat to which to secure the cords when the blind (shade) is raised.

Making up the blind (shade).

Cut out the fabric and join widths with French seams (see page 149) to make a panel twice the width of the window. Make 2.5cm (1in) side and lower hems. If you want a ruffle, add it at this stage (see page 153). Turn in 12mm ($\frac{1}{2}$in) along the top edge and tack.

Lay the blind (shade) flat, wrong side up. Mark double vertical lines with pins or tacking (basting) to position the tapes, placing the first and last tapes about 6mm ($\frac{1}{4}$in) in from the edges and the others spaced evenly between the tapes twice the intended width of the finished swag. These lines run from top to bottom of the blind (shade), not including any ruffle.

With the raw ends turned under at the bottom but not the top (where they will be covered by the heading tape), tack (baste) the

tape in place between the lines and machine stitch along both edges. Slip stitch (see page 148) the turned-under ends in place.

Sew the rings to the tapes by hand, positioning the top one about 15cm (6in) from the top, the bottom one about 6.5cm ($2\frac{1}{2}$in) from the bottom (not including any ruffle) and spacing the rest evenly at intervals of about 20cm (8in) apart, keeping them level horizontally.

Sew the curtain tape to the wrong side of the blind (shade) 6mm ($\frac{1}{4}$in) from the top edge. Gather it to fit the heading board.

Fix the screw eyes to the heading board as for Roman blinds (shades) then fix the track (rod) to the front of the heading board. Thread the cords through the rings and screw eyes as given for Roman blinds (shades) and attach the blind

BEDS AND BED LINEN

So many items in the bedroom can be made of or covered with fabric; there is really no other room in the house which offers such scope for individual styling to eager home sewers. With a bit of imagination and a good deal of hard work and plenty of time, the so-called co-ordinated bedroom which used to cost a fortune in interior decorator's fees, is now within everybody's grasp. Here is how to make the main ingredients. On page 109 you'll find instructions for curtains, and on pages 137–8 loose covers and a dressing table skirt.

Bedspreads

In a bedroom, it is usually the bed which first catches the eye because it is potentially the largest mass of colour and pattern in the room. How it is dressed – be it smartly tailored or canopied, ruffled and glamorous – is the key to setting the style and mood of the room.

Choosing the style
The simplest type of bedspread is the throwover cover which can either fall to just above the floor or can end just below the top of a valance (dust ruffle) (Fig 1). The corners can be square or rounded off and the edges can be plain, bound or ruffled. A quilted fabric is the most practical choice because it is wonderfully crease-resistant and it looks so opulent besides being as warm as an extra blanket.

For a more tailored bedspread, ideal for bed-sits (studio apartments), make a fitted cover to the size of the mattress and finish it off with either straight panels with kick pleats, box pleats or a frill (gathered skirt) (Figs 2–4).

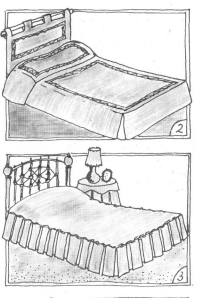

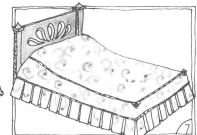
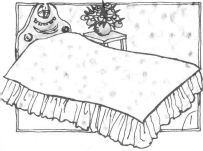

Valances (dust ruffles) cover the base of the bed and can either be separate from the bedspread or attached to it. They can be plain with kick pleats at the corners, ruffled or box-pleated (Figs 5–7). Whichever version of bedspread you choose, the main seams can be piped (corded) (see page 150) with matching or contrasting, plain or patterned fabric.

UNLINED THROWOVER BEDSPREAD
As well as being the simplest style visually this is, of course, the simplest cover to make and the most economical on fabric.

Measuring up
Always take measurements when the bed is made up with its usual quota of blankets and pillows and take the measurements from 2.5cm (1in) above floor level. Following Fig 1, measure the length and add 15cm (6in) for the tuck-in at the back of the pillows. Add a further 15cm (6in) if you like to tuck the bedspread in along the front of the pillows. Measure the width either from floor to floor as shown here or from higher up if there is to be a valance. If more than one width is necessary, add 5cm (2in) for each seam – even if you only need two widths, one

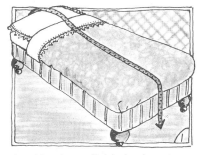

should be divided in two lengthways and each half added to each side of a centre panel (Fig 2), to balance the two seams. Finally, add 5cm (2in) all round for hems. If there is a pattern, allow extra for matching, i.e. the depth of one pattern repeat for each width.

Cutting out the fabric
Cut each width to the correct length, cutting each length from

the same point of any pattern repeat. If there are only two lengths, fold one in half, lengthways, and cut along the fold.

Making up the bedspread
Join the widths in a flat seam with a 2.5cm (1in) allowance, matching patterns where necessary (see page 150). Trim off the selvedges as these will pucker the seams because the weave is tighter than on the main body of the fabric. Alternatively, make notches along the selvedge at approximately 15cm (6in) intervals.
Press the seams open and finish any raw edges with zig-zag stitch. Turn in and press 5cm (2in) all round the bedspread, mitring the top two corners (see page 151). Make a double 2.5cm (1in) hem and slip stitch in place (see page 148).
To round off the bottom corners, before turning in the edges lay the bedspread flat, wrong side up, and use a saucer or a plate as a template to draw in the curve (Fig 1). Cut along the chalk line.
Alternatively, for a deeper curve, measure from the top of the mattress to 2.5cm (1in) above floor

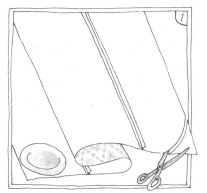

level to find the depth of the overhang. On the wrong side of the bottom corners of the bedspread mark, with tailor's chalk or pins, a square with sides measuring the same as the overhang (Fig 2).

Take a piece of string the same length as the overhang measure-

ment. Tie one end to a pencil and the other to a drawing pin (thumb tack) Place the drawing pin (tack) at the inside corner of the square and, keeping the string taut, draw a quarter circle as shown. Cut along the curve.

Turn in and press 2.5cm (1in) all round. At the curved corners, machine stitch close to the foldline

Above: The quilted throwover bedspread completes the co-ordinated look of this bedroom.

and cut notches along the edge to allow the fabric to lie flat (Fig 3). Turn in a further 2.5cm (1in) all round to make a double hem and slip stitch in place.

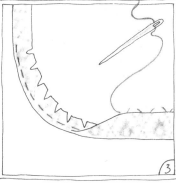

LINED THROWOVER BEDSPREAD

Lining a throwover bedspread makes a neater back to the bedspread and if you also line it in a quilted fabric, it will provide an extra layer of warmth.

When cutting out the fabric, allow only 2.5cm (1in) all round for turnings. Join the widths and

Above: The fitted bedspread with frilled valance gives this small room a tailored appearance.

shape the corners, if desired, as given for the unlined version. Make up the lining in the same way and to the same dimensions. Lay the bedspread and the lining flat, right sides together. Machine stitch 2.5cm (1in) from the edge all round, leaving a gap of about 60cm (24in) along the top edge (Fig 1).

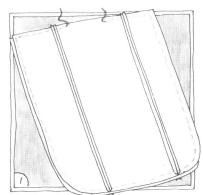

Trim square corners diagonally or notch curved corners, then turn the whole bedspread right side out and press. Slip stitch (see page 148) the opening together to finish off

FITTED BEDSPREAD WITH FRILLED VALANCE (GATHERED SKIRT)

This is the simplest of the fitted bedspreads to make and can be lined or unlined.

Centre panel

Measure the bed only to the edges of the mattress (Fig 1), add the pillow tuck as before and add 12mm ($\frac{1}{2}$in) all round for seams plus an extra 12mm ($\frac{1}{2}$in) allowance on the top edge only. Make up the widths as for the unlined throwover bedspread. Always round the corners using a saucer as a template; mattresses never have right-angled corners and,

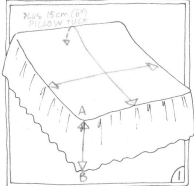

once made up, the blankets form a gentle curve at the corners, so a sharply angled corner on the bedspread would not fit.

Valance (skirt)

Measure from the top of the mattress to 2.5cm (1in) above floor level to find the depth of the valance (skirt) (A–B in Fig 1) and add 5cm (2in) for the lower hem and 12mm ($\frac{1}{2}$in) for the seam at the top. Cut the fabric to this depth. To work out the length of the valance (skirt), add twice the finished length to the finished width of the centre panel and multiply by 1$\frac{1}{2}$ then add 5cm (2in) for turnings (seams).

Making 2.5cm (1in) flat seams, join sufficient pieces together to make up to this measurement in one continuous length, finishing off the raw edges with zig-zag stitch.

Make two lines of gathering stitches 12mm ($\frac{1}{2}$in) from the top edge of the valance (skirt). Lay the centre panel of the bedspread flat and gather the valance (skirt) to fit round the side and bottom edges, spacing the gathers evenly. With right sides together, pin and tack (baste) the valance (skirt) to the panel. Machine stitch along the line of gathering stitches then zig-zag the raw edges of the seam allowance together.

Turn up 5cm (2in) along the lower edge of the valance (skirt) and make a double 2.5cm (1in) hem. On the top edge of the bedspread, turn in 2.5cm (1in) and make a double 12mm ($\frac{1}{2}$in) hem all the way across (Fig 2).

Remember when tucking the top of the bedspread under the pillows to fold the valance (skirt) under itself (Fig 3).

To line this bedspread, either make a lining for the centre panel only as for the throwover bedspread, slip stitching it in place once the valance (skirt) has been added, or make a lining for the centre panel and make a double ruffle (see page 153) for the valance (skirt) again adding the centre panel lining after the ruffle.

FITTED BEDSPREAD WITH BOX PLEAT VALANCE

This gives a more tailored look to a fitted bedspread. In a bed-sit (studio apartment) the bed will look like a sofa during the day, particularly if you add box or bolster cushions (see pages 135–6) along the wall backing the length of the bed and bolster cushions at either end.

Make a centre panel in the same way as for the version with the gathered valance (skirt). Before rounding off the bottom corners, fold them diagonally and mark the middle of each cover with tailor's chalk. Measure the depth of the valance (skirt) in the same way as for the gathered version. To find the length, measure round the side and lower edges of the centre panel, 12mm ($\frac{1}{2}$in) from the edge, and multiply by three. Cut and

join strips of fabric to make up to these measurements in the same way as for the gathered valance (skirt) and make the pleats (see page 154).

10cm (4in) is a convenient width for each pleat as it will fit most bed dimensions. For example, there would be eighteen pleats down the side of a 180cm (6ft) bed or nineteen pleats down a 190cm (6ft 4in) bed, but always double check the measurements of your bed before pleating the valance (skirt) in case it is not standard. Rounding the corners, for example, shortens the all round measurement by almost 5cm (2in). When checking the measurements, use the marked diagonal as the corner.

Lay the centre panel flat and pin the valance (skirt) to the panel, right sides facing. Stitch the valance (skirt) and finish off the bedspread in the same way as the gathered version. Lining, if any, is usually limited to the centre panel; if you want a valance (skirt) lining, tack (baste) it to the main piece at the cutting out stage and treat the two layers as one.

FITTED BEDSPREAD WITH STRAIGHT SKIRT AND KICK PLEATS

This is the most tailored of all the fitted bedspreads and also helps to make a bed-sit (studio apartment) look more like a sitting room during the day. The straight skirt

requires kick pleats at the corners. Make a centre panel in the same way as for the version with the gathered valance (skirt). Round off the corners, first folding them diagonally and marking the centre of the curve as in the box pleat version.

Cut two side panels and one end panel to match the measurements of the centre panel as shown in Fig 1 plus 15cm (6in) to each side panel and 30cm (12in) to the end panel for the kick pleats. Measure for the depth of the panels as for the frilled valance (gathered skirt), adding 6.5cm (2$\frac{1}{2}$in) for the hem and top seam allowance.

Cut two pieces of fabric for the corner pleats, each 30cm (12in) long and the same depth as the side and end panels. With right sides facing and using 12mm ($\frac{1}{2}$in) flat seams, join one side of each corner pleat to a side panel and the other to the end panel (Fig 2).

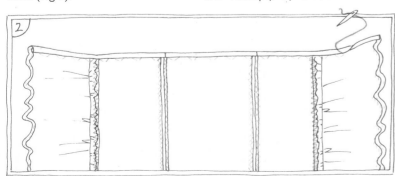

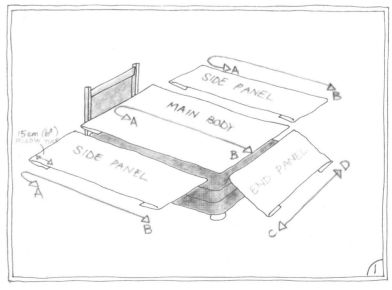

With pins or tailor's chalk, mark a line 14cm (5½in) to each side of the pleat sections as shown. Fold the side and end panels along these lines and position the fold together over the pleat sections (Fig 3). With right sides facing and positioning the pleats exactly at the corners, join the valance (skirt) to the centre panel and finish off as for the gathered version.

Lining, if any, is usually limited to the centre panel. If you want a

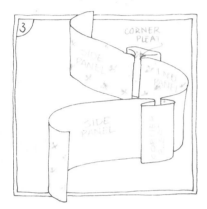

valance (skirt) lining, it can be tacked to the fabric at the cutting out stage and the double thickness worked as one.

TAILORED BEDSPREAD

This is made with a boxed top which fits over the mattress and the valance (skirt) is added below. First make a centre panel as for the fitted bedspread, remembering to mark the diagonals before rounding off the corners.

Cut three strips of fabric, two to fit the side edges of the centre

panel and one to fit the bottom edge, all measuring the depth of the mattress plus 12mm (½in) all round for seam allowances (Fig 1). Join the strips, in the correct sequence, with 12mm (½in) seams to make a continuous piece. With right sides facing, stitch the box strip to the centre panel with a 12mm (½in) seam, matching the seams to the corners. Clip the corners as shown in Fig 2.

To find the depth of the valance (skirt), measure from the bottom of the mattress to 2.5cm (1in) off the floor and add 5cm (2in) for the hem and 12mm (½in) for the top seam. It can be any of the styles given for the fitted bedspreads and is made up in the same way, joining it to the lower edges of the box sides of the centre panel.

Valances

A separate valance (dust ruffle) which covers the bed base (frame) at all times is designed to sit below the mattress and finishes just above floor level.

Choosing the style

The valance (dust ruffle) can be gathered, box-pleated or have straight sides with kick pleats. For the part which never shows — under the mattress — you can use an inexpensive lining fabric. If there is a fitted bottom sheet and duvet (continental quilt) on the bed, a frilled valance (dust ruffle) made in much the same way as a bedspread is practical. The centre panel will require a border about 15cm (6in) wide to match the valance (skirt) (Fig 1). Otherwise, the most practical design is one with a fitted top (the shaded area

Below: A simple valance.

in Fig 2) so that when you make the bed, the valance (dust ruffle) does not get scooped up along with the sheets and blankets and tucked under the mattress.

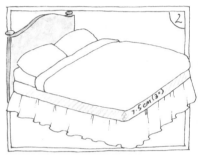

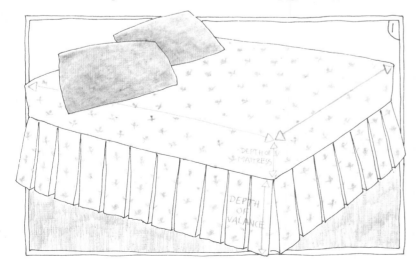

SIMPLE VALANCE (DUST RUFFLE)

Measure the exact length and width of the mattress. Deduct 30cm (12in) from each measurement to find the finished size of the centre panel. Cut out or make up the lining fabric to these measurements plus 12mm ($\frac{1}{2}$in) all round.

Cut two strips of the main fabric each 18cm (7in) wide and the same length as the mattress plus 2.5cm (1in) for seam allowances. Cut another two strips each 18cm (7in) wide to the same measurement as the width of the bed plus 2.5cm (1in) for seam allowances. Cut the ends of each strip to an angle of 45 degrees to mitre the corners as shown in Fig 1. With right sides

facing, join the four corners with a 12mm ($\frac{1}{2}$in) seam to form a rectangle. Press all four seams open. Turn in and tack (baste) 6mm ($\frac{1}{4}$in) all round the inner edge of the rectangle. Lay the centre panel flat, right side up, and lay the rectangle over it, also right side up, overlapping the edges evenly all round by 12mm ($\frac{1}{2}$in). Machine stitch in place. Turn in and press 12mm ($\frac{1}{2}$in) along the bedhead edge of the border and make a double 6mm ($\frac{1}{4}$in) hem.

Complete the valance (dust ruffle) in the same way as for the fitted bedspread with frilled valance (see page 124).

FITTED VALANCE (DUST RUFFLE)

This is made in the same way as the simple valance (dust ruffle) but follow the instructions for the tailored bedspread (see page 126) to complete the valance.

Headboards

No bed is really complete without a headboard. A successful design should not only look good, matching or blending with your colour scheme, but also be comfortable to lean against and stop the pillows falling backwards onto the floor.

Choosing the style

There are lots of shapes to choose from, but your choice will depend on your style and how complicated a shape you want to tackle. If you lack inspiration you could copy an existing shape in the room, like the top of a window or mirror, or trace the outline pattern in your fabric.

To make the headboard

You will need a piece of 2.5cm (1in) blockboard (plywood) the same width as the bed and about 92cm (36in) deep. You can leave the board as a simple rectangle or round off the corners (Fig 1) using

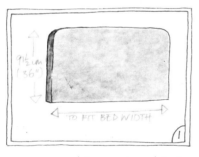

a saucer or plate as a template to draw the shape on the board before cutting. For a more ornate shape (Fig 2a–c) make a paper pattern. Cut the paper to the same size as the board, fold it in half widthways and draw out the shape for cutting out. Open up the pattern and pin it onto the board. Draw round the shape with a pencil before cutting it out.

To give a depth and softness to the headboard, cover it with foam rubber 2.5–5cm (1–2in) thick. Cut the foam to the same shape as the board and glue it to the front.

Fix the headboard to the bed with strips of wood, each 7.5 × 2.5cm (3 × 1in). Notch one end of each strip to fit over the screws at the back of the bed (Fig 3).

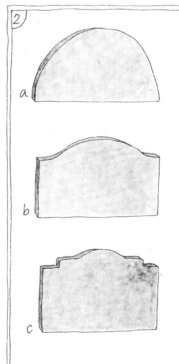

PLAIN HEADBOARD COVER

The slip-over cover is made in much the same way as a pillowcase, with an opening along the lower edge. Quilted fabric and piped (corded) seams (see page 150) look best.

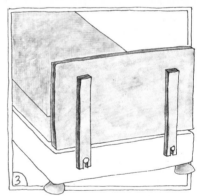

Cut a piece of the main fabric to the same dimensions as the headboard and add 12mm ($\frac{1}{2}$in) all round for turnings (seams). Cut a second piece the same size from lining fabric to back the headboard.

Cut a strip of main fabric, or a contrasting one, to fit round the side and top edges of the

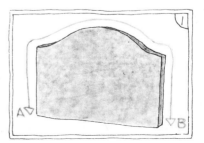

headboard (Fig 1) plus 2.5cm (1in) for turnings, making it as deep as the headboard (front to back) plus 2.5cm (1in) for turnings.

With right sides facing, join this strip to the side and top edges of the front section with a 12mm ($\frac{1}{2}$in) flat seam and include the piping (cording) if any. Notch curves and trim corners (Fig 2) then trim the seam allowances to about 6mm ($\frac{1}{4}$in) from the stitching.

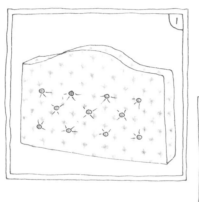

Join this gusset strip to the back section of the cover in the same way. (The alternative to having a gusset is to taper the front edge of the foam rubber by snipping with scissors [Fig 3] then the front and back sections can be stitched directly to one another.)

Turn in 12mm ($\frac{1}{2}$in) along the open edges and make a double 6mm ($\frac{1}{4}$in) hem. Turn right side out and slip the cover over the headboard.

BUTTONED HEADBOARD COVER

Cut a piece of 5cm (2in) or 7.5cm (3in) thick foam to the same size as the headboard. Add the depth of the foam (front to back) to the width of the gusset strip. Mark the positions of the buttons on the front fabric (Fig 1). Join the gusset strip to the front fabric as described for the plain cover.

Position the foam against the wrong side of the front fabric. Sew the buttons in place, taking the needle through both the fabric and the foam and pulling the thread tight so that the button makes an indentation.

Join the back section of the cover to the gusset and finish off as for the plain cover.

Bedhangings

There are literally dozens of different ways to dress up your bed and your choice will depend as much on the structure and style of the bed as on the amount of fabric your budget will allow. Even if you do not own a traditional four poster bed, you can achieve a similar effect with corona bed drapes.

Choosing the style

There are three possible ways of dressing a four poster bed and you can choose any combination. There are drapes, which hang down the length of each post; valances, which are suspended at the top between the posts; and the canopy, which forms a 'roof' over the bed (see photograph opposite).

Most four posters are made of either brass or wood. Some have poles between the posts, some

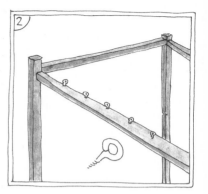

canopy and/or a valance.

An ordinary bed can be made to look almost as grand as a four poster with corona drapes. These are suspended either from a straight pole or a coronet positioned centrally above the bedhead (it does mean that the bed must be directly under a ceiling joist). The fabric can be hung flat or gathered or, from a pole, it can be festooned. Tiebacks hold the drapes in place at either side of the bed.

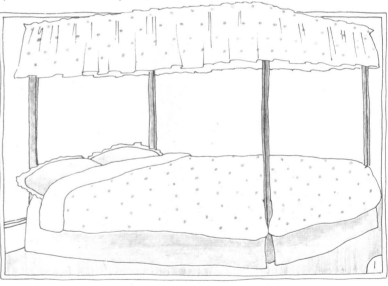

come complete with curtain rings and others have a built-in or concealed curtain track (rod).

For a bed with poles only (Fig. 1), a cased heading can be slotted directly onto the pole or hung from curtain rings suspended from the pole. If the bed has a wooden frame and is not a valuable family heirloom, fix a line of screw eyes at 7.5cm (3in) intervals along the top of the frame (Fig 2). Onto these you could fix a ruched

VALANCES

There are two methods of making valances — with a cased heading if there are detachable poles between the four posts and, if not, with curtain tape. Both versions should be lined because they are seen from both sides. This gives you a choice of using matching fabric or a contrasting plain colour for the lining. The bottom edges can be finished off with any number of different trimmings from a plain binding to double ruffles with broderie anglaise (eyelet) trim.

Valance with cased heading

Multiply the lengths of the poles by one-and-a-half to two times for fullness. Decide on the depth of the valance (30cm [12in] is about average) and add 2.5cm (1in) for the top turnings (seams) plus the circumference of the pole. Cut four strips of fabric to this depth – two to the side lengths and two to the end lengths. Cut four strips of lining to correspond. Make each of the four valances in the same way. With right sides facing, tack (baste) the lining to the main fabric all round; stitch 2.5cm (1in) from the edge round the side and bottom edges. Trim corners (Fig 1). Turn right side out and press. Turn in and press 2.5cm (1in) along the top edge to the lining side. Make a second turning, this time to the depth of half the pole circumference and tack (baste). Machine stitch close to the lower edge of the casing (Fig 2). Slot the pole through the casing and space the gathers evenly (Fig 3). Or, allow 5cm (2in) top turning (seam)

instead of 2.5cm (1in), turn 12mm ($\frac{1}{2}$in) to the inside at the top edges and slip stitch them together. Make two lines of stitching for the casing, the top one 4cm (1$\frac{1}{2}$in) down from the top edge to create

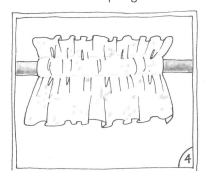

a small ruffle to decorate the pole (Fig 4).

Valance with curtain tape

This version looks particularly pretty with bound edges so there are no allowances for top and bottom turnings.

Measure the length of each valance as for the version with the cased heading. Decide on the finished depth and add 7.5cm (3in) for the top ruffle. (If you prefer to make the valance plain, add a further 2.5cm [1in] for the lower hem and 12mm [$\frac{1}{2}$in] for the top turning.) Cut out the four strips of fabric to the correct measurements and

four lining pieces to correspond and make the four valances in the same way.

With right sides facing, stitch the lining to the fabric 12mm ($\frac{1}{2}$in) from the side edges only (Fig 5). (For the unbound version, stitch along the lower edge too.) Turn right sides out and press.

Using 5cm (2in) bias binding either homemade (see page 152) in contrasting fabric or purchased, fold the binding in half lengthways and, turning in the raw ends, tack (baste) it over the raw edges of the valance, top and bottom (Fig 6).

Below: A four poster with hangings.

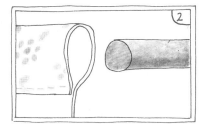

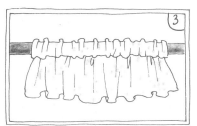

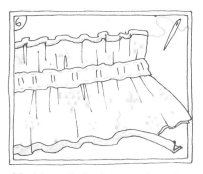

Machine stitch close to the edges and slip stitch the ends closed. (For the unbound version, turn 12mm [½in] to the inside along the top edges and slip stitch together.)

Prepare standard gathering curtain tape as for curtains (see page 110) and stitch it to the lining side of the valance, 7.5cm (3in) from the top edge. Draw up the cords to fit the poles. Using curtain hooks, attach the valance to curtain rings or screw eyes fixed to the top of the frame.

CANOPIES

The traditional 'roof' over a four poster bed is very romantic and can be simply made, in much the same way as a bedspread with a frilled valance (gathered skirt).

The edges of the canopy sit on top of the horizontal poles and the valances are attached to it (Fig 1).

Plain canopy

Make four valances in the same way as the valance with a cased heading but leave out the casing. Make two lines of gathering stitches through both thicknesses along the top of the valance, the lower one 2.5cm (1in) from the raw edges (Fig 2).

Make up two pieces of fabric to the finished size of the canopy plus 2.5cm (1in) all round. The top fabric of the canopy could be made with lining fabric if the bed posts will hide it from any angle.

Lay the underside of the canopy flat and draw up the valances to fit, keeping the ends of the valances *within* the seam allowances of the canopy (Fig 3). Space the gathers evenly and tack (baste) the valance to the canopy, the lining side of the valance facing the right side of the canopy, raw edges together. Stitch 2.5cm (1in) from the edge. Press the seam towards the canopy.

Lay the top section of the canopy flat and turn in and press 2.5cm (1in) all round to the wrong side, pressing in a mitre at each corner (see page 151). Tack (baste).

Pin the two canopy sections together, wrong sides facing, enclosing the seam allowances. Top stitch all round, as close to the edge as possible (Fig 4).

Ruched canopy

This is made in the same way as the plain canopy except that the underside of the canopy is cut to one-and-a-half times its finished length and gathered down the side edges before joining it to the valances (Fig 5).

Ruched canopy with curtain tape

If you can fix screw eyes to the top of the frame, this is a quicker way to make a ruched canopy.

Cut two pieces of fabric to one-and-a-half times the finished length of the canopy by the finished width. Place them right sides together and stitch all round, 2.5cm (1in) from the edge, leaving an opening of 60cm (24in) on one end (Fig 6). Trim corners and turn

right sides out. Turn in 2.5cm (1in) along the opening and slip stitch together. Press.

Prepare standard gathering tape as for curtains (see page 110) and stitch it as close as possible to the long edges of the canopy on the underside. Draw up the cords to the correct length, spacing the gathers evenly.

Place curtain hooks at 7.5cm (3in)

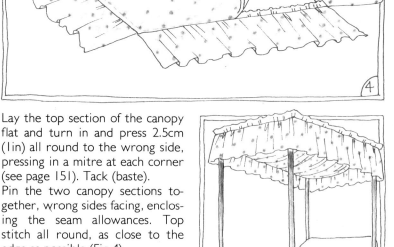

intervals along the tape and hook them onto the screw eyes.

Make a valance with a top ruffle to hide the line of hooks.

DRAPES

Bed drapes are made in exactly the same way as loose lined curtains (see page 111) except that the lining is exactly the same width as the main fabric so that the inside view from the bed looks as smartly tailored as the outside. This construction also makes it easy to insert ruffles down the sides of the curtains.

For drapes with ruffles along the side and bottom edges, treat each curtain as if you were making a huge pillowcase with ruffles on

three sides, the only difference is that you do not need an envelope opening (see page 133). Ruffles could be inserted at side edges only (Fig 1).

Allow an extra 2.5cm (1in) along

the top edge of both lining and main fabric and turn in this allowance *before* joining the two fabrics together. This gives a neat edge in line with the edge of the ruffle once the curtain is turned right side out (Fig 2). Slip stitch the edges together. Stitch the curtain tape to the wrong side about 6mm (¼in) from the top edge.

Tie-backs

Tie-backs for bed hangings are made in the same way as curtain tie-backs (see page 114).

Corona drapes

There are several variations of corona drapes which, as the word suggests, centre above the head of the bed. The simplest method of

hanging them is from a pole fixed to a curtain pole holder screwed to a ceiling joist (Fig 1). The drapes then loop back into tie-backs at either side of the bed. Alternatively, you can attach a bracket to the wall behind the bed and slot one end of the pole into it (Fig 2). Some old-fashioned brass or wrought iron beds are specially designed for corona drapes: they have a metal pole cantilevered from the headboard. The drapes are suspended about 112–152cm (4–5ft) above the bed and tied back on either side.

Above: Coronet-fixed corona drapes.

Simple corona drapes

Measure from the top of the pole to the floor (Fig 3, A–B), add at least 30cm (12in) for looping the drapes into the tie-back plus 2.5cm (1in) for the hem and 12mm (½in) for the top turning (seam). Double this measurement and multiply by the number of widths required to find how much fabric is needed.

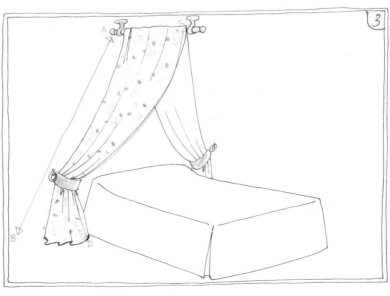

The pole should be about 60cm (2ft) long and one width of 120cm (48in) fabric should be enough.

Cut the fabric into two equal lengths or four if using two widths per side. You may prefer to use two widths for extra fullness. If so, join them in pairs, lengthways, right sides facing and with a 12mm (½in) seam. Match any patterning (see page 150). Remove the selvedges or notch as for curtains (see

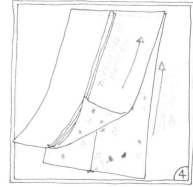

page 110) and press the seams open.

Lay the two pieces flat, right sides together, and join them across the top with a 12mm (½in) seam (Fig 4). If the fabric has a directional pattern, make sure that it runs upwards towards the seam from either side.

Make the lining in the same way.

With right sides facing, stitch the lining to the main fabric along the side edges with a 12mm ($\frac{1}{2}$in) seam. Turn right sides out and press. Turn 2.5cm (1in) to the inside along the bottom edges and slip stitch them together.

Prepare standard gathering tape as for curtains (see page 110) and, on the wrong side of the drapes, position it over the centre seam and stitch in place. Draw up the cords to fit the pole.

Hang the drapes over the pole with the tape along the top of the pole. To attach the tie-backs fix brass hooks to the wall on either side of the bed, just above the level of the top of the mattress.

For a softer look, edge the drapes with a ruffle or fringing.

Festooned corona drapes

These are made in the same way as the simple drapes with the addition of two or more rows of gathering tape sewn at intervals across the inside of the drapes. They are drawn up to create the festooned effect as shown in Fig 5. The front bottom corners of the drapes should be curved.

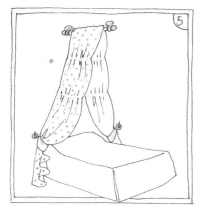

Coronet-fixed corona drapes

These drapes hang from a special coronet or a semi-circular bracket which is fixed to the wall 120–150cm (4–5ft) above the centre of the bed (Fig 6). They include a third curtain which hangs against the wall. Because the bracket has a curtain track (rod)

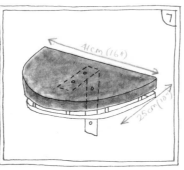

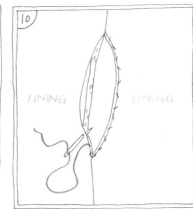

fixed to it (Fig 7), the drapes are made in the same way as conventional curtains, using standard gathering tape (see page 110).

The bracket illustrated is made of 2.5cm (1in) chipboard, 41cm (16in) across and 25cm (10in) deep, and is mounted on the wall with angle irons. The drapes have a pelmet (valance) across the top which hides the curtain track (rod).

For a single (twin) bed, allow two widths of fabric for the curtain which hangs against the wall; for a double, allow three. Allow one or one-and-a-half widths for each side curtain, depending on the fullness preferred.

Fix the coronet bracket to the wall

and measure the length of the drapes from the track (rod) to the floor in the same way as for simple drapes (Fig 6). If the drapes are to be level with the floor (Fig 8), measure C–D instead of A–B. Otherwise the curtains will fall in staggered folds (Fig 9). Add 2.5cm (1in) for the top turning and 5cm (2in) for the hem.

Make up the back and two side curtains as one enormous lined curtain as given for loose lined curtains (see page 111) but leave the hem unfinished if it is to hang level with the floor.

Make the tie-backs (see page 114).

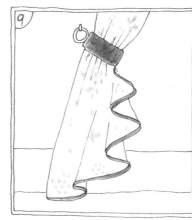

Attach hooks to the curtain tape, draw up the cords to fit the coronet and hang the curtains in place. Screw the ring holders for the tie-backs to the wall.

Mark on the seamline between each side curtain and the back curtain where the tie-backs will come. Take the curtains down and unpick (open) the seam at the marks for 15cm (6in). Slip stitch the curtain fabric to the lining on

either side of the slot (Fig 10). Rehang the curtains and slot the tie-backs through.

For curtains which are to hang level with the floor, mark the hem foldline with pins (Fig 11). Remove the curtains from the track (rod) and cut 5cm (2in) below the pins. Turn up and press the fabric along the pinline and make a double 2.5cm (1in) hem.

Make a pelmet (valance) to fit the

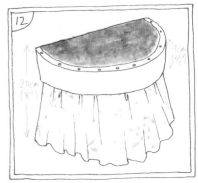

corona bracket with a straight flat panel about 9cm (3$\frac{1}{2}$in) deep at the top and a gathered ruffle about 20cm (8in) deep below (Fig 12).

132

Bed linen

Making your own sheets, pillow-cases and duvet (continental quilt) covers provides yet another opportunity to extend the scope of the co-ordinated bedroom colour scheme. Extra wide sheeting fabrics on the market, help make the job that much easier. Even a simple border of fabric to match curtains, or bedspread, sewn to the top of an existing sheet, will add to the co-ordinated look.

PLAIN PILLOWCASES

The simplest method is to cut the pillowcase out of a single piece of extra-wide sheeting fabric. Otherwise you can make it in two or three sections as for a ruffled pillowcase.

Measure the width and length of the pillow. Cut a single piece of fabric double the length plus 23cm (9in) for turnings and the envelope flap, the same width plus 5cm (2in) for turnings (seams), with one short end having the selvedge.

Turn in and press 6.5cm (2½in)

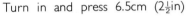

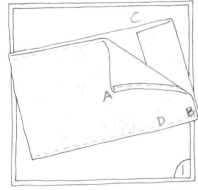

across the non-selvedge end (Fig 1, A–B) and turn in 6mm (¼in) of that to make a double hem, machine stitching close to the edge.

With wrong sides together, fold the selvedge end (C–D) to make a 15cm (6in) pocket. Still with wrong sides together, fold the fabric in half widthways. Stitch the side edges 6mm (¼in) from the edge and trim to 3mm (⅛in). Turn wrong side out and press. Stitch along the side edges again, 6mm (¼in) from the edge, to form a French seam. Turn right side out and press.

Right: Matching reversible bed linen.

RUFFLED PILLOWCASES

Cut two pieces of fabric each the length and width of the pillow plus 2.5cm (1in) all round. Cut a separate pocket piece to the same width as the main sections by 20cm (8in) across.

Make a ruffle (see page 153) to fit round the pillow. Pin and tack (baste) it in place, right sides together, to the top section of the pillowcase.

Press 12mm (½in) to the wrong side along one long edge of the pocket piece, make a double 6mm (¼in) hem and machine stitch in place. Lay the pocket piece over the top section of the pillowcase with the ruffle between and right sides together, as shown in Fig 1.

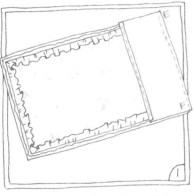

Machine stitch from E to F. Turn right side out and press.

On the second pillowcase section press 12mm (½in) to the wrong side along one short edge, make a double 6mm (¼in) hem and machine stitch.

Place the two sections of the pillowcase right sides together and stitch round three sides 12mm (½in) from the raw edges (Fig 2),

keeping the ruffle turned in as shown. Trim the corners then zig-zag the raw edges to neaten them. Turn right sides out and press.

DUVET (CONTINENTAL QUILT) COVERS

Measure the width and length of the duvet and add 12mm (½in) all round for seam allowances. Cut two pieces of fabric to these measurements.

With wrong sides facing, stitch round three sides 6mm (¼in) from the edge, leaving one short end open (Fig 1). Trim the seam to 3mm (⅛in). Turn wrong sides out and press. Stitch again, 6mm (¼in) from the edge to form a French seam. Around the open end press 12mm (½in) to the wrong side,

make a double 6mm (¼in) hem and machine stitch. Turn right sides out and press all seams.

Sew a line of press-studs (snaps) to the inside of the opening, spaced at about 15cm (6in) intervals.

SOFT FURNISHING

New loose (slip) covers for cushions, sofas and armchairs have a revitalising effect on the look of a room, but the actual job of making them takes a lot of time. Even so, it is not a task to dismiss as being too difficult. Making a dress is generally considered more complicated. And the satisfaction of seeing a favourite jaded armchair transformed, makes all the effort worthwhile. It is also considerably cheaper than having them all made professionally.

Cushions

Cushions (usually known as pillows in the US) are immensely decorative as well as practical. They can provide contrasting colours to a room, introduce pattern or inject vibrant primary colours into an otherwise monotone colour scheme. And, of course, even if a bed or chair does not actually *need* them, a great pile of cushions will create a plushness that is always psychologically satisfying.

All the shapes described in this chapter can be made plain or with piped (corded) or ruffled edges (see pages 150 and 153).

RECTANGULAR CUSHION COVER

Without zip opening. Measure both the width and the length of the cushion pad (form) across the centre as shown in Fig 1. Never measure the side seams – some cushions may look square when they are, in fact, rectangular! Add 12mm ($\frac{1}{2}$in) all round and cut two pieces of fabric to these dimensions. If several cushion covers are to be made out of one large piece of fabric, make a paper pattern first so that the fabric can be cut in the most economical way.

With right sides facing, stitch the two pieces together all round, 12mm ($\frac{1}{2}$in) from the edge, leaving an opening on one side (Fig 2). Clip the corners, turn right side out and press.

Insert the cushion pad (form), taking care to fill out the corners. Along the opening turn in 12mm ($\frac{1}{2}$in) and slip stitch (see page 148) together (Fig 3), using fairly long stitches so that they will undo easily when removing the covers for cleaning.

With zip opening. Measure the cushion pad (form) and cut out the fabric as for the cover without an opening.

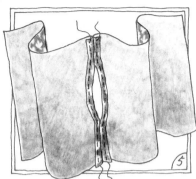

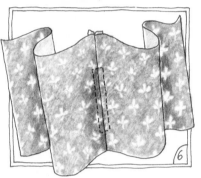

Below: Co-ordinating cushions.

With right sides facing, tack (baste) the seamline on one side only and machine stitch, leaving a centrally positioned space for the zip opening (Fig 4). On a 30cm (12in) square cushion, for example, a 20cm (8in) zip would be about right.

Lay the two pieces of fabric flat, wrong sides up, and press the seam open. Tack (baste) the seam allowances in place (Fig 5).

Tack (baste) the zip in place centrally over the seam and between the machine stitching. Machine stitch all round the zip teeth as shown in Fig. 6.

Open the zip and, with right sides facing, join the back and front of the cover by stitching the remaining three sides. Trim corners, turn right side out and press.

ROUND CUSHION COVER

Without zip opening. Measure the diameter of the cushion pad (form)

and add 2.5cm (1in). Cut a square of brown paper slightly larger than this measurement and fold it in four (Fig 1).

Tie a pencil with a piece of string and push a drawing pin (thumbtack) through the string at the same distance from the pencil as the radius of the cushion pad (form) plus 12mm ($\frac{1}{2}$in). Push the drawing pin into a firm surface at the folded corner of the pattern

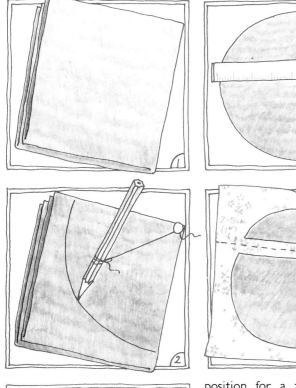

and, keeping the string taut, draw a quarter circle (Fig 2). Cut round the pencil line through all thicknesses then open up the pattern. Using the pattern, cut two pieces of fabric – if there is a large motif, place it centrally.

With right sides facing, stitch the

fabric together leaving an opening of just over one third of the seam (Fig 3). Notch the seam allowance all round then turn back the seam allowance on either side of the opening and tack (baste) it in place. Turn right sides out and press.

Insert the cushion pad (form) and slip stitch the opening as for the rectangular cushion cover.

With zip opening. The neatest

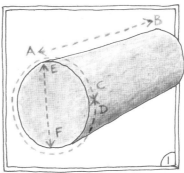

position for a zip on a round cushion cover is across the back. Once the front fabric has been cut out, lay the paper pattern flat and draw a line across it about a third of the way down (Fig 4). Cut along the pencil line and lay the two pieces on the fabric leaving a 2.5cm (1in) gap between them. Draw a line on the fabric down the middle of this gap (Fig 5). Cut round the pattern and across on the line marked on the fabric.

With right sides facing, tack the pieces together 12mm ($\frac{1}{2}$in) from the edge and machine stitch a short seam at each end, leaving the correct space for the zip. Press the seam open and tack the seam allowances in place as for the square cushion cover.

Tack the zip in place centrally over the seam and between the two short seams. Machine stitch all the way round.

Open the zip and, with right sides facing, stitch the back and front of the cover together all the way round, 12mm ($\frac{1}{2}$in) from the edge. Notch the seam allowances, turn right sides out and press.

BOLSTER CUSHION COVER

The bolster cushion is long, thin and sausage-shaped. Traditionally it is used to soften the ends of sofas or bolster pillows at the head of a bed. They are often used to provide extra back support on a day bed.

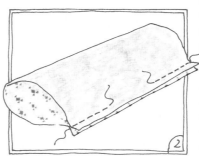

Measure the length (A–B) and the circumference (C–D) of the bolster (Fig 1) and cut out a piece of fabric to these dimensions plus 12mm ($\frac{1}{2}$in) all round. Measure the diameter of the end of the cushion pad (form) (Fig 1, E–F). Make a paper pattern for the end pieces as for the circular cushion and cut two pieces of fabric with it, remembering to allow for the seams. With right sides facing, fold the main section in half lengthways; tack (baste) it together 12mm ($\frac{1}{2}$in) from the edge. Machine stitch 10cm (4in) from each end making the zip opening 20cm (8in) shorter

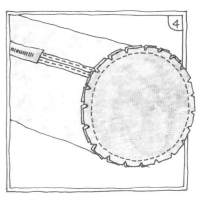

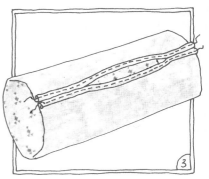

than the bolster (Fig 2). Press the seam open, turn under 6mm ($\frac{1}{4}$in) on each seam allowance and machine stitch the edge (Fig 3).

Stitch the zip in place as for the square cushion cover except that the fabric cannot be opened out flat.

Open the zip and, with right sides facing, sew the end pieces in place. Notch the seam allowance before machine stitching (Fig 4).

Turn right sides out, press all seams and insert the bolster.

SQUAB CUSHION COVER

The squab cushion is designed to fit and tie onto a straight chair. The cover is made in the same way as square or round cushion covers except that the pattern is taken from the seat or back of the chair. Lay a large piece of tracing paper over the chair seat (or back) and, with a thick felt pen, mark out its shape. Cut out the pattern 12mm ($\frac{1}{2}$in) outside the outline. If the ties are to attach a square cushion to the chair, mark their positions on the pattern (Fig 1 p 136), two ties for each arm or leg (Fig 2 p 136). If they are round, one double-ended tie positioned centrally will do for each. Transfer these marks with

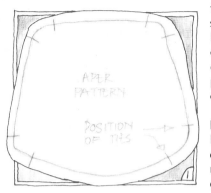

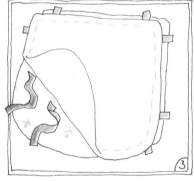

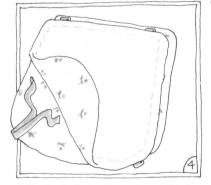

them (Figs 3 and 4). The ties should be long enough to tie in a bow round the appropriate arm or leg. To make a squab cushion cover with a zip opening, cut the pattern in half and insert the zip on the back as for a round cushion.

BOX CUSHION COVERS

Box cushions, also called welted cushions, can be rectangular or round. The welt runs round the circumference of the cushion, forming the sides of the box.

Rectangular

Measure both the width and length of the cushion pad (form) – some square-looking cushions turn out to be rectangular – (Fig 1). Measure A–B for the length of

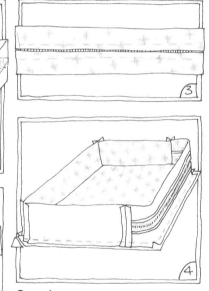

the zip which should be long enough to turn each of the two adjoining corners by 5cm (2in). The zip welt is made up of two strips of fabric each 2.5cm (1in) longer than the zip and half the depth of the cushion plus 2.5cm (1in). The rest of the welt is made of three sections, a seam at each corner and making up to the A–B measurement in Fig 2 with 12mm ($\frac{1}{2}$in) allowances all round. Cut out

all the welt pieces and the top and bottom sections of the cushion cover – the last two also have 12mm ($\frac{1}{2}$in) allowances all round. Apply the zip to the narrow welt pieces as for a square cushion (Fig 3). With right sides facing, join the other three welt pieces with 12mm ($\frac{1}{2}$in) seams then join in the zip section in the same way. Press the seams open.

With right sides facing, attach the welt to the bottom of the cushion cover (Fig 4) with a 12mm ($\frac{1}{2}$in) seam. Clip the seam allowance of the welt at each corner and trim diagonally across the corners through both thicknesses. Open the zip and join the top of the cover to the welt in the same way. Turn right side out and press.

Round

Make a paper pattern for the top and bottom of the cover as for a simple round cushion cover. Measure the depth and circumference of the cushion. Cut one strip of fabric to the full depth and half the circumference plus 12mm ($\frac{1}{2}$in) all round; cut two other strips to half of the depth and half of the circumference with 12mm ($\frac{1}{2}$in) extra all round. The zip should also measure half the circumference.

Apply the zip to the narrow welt pieces as for a square cushion cover and then, with right sides facing, join the two halves of the

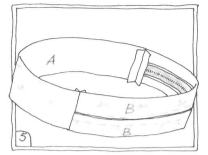

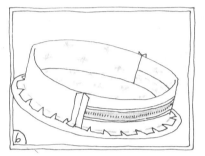

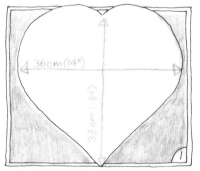

welt with 12mm ($\frac{1}{2}$in) seams (Fig 5). Press seams open.

With right sides facing, join the welt to one of the circular pieces with a 12mm ($\frac{1}{2}$in) seam and notch the allowance all round (Fig 6). Open the zip and join the welt to the other circular piece in the same way. Turn right side out and press.

HEART-SHAPED CUSHION

As they are not always easy to come by, you may need to make

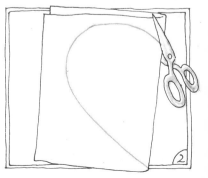

tailor's chalk to the cut-out fabric. Make the cushion cover as for the rectangular or round cover without zip openings except that before joining the back and front pieces, place the ties between the heart-shaped cushion pad (form) as well as the cover.

Cut a piece of paper a little larger than the intended cushion – 36cm (14in) across and 33cm (13in) long would be a good size (Fig 1). Fold the paper in half lengthways and draw half a heart against the fold.

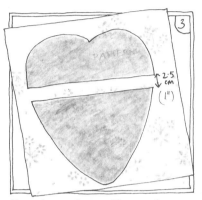

Cut along the outline and open out the pattern (Fig 2).

Make up the pad following the instructions for cushions without openings, inserting the stuffing before slipstitching the opening together. Make up the cover following the instructions for a round cushion with an opening, cutting the paper across the heart as shown in Fig 3. The zip should be the full width of the cover.

BUTTONED CUSHIONS

Make up a cover without a zip opening and insert the cushion pad.

Lay the cushion flat to mark the positions of the buttons with pins, making a regular, criss-cross pattern as shown in buttoned headboard covers (see page 128). Two buttons, one on each side, will be required for each mark. Covered ones look best, preferably made of plastic, not metal which, so that the cushion can be washed.

Take a tracing of the front of the cushion including the button positions and use it to mark the reverse side to correspond.

Sew the buttons in place on the front, stitching right through the cushion pad. Pull tightly and secure the thread on the back then sew each button on the back over the securing stitches, winding the thread round the button to finish.

Loose covers

Lots of people who would think nothing of making a bedspread would never dream of attempting loose (slip) covers. But once you know how to make a pattern for cutting out the fabric, they are not much more difficult than a bedspread. More time and work are involved, however, simply because there are more pieces to sew together.

Working out the pattern

Measure each section of the chair or sofa (Fig 1) at its maximum points and cut a rectangle of calico (muslin) to correspond, allowing extra for seams and tuck-ins. Pin each piece in place and mark its exact shape with pencil or felt pen. Remove the pieces and add 2.5cm (1in) all round each piece for turnings (seams) and 15cm (6in) tuck-in on the inside of arms, seat and back pieces (Fig 2).

There are several ways of finishing off the bottom edges of loose (slip) covers and you must make your choice before cutting out the fabric pattern. Flaps can be stitched to the bottom of the cover and tied in place under the piece of furniture to give a completely fitted look (Fig 3). Or you can make a flat skirt with kick pleats (Fig 4), or a gathered (Fig 5) or box pleated skirt (Fig 6).

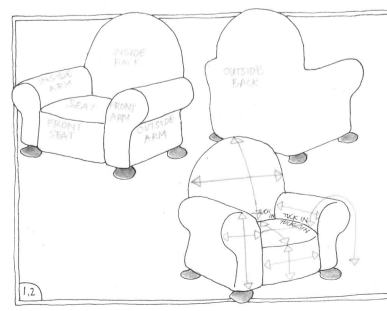

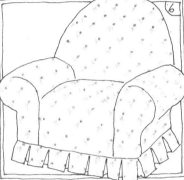

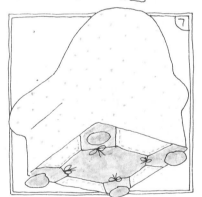

To make a pattern for bottom flaps, turn the piece of furniture upside down and measure the distance between the legs. Cut a strip of calico (muslin) to the same length by about 20 cm (8in) wide, plus 2.5cm (1in) all round. Eight pieces of tape are used to tie the flaps in place (Fig 7).

To make a pattern for a straight skirt with kick pleats, measure A–B (Fig 8) and cut a strip of calico

(muslin) to this length by 22cm (8½in) deep, plus 2.5cm (1in) all round. In the same way, measure and cut a pattern for each side and the back of the piece of furniture. The pattern for the pleat should

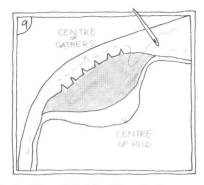

be 30cm (12in) by 22cm (8in) deep, plus seam allowances.

Make up the skirt as given on page 124. There are also instructions for gathered and box-pleated skirts on pages 124 and 125. If there is a separate seat cushion (or cushions), make calico (muslin) patterns for these as well.

Once all the pattern pieces have been made, pin each piece in place onto the chair or sofa, wrong side out, and then pin the pieces to one another, right sides facing, in the following order: outside back to inside back, inside back to seat, seat to front seat, seat to inside arm, inside arm to outside arm, then finally pin the front arms in place. On curved edges, such as the top of scroll arms or rounded backs, gather the inside section to

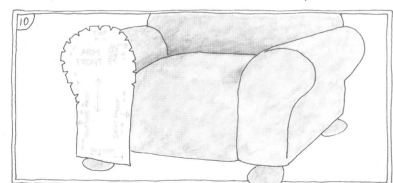

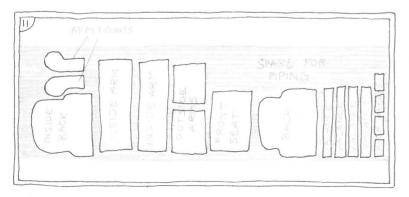

its adjoining section by marking where the gathers begin and end, the centre of the gathering line and the corresponding centre on the ungathered section. Match up these centre marks when pinning the fabric pieces together (Fig 9). Push the tuck-in areas in place and adjust if necessary. Before unpinning the pattern, mark on each piece its identity, the direction of the grain (Fig 10), the wrong side, top, bottom, the pinned seamline and, along each seamline, indicate which section it is to be joined to.

Estimating fabric quantities

Mark two lines on a clean floor with chalk, the width of the upholstery fabric apart, usually 122cm (48in). Unpin the pattern pieces and lay them out on the floor between the lines. Place them wrong sides down and with all the grain lines running in the right direction, juggling them for the most economic fit (Fig 11). If the fabric has a large pattern, position the pieces so that the outside back, inside back, outside arm, seat and front seat centre on the centre of the pattern. Include the skirt pieces.

Measure all the prominent seam

lines (Fig 12) to find how much piping cord (cable cord) is required and allow sufficient fabric for covering the cord — on average, 1m (1⅛yd) for a sofa and 0.75m (⅞yd) for an armchair.

On a small sofa, position any seams in the inside back, seat and front seat pieces in the middle; on

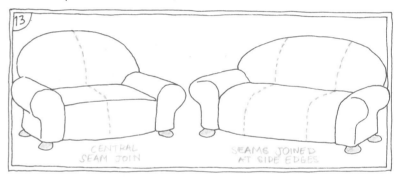

a large sofa, place them at either side (Fig 13).

Cutting out the fabric

Lay out the fabric, right side up, and pin the pattern pieces on it, also right side up. Keep all the grain lines parallel with the selvedges. As each piece is cut out, pin a label to it for identification and mark top, bottom and grainline.

Making up the cover

Pin the pieces together on the chair or sofa to check that they fit, working in the same sequence as for the pattern. Gather between the gathering points and fit and pin curves together.

Remove the cover; tack (baste) the seams, inserting any piping (cording) (see page 150). Stitch the pieces together leaving an opening of between 30cm (12in) and 46cm (18in) on one of the back seams for

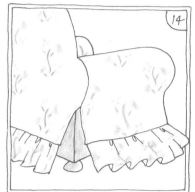

a zip (Fig 14). Put in the zip. Alternatively, if you prefer, hem the edges of the opening and sew hooks and eyes at 10cm (4in) intervals.

Clip all the curved seams (Fig 15). Turn the cover right sides out and press.

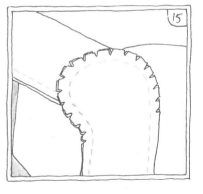

DRESSING TABLE SKIRT

The traditional kidney-shaped dressing table provides an old fashioned charm and yet another opportunity to introduce still more soft fabric folds into a bedroom. Adding a fabric top edged with a valance and a skirt will hide any old ugly piece of furniture — even an office desk. These instructioncs can be adapted to suit a rectangular shaped top as well.

Making up the skirt

To find how many widths of fabric will be needed for the main skirt, measure the circumference of the dressing table top and multiply by one-and-a-half. The depth is measured from the curtain track (rod) to just above floor level. Here, the edges of skirt and valance have been bound (see page 152) which makes them flare prettily (Fig 1). Otherwise, add an allowance for a bottom hem.

Make the skirt in one piece as for loose lined curtains (see page 111). The edges meet at the centre front to give an opening into the space below the dressing table.

To make the top, cut a piece of brown paper to cover the entire surface and trace the outline onto it. Cut out the fabric to this shape adding an extra 2.5cm (1in) all round.

Make up the top as for a fitted bedspread with a frilled valance (gathered skirt) (see page 124) except that the valance will be continuous all the way round the centre panel. The valance should be at least 15cm (6in) deep, either with a bound edge or with a hem. Either use quilted fabric for the main section of the top or line the top of the dressing table with terylene wadding (fiberfill batting) cut out to the shape and laid in place. Pipe (cord) the seam (see page 150) where the gathered valance joins the top cover (Fig 2).

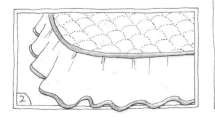

Table linen

Apart from protecting the table, a well-designed cloth can inject a cheering dollop of extra colour and prettiness into your room. The bigger the table, the better the impact. By making your own, you can choose a fabric to match others in the room.

Choosing the style

As always, the variety is endless, and choice depends on what you want to achieve. To hide a table with ugly legs, a floor length cloth is an obvious answer. If your table top is precious, then lining the tablecloth with heat proof foam, or making it out of a quilted fabric, will protect it from hot plates and casseroles. For extra extravagant, soft effects, you can layer a table with two or even three tablecloths. Lace on plain, and rectangular cloths topping full length round cloths look particularly pretty. To decorate the edges, you can use a frill, appliqué pattern, border, binding, or scallop shape — the scope is limitless.

RECTANGULAR TABLECLOTH

If you have a cloth which fits the table, simply copy it by measuring its length and width and add seams and hems. Otherwise, measure the table top. To find the required length of overhang, sit at the table and measure the distance from the top edge of the table either to your lap or to the floor. Double this measurement and add it to each of the length and the width of the table. Add a further 2.5cm (1in) all round for a narrow hem or 5cm (2in) for a wider hem.

If a seam is necessary in the fabric,

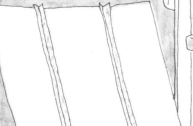

never place it down the centre of the cloth. Instead, add half the extra at either side (Fig 1). Make either a flat seam or a flat fell seam (see page 149). Neaten a flat seam with a zig-zag stitch.

The neatest way to finish rectangular corners on the tablecloth is with a mitre (see page 151). On the narrow hem, turn in first 6mm ($\frac{1}{4}$in) then 2cm ($\frac{3}{4}$in); on the wide hem turn in first 12mm ($\frac{1}{2}$in) then 3.75cm ($1\frac{1}{2}$in). Once the mitre is stitched, finish off the hems either with a slip stitch (see page 148), with straight machine stitching close to the edge or satin stitch (Fig 2). Alternatively, finish off the edges with a simple binding in a matching or contrasting colour (see page 152).

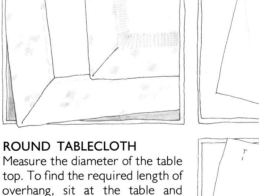

ROUND TABLECLOTH

Measure the diameter of the table top. To find the required length of overhang, sit at the table and measure the distance from the top edge of the table either to your lap (Fig 1 A–B) or to the floor (C–D). Double this measurement and add it to the diameter of the table top. Add a further 12mm ($\frac{1}{2}$in) all round for a simple hem or 6mm ($\frac{1}{4}$in) for a bias binding hem.

Stitch together enough fabric to

form a square with sides equal to the diameter of the cloth, plus hems. Make sure that any seams do not fall right across the centre of the cloth — it is better to have one at each side with a large panel in the middle. Fold the fabric into quarters, wrong side out. Cut a piece of paper the same size as the folded fabric. Lay the paper flat on a surface into which you can push a drawing pin (thumb tack). Tie some string to a pencil and push a drawing pin (tack) through it at the same distance from the pencil as the radius of the tablecloth plus the seam allowance. With the drawing pin (tack) in one corner of the paper and the string taut, draw a quarter circle (Fig 2). Cut round the pencil line.

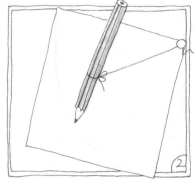

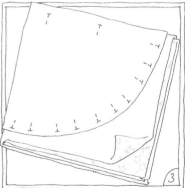

Pin the pattern to the folded fabric, placing the corner where the drawing pin was at the folded corner (Fig 3). Position the pins at right angles to the curved edge. Cut along the curved edge of the pattern through all thicknesses of the fabric, remove the pattern and open out the fabric.

Snip V notches into the raw edges all round making them about 6mm

($\frac{1}{4}$in) deep and spacing them at about 2.5cm (1in) intervals (Fig 4). Turn under 5mm (just under $\frac{1}{4}$in) and tack (baste). The notches will close up to allow the fabric to lie flat round the curve (Fig 5).

For a simple hem, turn under a further 6mm ($\frac{1}{4}$in) and stitch in

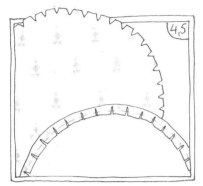

place. Alternatively, stitch bias binding on the wrong side of the cloth to cover the raw edge.

TABLECLOTH WITH GATHERED SKIRT

This cloth has a smooth, fitted top, cut to match the shape and size of the table and at the edge of the table, where the overhang usually starts, it is joined to a gathered skirt (valance).

For a square or rectangular table, measure the length and width of the top. Cut and make up a piece of fabric to that size, adding 12mm ($\frac{1}{2}$in) all the way round. For a round table top, make a paper pattern first, following the instructions on page 136 for the round cushion cover; add 12mm ($\frac{1}{2}$in) all the way round and cut out.

To find the length of the skirt (valance), measure the distance from the top edge of the table to the floor. Add a further 2.5cm (1in) for a narrow hem, or 5cm (2in) for a wider hem. To find out the width of the skirt (valance), measure the circumference of the table and multiply by one-and-a-half. Allow 2.5cm (1in) extra for each seam. Make up the skirt (valance) to these measurements. With right sides' facing, join the skirt (valance) along the edges lengthways to make a complete circle. Gather along one side of this circle (the side to be joined to

the table top) and make a 2.5cm (1in) or 5cm (2in) turn under along the other edge, and then a 12mm ($\frac{1}{2}$in) or 2.5cm (1in) fold and hem. With right sides facing, join the gathered edge to the circumference of the table top, 12mm ($\frac{1}{2}$in) in from the outside edge. Ease the gathers to spread them evenly. Tack (baste) and then seam the skirt (valance) to the top, making sure that the skirt (valance) finishes 12mm ($\frac{1}{2}$in) above floor level. For added smartness, you can pipe the seam joining the table top to its skirt.

SPECIAL EDGES
Ruffled edge
This creates a soft, feminine effect as well as a certain opulence. The added weight also makes the cloth hang better. Make the ruffle either in matching fabric or in a contrast to add a new colour to the scheme; or finish the edges of the ruffle with a plain contrast binding – the combinations are endless.

To estimate the length of ruffle required for a circular cloth, multiply the diameter by $3\frac{1}{2}$ and then double that figure. For example, a 175cm (or say 70in) diameter multiplied by $3\frac{1}{2}$ equals 550cm (220in) so that the length of the ruffle must be 11m (440in).

For a rectangular cloth, measure the circumference and double it for the ruffle length. Make up the ruffle as given on page 153.

Double ruffle
The double-sided ruffle gives an even frothier, more extravagant finish to a tablecloth (Fig 1). Follow the instructions on page 154.

Bias bound ruffle
This takes time to make but gives a tailored finish which looks particularly pretty combined with a

small print (Fig 2). Bind both edges of the ruffle (see page 152) and make it up as a double ruffle.

Scalloped edge
To scallop the edge of a round tablecloth, do not unfold it after cutting out the quarter circle shape but fold it in half, then half again. Lay a piece of tracing paper over this sixteenth segment, trace its shape with a felt pen and cut it out. Fold the paper in two. Mark point A (Fig 3) about 15cm (6in) from the curved edge then, using a plate as a template, or compasses, draw a gentle curve from A to B. Cut along the curve and open out the pattern.

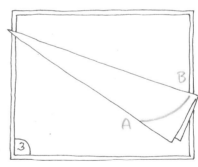

With the tablecloth still folded to correspond to the pattern, pin the pattern to it, pins at right angles to the curve, and draw the outline on the fabric with tailor's chalk or pencil. Tack (baste) lightly through all the layers of fabric along the inside of the outline to keep the segments even while cutting round the shape. With a thick fabric it may not be possible to cut through sixteen layers all at once in which case open out the cloth into eighths or quarters and trace more scallops as required.

The edges can be finished off with a simple bias binding (see page 152). However, a more professional finish would be to make facings. Fold the cloth in quarters

and, using it as a template, cut four quarter circle facings each 20cm (8in) deep with 6mm ($\frac{1}{4}$in) extra on all the straight edges (Fig 4). With right sides facing, stitch the four facings together to make a complete circle. Turn in and press 6mm ($\frac{1}{4}$in) to the wrong side on the inner edge. Notch the raw edge so that it can lie flat. Pin the facing to the cloth, right sides facing, round the scallops. Machine

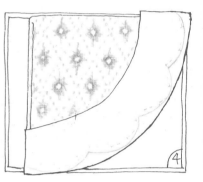

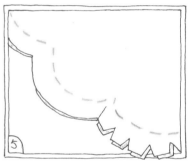

stitch 6mm ($\frac{1}{4}$in) from the edge then notch curves and clip close to the stitching at the points between the scallops (Fig 5). Turn right sides out and press. Lightly slip stitch the facing to the cloth at 20cm (8in) intervals.

Appliquéd edge
This is one of the most original and extravagant-looking ways of finishing a cloth. It is a painstaking job but really well worth it. Either cut flower shapes out of plain fabric or use an already printed floral pattern to cut out individual flowers. Leave a 3mm ($\frac{1}{8}$in) margin all round the shapes (Fig 6).

Arrange the flowers along the edge of the cloth, overlapping them in some places and grouping large clusters in the corners. Pin and tack (baste) round the edge of each shape (Fig 7).

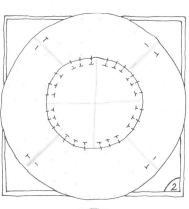

Choose a thread to match the dominant colour of the flowers, set the machine to zig-zag stitch and very carefully satin stitch round each flower shape to cover the raw edges completely. For a neat finish along the outer edges where the flowers project beyond the cloth, cut a piece of extra lightweight Vilene (non-woven interfacing) as a backing for the outside flowers. Satin stitch round the outline through both the top fabric and the Vilene (interfacing). When all the satin stitching is completed, cut away the Vilene close to the stitching.

If you have not got a machine which will do satin stitch, it is posssible, but a lengthy pro-

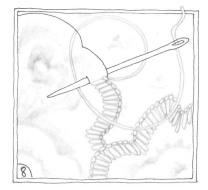

cess, to work by hand, using buttonhole stitch (Fig 8).

TOP LAYER CLOTHS

These are sometimes called throw-over cloths and are usually designed to cover about a third of the full-length one underneath. The edge, being much more noticeable than the floor-level one, usually has special edging treatment. But there are no hard and fast rules; have fun experimenting to find what looks good to you. Even the shapes need not be limited to the traditional rectangles or circles. Why not make one shaped like a star.

Star-shaped top layer cloth

The centre of the star exactly covers the top of a round table and the points cascade to about 20cm (8in) above floor level.

To make a star-shaped cloth, begin by measuring the diameter of the table top. Cut a paper pattern to fit the top exactly. Fold it into four to mark the quarter circles with creases.

Take the full-length circular cloth which the star-shaped cloth is to cover and fold it into four, pressing in the creases lightly. Open up the cloth and mark each crease line with a pin, 20cm (8in) up from the hemline (Fig 1).

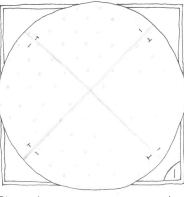

Place the paper pattern on the cloth so that its quarter foldlines exactly divide the quarter sections of the cloth in half (Fig 2), pinning at right angles to the edge.

Cut a piece of brown paper to cover one full quarter of the tablecloth except for 20cm (8in) round the hem. Place this pattern

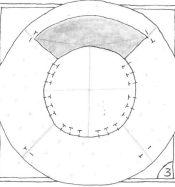

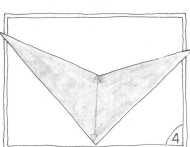

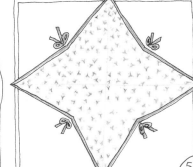

between the circular pattern and the cloth as shown in Fig 3, pinning it in place. With a ruler, draw a straight line from each of the pin marks on the cloth to the foldline on the circular pattern between them (Fig 3). Cut along these lines to give a quarter star shape (Fig 4).

Place this template on the over-cloth fabric, centred on the straight of the grain, and cut out leaving an extra 12mm ($\frac{1}{2}$in) all round. Cut three more pieces the same.

With wrong sides facing, join the pieces to make the star shape (Fig 5). Press seams open. Bind the edges (see page 152). Make four bows to match the binding and sew them to the inner points of the star. These bows will sit on the edge of the table.

NAPKINS AND MATS

Napkins are usually square and measure anything from 25cm (10in) to double that size. On 122cm (48in) fabric, either of those sizes will cut out quite economically, leaving just enough over for hems.

Mats, on the other hand, are usually rectangular measuring about 20 x 30cm (8 x 12in) or round measuring between 20cm and 25cm (8in and 10in) across. In the USA they tend to be larger — usually about 30 x 45cm (12 x 18in) or circular, between 30cm and 38cm (12in and 15in) across.

One of the most practical fabrics is quilting and reversible quilting will also give you a change of pattern. The other bonus of quilted fabric is that the raw edges only need simple binding to finish them (see page 152).

Cut out a rectangle of about 30cm (12in) wide by 20cm (8in) deep in quilted fabric. This is a good average size but, of course, the mat could be much larger if desired. Gently round off the corners (Fig 1).

Use either purchased or made up binding about 5cm (2in) wide to bind the raw edge (see page 152).

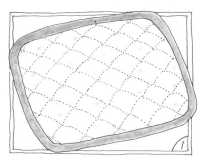

ACCESSORIES

Most people think of home sewing in terms of large projects such as making curtains or loose (slip) covers. However, there are lots of smaller things which are ideally suited to furnishing fabrics (especially quilting). Many are extremely easy to make either for your own use or as gifts. And, like everything you can make yourself, they work out much cheaper than if you bought them.

TEA COSY

Make a paper pattern using the chart in Fig 1, scaling it up to the size required. An average size would be 23cm (9in) high by 30cm (12in) across. Check the dimensions of your teapot and adjust the scale accordingly.

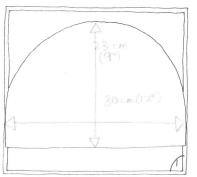

Using the pattern, cut two pieces of reversible quilted fabric, adding 12mm ($\frac{1}{2}$in) all round. Make up enough piping (cording) (see page 150) in a contrasting plain colour to edge the seam and trim the lower edge.

Cut a strip of fabric to match the piping (cording), to make a loop for the top of the cosy. For an average pot it should be about 6.5cm (2$\frac{1}{2}$in) wide by 15cm (6in) long but the dimensions, particularly the width, should be adjusted to look in proportion to the tea cosy. Fold and press 6mm ($\frac{1}{4}$in) to the wrong side down each long edge then fold the strip in half lengthways (Fig 2) and slip stitch the edges together (see page 148). Fold the strip in half and pin the edges on either side of the piping (cording) to the right side of one section of the cosy, centring it with raw edges matching (Fig 3). With right sides facing stitch the

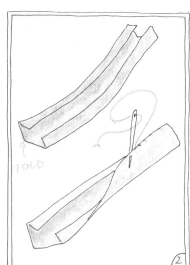

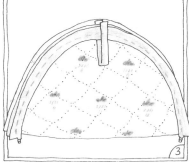

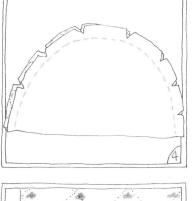

loop, piping (cording) and two halves of the tea cosy together

with a 12mm ($\frac{1}{2}$in) seam (Fig 4). Notch the seam allowance.

Turn right side out and press. Pin the piping (cording) round the lower edge of the cosy, matching the raw edges (Fig 5). Turn the raw edges of the piping (cording) to the wrong side of the cosy and slip stitch in place to bind the raw edge of the cosy (Fig 6).

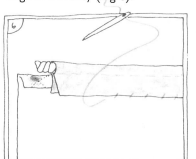

EGG COSY

An egg cosy is made in exactly the same way as the tea cosy but the chart is scaled down to 11.5cm (4$\frac{1}{2}$in) high by 9cm (3$\frac{1}{2}$in) across. Omit the top loop.

COASTERS

Cut out a 10cm (4in) square of quilted fabric and gently round off the corners. Finish off as for tablemats.

POT HOLDERS

Cut out either a 20cm (8in) diameter circle or a 20cm (8in) square of quilted fabric. For a square pot holder, gently round off the corners.

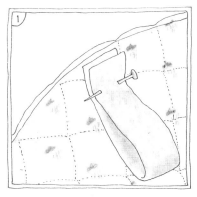

Finish off the holders as for tablemats but cut a 7.5cm (3in) strip of fabric to make a loop as for the tea cosy; attach it to the edge of the holder before binding (Fig 1).

COFFEE POT/BLENDER COVER

This is made in the same way as the tea cosy except that it has four sides. Cut two pieces of quilting for the back and front to the width and height required and round off the top (Fig 1a). Cut two rectangular pieces for the gusset (Fig 1b). Make a tab as for the tea

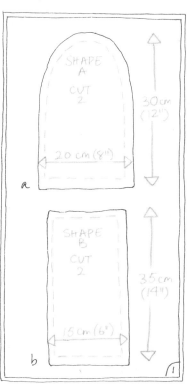

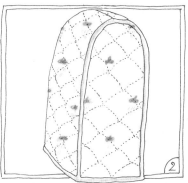

cosy and tuck the ends into the top gusset seam. Join the pieces together, piping (cording) the curved seams at back and front and round the base as for the tea cosy (Fig 2).

TOASTER COVER

A toaster cover is made in the same way as the coffee pot/blender cover with the dimensions of the toaster but making the gusset in one piece and omitting the loop. Pipe the curved seams at front and back and round the base (Fig 1).

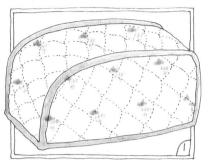

TISSUE BOX

Cut a piece of quilted fabric to the same width and length as the tissue box plus 12mm ($\frac{1}{2}$in) all round for the top section. Measure the perimeter and depth of the box and cut a strip of fabric to these dimensions plus 12mm ($\frac{1}{2}$in) all round to make the gusset of the cover.

Make up two lengths of piping (cording) each long enough to go round the top edges of the box.

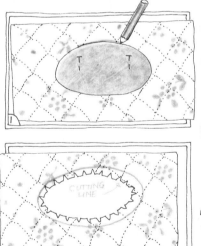

Using the top of an empty tissue box as a template, mark the top opening on the fabric with tailor's chalk or pencil (Fig 1). Cut out the hole 12mm ($\frac{1}{2}$in) inside the opening and notch round the edge (Fig 2). Bind the opening with bias binding (see page 152).

With right sides together, join the short ends of the gusset piece with a 12mm ($\frac{1}{2}$in) seam. With right

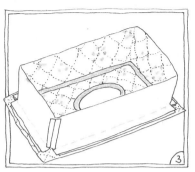

sides together and the piping (cording) placed between, join the top and gusset sections, placing the gusset seam at the centre back and snipping into the gusset seam allowance at each corner almost to the stitching (Fig 3). Trim the seam allowance close to the stitching.

Turn right side out and apply the piping (cording) round the lower edge; finish off as for the tea cosy.

COATHANGER COVER

Cut a strip of quilting 14cm (5$\frac{1}{2}$in) deep and 10cm (4in) longer than the hanger (Fig 1).

With right sides facing, fold the fabric in half lengthways and, using

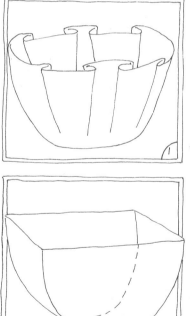

an egg cup or glass as a template, draw a semicircle about 6mm ($\frac{1}{4}$in) from each end (Fig 2).

Turn down and tack (baste) 6mm ($\frac{1}{4}$in) along each of the top edges

then machine stitch along the semicircles (Fig 3). Trim the seams close to the stitching.

Turn right side out and insert the hanger. Stitch the top edges together with a firm running stitch, gently gathering the fabric to fit (Fig 4).

LINING FOR A WICKER BASKET

Quilting is the ideal fabric to line a basket with but PVC (vinyl-coated fabric) may be more practical, especially if the basket is intended to be used for something like picnics. If the basket has a curved bottom, make a paper pattern. First make a rectangle of brown paper large enough to cover the outside of the basket then place it inside the basket, pleating the paper to fit (Fig 1), Dart the fabric to correspond, adding 12mm ($\frac{1}{2}$in) all round the top edge.

Alternatively, put tracing paper inside the basket and draw the basket in sections (Fig 2). Cut the fabric to correspond, adding 12mm ($\frac{1}{2}$in) all round each section. If the basket is flat-bottomed, measure the width and length of the base and the width and depth of each side (Fig 3). Cut out five

sections to correspond, adding 12mm ($\frac{1}{2}$in) all round each.

For the round-bottomed basket lining, either stitch the darts or join the sections together with 12mm ($\frac{1}{2}$in) seams, notching the curves.

For the rectangular basket, stitch the side pieces together in the correct sequence, with 12m ($\frac{1}{2}$in) seams. Press the seams open. Stitch the base to the side pieces, curving the seams at the corners and notching the side pieces at the corners (Fig 4).

Turn the lining right side inwards and fit it into the basket. With

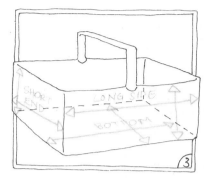

pins or tailor's chalk, mark the width of the handle at each side (Fig 5) and clip into the seam allowance at each mark. Between the clips, make a double 6mm ($\frac{1}{4}$in) hem on the wrong side of the

fabric. Make close zig-zag stitches over the raw ends (Fig 6).
Measure round the top of the basket from one side of the handle

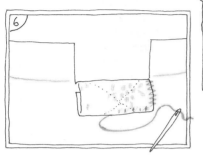

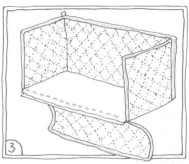

to the other (Fig 7, A–B) and make two ruffles each to one-and-a-half times this measurement (see page 153), adding 12mm ($\frac{1}{2}$in) seam allowance along the top. Bind the side and bottom edges of the ruffles (see page 152).
Cut four 20cm (8in) lengths of ribbon; tack (baste) them to the seamline of the top edge of the lining, one to each side of the hemmed sections behind the handles on the right side of the fabric, matching the raw edges (Fig 8).
Gather up each ruffle to fit and stitch it to the top of the lining (Fig

9), right sides together, stitching the ends of the ribbons in with the 12mm ($\frac{1}{2}$in) seam.
Place the lining in the basket and turn the ruffles to the outside.

Secure the lining by tying the ribbons to the handle.

COT (CRIB) LINING

As well as making a cot (crib) prettier and more cosy, a lining will protect the baby from the hard sides of the cot (crib) and also keep out draughts. Measure the width and length of the cot (crib) base. The sides should not be too high or the baby will be unable to see out and may feel enclosed. Measure from the lower edge of the mattress to the height you wish the finished lining to be.
Cut four pieces of reversible quilted fabric, two for the sides and two for the ends, all with 12mm ($\frac{1}{2}$in) added all round. As the bottom section goes under the mattress, it can be cut from less expensive lining fabric, again adding 12mm ($\frac{1}{2}$in) all round.
With right sides facing and taking 12mm ($\frac{1}{2}$in) seams, join a short end piece to each end of one of the side sections. Trim the seam allowances slightly, press them open and cover each seam with 2.5cm (1in) binding (see page 152). Bind the remaining raw edge of each

short end then bind right round the top edge of the lining (Fig 1). On the remaining side section, bind the top and side edges.
With wrong sides together, join the base to the three-sided section with a 12mm ($\frac{1}{2}$in) seam, notching the sides at the corners as shown in Fig 2. Turn right sides out and join the fourth side to the base, wrong sides together (Fig 3).
Cut six 40cm (16in) lengths of

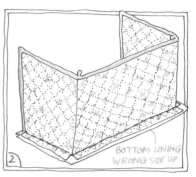

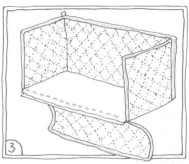

ribbon and stitch three of them to each side section of the cot (crib) lining, one at each end and one in the centre, their exact positions corresponding to an upright to which they can be tied on the outside (Fig 4).

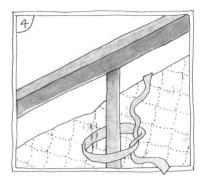

MOSES BASKET LINING

Measure the width and the length of the inside of the basket at their widest points. Add 2.5cm (1in) to each measurement and cut a rectangle of quilted fabric to these dimensions. Place it inside the basket, right side up, press it into the edges of the base where it joins the sides and mark the exact outline of the base with pins. Trim the fabric to 12mm ($\frac{1}{2}$in) from the pin line. Fold the fabric in two lengthways and mark with pins the centre at each end (Fig 1).
Measure the inside depth of the basket. Cut two pieces of fabric each with a width of twice the basket depth measurement and as long as half the perimeter (Fig 2, A–B) plus 2.5cm (1in).

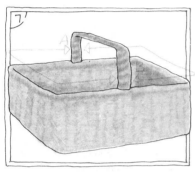

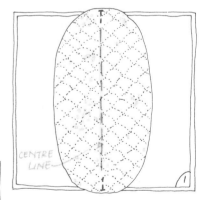

With right sides facing, join the two pieces at the short ends with 12mm (½in) seams. Press seams open.

Notch into the 12mm (½in) seam allowance round one edge of this section then join that edge, right sides facing, to the base, aligning the centre pin marks on the base with the seams on the side section (Fig 3).

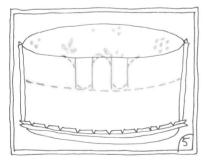

Place the lining in the basket and, with pins or tailor's chalk, mark the positions of the outer edges of the handles and the rim of the basket (Fig 4).

Remove the lining from the basket and fold it in half lengthways. On each side draw a line down from each of the four pins marking the handle, placing them at right angles to the pin line marking the top edge of the basket

and taking them to the edge of the fabric. Join the lines with curves and round off the lower edge of the outer lines as shown in Fig 5. Cut the lining as marked. Bind the raw edge (see page 152).

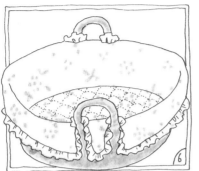

Make a double ruffle (see page 153) to fit the edge of the lining and stitch it in place.

Put the lining in the basket, folding the surplus over the top and slotting it through the handles (Fig 6).

HANGING POCKET WALL STORAGE

These are usually intended for strong shoes but, of course, they could contain other things such as small articles of clothing, toys, jewellery or toiletries. PVC (vinyl-coated fabric) is a good practical choice of fabric but this depends on the intended contents.

To make a pocket, decide on its finished size and add 12.5cm (5in) to the width and 2.5cm (1in) to the depth. Cut a piece of fabric to these dimensions.

Turn in and press 12mm (½in) all round the fabric to the wrong side and make a double 6mm (¼in) hem. Alternatively, cut the pocket 12mm (½in) smaller all round and bind the edges (see page 152) with 2.5cm (1in) binding.

Lay the fabric flat, right side up, and with pins or tailor's chalk mark a line 5cm (2in) in from each side edge. Make a fold along each of these lines and place it along the side edge. Pin the pleats in place and tack along the bottom of the pocket (Fig 1).

Make as many pockets as are required in the same way or make one long strip.

Cut a piece of fabric for the backing, making it large enough to take the arrangement of pockets plus 12mm (½in) to either side for a bound edge or 2.5cm (1in) for a hemmed edge and adding 20cm (8in) above the top row of pockets and the same allowance between the bottom row as for the sides.

Finish off the edges.

Pin the pockets in place on the backing and top stitch them down the side edges and across the bottom as close to the edges as possible (Fig 2).

Sew two, three or four loops to the top of the backing for fixing it to the wall.

HAMMOCK

For safety's sake, only hardwearing fabrics like canvas are a suitable choice for a hammock. So before

you start on this project, check that your sewing machine is capable of handling the extra thickness. (Small portable sewing machines are unlikely to be able to cope.) For extra comfort, you could line the inside of the hammock with a quilted fabric, or use a soft summery print. Cut one piece of canvas 120cm (48in) wide and 211cm (83in) long. Cut a piece of quilted fabric or lining fabric to

the same size. With right sides together, place pieces on top of each other, and seam the ends together, 12mm (½in) in from the edge. Turn right side out and press.

Along the long sides, make a 6mm (¼in) turn and a second 2.5cm (1in) turn to enclose the raw edges. The plain canvas forming a border to the lining, press, tack and top stitch in place (Fig 1).

To make loops through which to slot poles at either end, cut 22 pieces of canvas, each 4.5cm (1¾in) by 14.5cm (5¾in). Fold each piece in half lengthways. Turn in a 6mm (¼in) turn along the raw edges. Press and seam around all four sides as close to the edges as possible. Space each tab along the ends of the hammock, eleven for

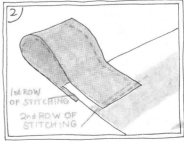

one end and eleven at the other, leaving about 10cm (4in) gap between each. Sew one end of the tab to the front of the hammock, and the other end to the back, to form a loop. As it is difficult to sew through all six layers at once, place one end of each tab below the other, as shown in Fig 2.

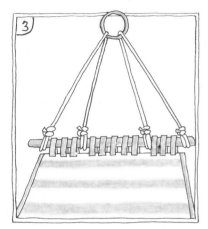

Cut two wooden poles 5cm (2in) in diameter and 63cm (25in) long. Slide one through the top, and the other through the bottom line of loops. Cut a length of strong (preferably nylon) rope into four 123cm (50in) lengths. Tie two to one pole and two to the other copying the positions shown in Fig 3, and threading the rope through a 8cm (3in) diameter steel ring. To knot the rope to the pole, use a round turn and two half hitches (Fig 4). Tie the hammock between two conveniently placed trees, using the same knots and strong rope.

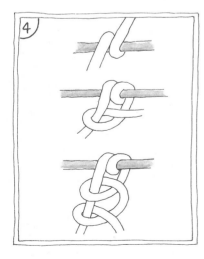

PICNIC HOLD-ALL
This ingenious design to take with you on picnics doubles up as ground sheet, tablecloth, cutlery holder and cushion holder and has handles for easy carrying.

You will need 2.25m (2½yd) of 120cm (48in) PVC (vinyl); 1.25m (1½yd) of 120cm (48in) fabric; 8.5m (9¼yd) of 2.5cm (1in) bias binding; 2.5m (2¾yd) of 12mm (½in) bias binding; matching thread; four cushion pads (forms) each 38cm (15in) square; either 2m (2¼yd) cushion fabric or 1m (1yd) cushion fabric and 1m (1yd) PVC (vinyl) to make cushions with waterproof backings. For information on working with PVC (vinyl), see Shower Curtains, page 114.

Hold-all
Following Fig 1, cut one piece of PVC (vinyl) for the base measuring 119cm (47in) square, four pieces A each 43cm (17in) square, four pieces B each 33 × 21.5cm (13 × 8½in) and two pieces C each 41 × 10cm (16 × 4in).
Bind two adjoining edges of each A

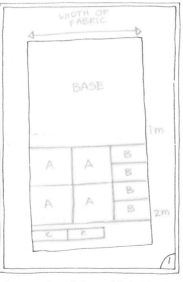

piece using 2.5cm (1in) binding (see page 152). On two of the B pieces, bind the top and right-hand edges and on the other two bind the bottom and left-hand edges using 12mm (½in) binding.
Lay the four A pieces flat, right sides up, two with their bound edges to the right and two with their bound edges to the left. Place

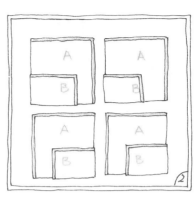

the B pieces over them, right sides up and raw edges matching as shown in Fig 2. Stitch each B piece to its A backing as indicated by the dotted lines (Fig 3), making the cutlery slots 3cm (1¼in) apart.
Fold each C piece in half lengthways, right sides together, and stitch 6mm (¼in) from the long edge. Turn right side out and top stitch 6mm (¼in) from the same edge.
Lay the base section flat, right side up, and position the four A pieces as shown in Fig 4, raw edges together. Stitch the A pieces in place as indicated by the dotted lines. Tape the handles in place as shown.
Cut a piece of fabric to the same

size as the base and lay it flat, wrong side up. Place the PVC base over it, right side up, and bind the edges together all round with 2.5cm (1in) bias binding. The tape can be removed once the handles are held in place by the binding.

Cushions
To make the ruffled cushion covers for the cushion pads, see page 134. These slot into the A pockets for carrying. Fold the cloth in half parallel with the top edges of handles, then fold in half again in the opposite direction, keeping the handles to the outside.

FITTED CUSHIONED WICKER CHAIR
To make a cushioned lining to a wicker chair, follow the instructions give for making a squab cushion cover (see page 135). Make a separate paper pattern for the seat and back. Cut the seat cushion about 15cm (6in) deeper than the seat to hang over the outside edge. Wicker can be lethal to the life of stockings and uncomfortable to lean legs against.) Fill the cushion covers with foam chips, or feathers (or a combination of both) and button them following the instructions for buttoned cushions (see page 137).
The cushions should be held in place by ties slotted through gaps in the wicker and tied at the back of the chair, in the same way as squab cushions are tied.

Lampshades

Fortunately an increasing number of fabric firms now include matching lampshades in their range, because conventional fitted shades are quite difficult to make – you either have nimble enough fingers to make them or you don't. If not, here are two of the simplest do it yourself designs – a Tiffany shade and a handkerchief shade – neither of which require careful fitting.

HANDKERCHIEF LAMPSHADE

By far the simplest lampshade to make is the handkershief lampshade. You will need a lampshade utility ring (Fig I) 20cm (8in) across. This will fit between the two washers of a bulb holder.

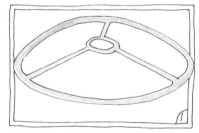

Cut a piece of fabric 90cm (36in) square. Make a narrow double hem all round the edge. Alternatively, make a scalloped edging bound with satin stitch (see page 153) as shown in Fig 2.
Fold the fabric in four to find the centre and, using a coin as a template, draw a small 6mm ($\frac{1}{4}$in) deep semicircle at the folded corner (Fig 3). Cut round the pencil line and open out the fabric to check that the hole is big enough to thread the electric flex through. Bind the hole with zig-zag stitch or bias binding.

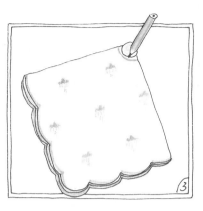

Take the flex through the hole and connect the utility ring and light bulb holder.

TIFFANY SHADE

You will need a Tiffany frame which in the UK are available in various sizes (Fig I). You can of course re-use the frame from an old lampshade if you have one. Measure the depth of the frame and add 12.5cm (5in) for turnings. Measure the circumference of the shade at the bottom and add 2.5cm (1in). Cut a piece of fabric to these dimensions. Cut a piece of lining fabric to the same size. Put both pieces together, wrong sides facing, and treat as one.
With right sides facing, join the short edges with a 6mm ($\frac{1}{4}$in)

French seam. Press the seam open and finish the edges with zig-zag stitch. Along the top and bottom edges turn in and press first 12mm ($\frac{1}{2}$in) then a further 2.5cm (1in) and slip stitch in place leaving a small gap on each hem to insert the elastic (Fig 2).

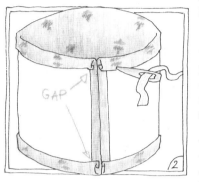

If there is to be a ruffle, top stitch it to the right side of the fabric at this stage, 2.5cm (1in) above the slip stitching.
Place the fabric over the frame. Thread 3mm ($\frac{1}{8}$in) elastic through top and bottom casings and draw it up so that the shade fits snugly round the frame, the edges overlapping each of the top and bottom edges of the frame by 2.5cm (1in) as shown in Fig 3. Sew the ends of the elastic securely together and slip stitch the gaps in the hems closed.

Recovering folding chairs

Putting on a new cover is very simple to do, and will extend the life of an old deck or director's chair. Make sure the frame is quite sound and give it a thorough clean before you start.

DECK CHAIRS

First pull out the old tacks from both ends of the frame, and remove the old canvas. Take the measurements of the old cover, and buy new canvas to the same length. (Alternatively you can use a tightly woven upholstery weight fabric, binding the side edges for extra strength.)
Turn under and tack (baste) a 2.5cm (1in) fold across both short edges of the cover. Lay the fabric on the ground or floor, wrong side up, and then lay the deck chair frame over it, front face down. Pull the canvas over the top bar of the chair frame, and tuck in around the back (Fig I). Hammer one tack in the centre of the bar.

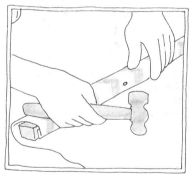

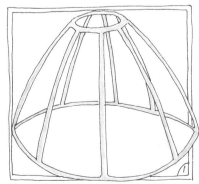

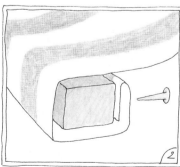

Then hammer in six more tacks spacing them equally across the width of the canvas. Repeat this procedure for the bottom end of the chair frame (Fig 2).

As the bottom end of most deck chairs is slightly narrower than the top end, you may need to fold the corners under to taper the width of the fabric. If you make up your own cover rather than using special deck chair width canvas, you can take this discrepancy into account before deciding on the width.

DIRECTOR'S CHAIRS
Use a sharp knife to cut through the old canvas along both seat edges (Fig 1).

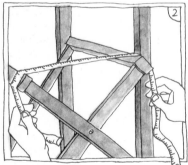

Cut the cover away from any nails, but do not attempt to remove them, as you may split the frame. Gently hammer them below the top surface of the wood.

Open up the chair and measure the distance between the outside edge of one rail across the chair to the outside of the other, adding 5cm (2in) to the total (Fig 2).

Cut a seat cover to fit this measurement using the old cover to determine the width of the seat canvas. Fold in a 2.5cm (1in) turn at both ends. Hammer to crease the folds. Next lay the folded end onto the outside edge of one seat rail. Collapse the chair and fix the cover by hammering six tacks in a row along the folded edge. Repeat

this process at the other side of the seat.

To fit a new back cover, slide the cover off both uprights (Fig 3). Measure the old cover, including the turned over ends, and add 5cm (2in) to the length and 4cm (1½in) to the width. Use a selvedge for one of the longer sides. Fold this over 12mm (½in) to the wrong side. At the other long side, turn in two 12mm (½in) folds. Machine stitch the hems along both these sides. Make a 12mm (½in) fold along both of the shorter sides of the cover and a second larger fold to form a slot or casing, big enough to fit over the wooden uprights. Machine stitch the casing and slot the cover back (Fig 4).

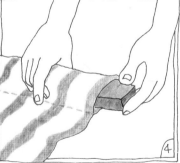

Some director's chairs, especially in the United States, have fabric-covered dowels that slide into slots in the frame. A new seat cover can be made with cased ends in the same way as the back cover.

Home sewing is like any other skill – once you have the basic know-how you are well on the way to successful results; not forgetting, of course, that practice makes perfect. In this chapter you will find basic know-how and some easy tricks of the trade to help you achieve a more professional finish to your work.

STITCHES
You can get by just knowing how to tack, seam and hem. But for the best results, it's really worth adding these stitches to your repertoire.

Slip stitch
This is an almost invisible method of stitching. To stitch a folded edge to a flat area of fabric, such as on a hem, bring the needle out on the fold. With the thread at an angle, pick up a single thread of the main fabric about 6mm (¼in) along from where the needle first emerged and draw the thread through. About another 6mm (¼in) along, insert the needle into the fold and slide it along inside before bringing it out on the fold again. Continue in this way all along the hem (Fig 1).

To slip stitch two folded edges

together, first bring the needle out on the fold of one of the edges. Insert the needle into the fold on the other edge, directly across from where it emerged and slide it down inside the fold to re-emerge on the foldline about 6mm (¼in) down (Fig 2). Continue in this way so that the stitching is practically invisible.

Hem stitch
This is the traditional method of finishing raw edges. It is not as unobtrusive as slipstitch but preferable on heavier fabrics.

Bring the needle out on the folded edge of the hem. About 6mm (¼in) along, pick up a single thread of the fabric with the needle point just above the hem and draw the thread through. Another 6mm (¼in) along, insert the needle into the back of the folded edge and draw the thread through. Continue in this way (Fig 3) along the hem, keeping the stitches even

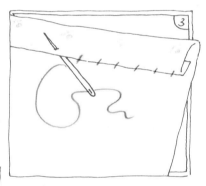

and not too taut, otherwise the hem will pucker. The hem should be invisible on the right side of the fabric. Never press along the stitching.

Lock stitch
This stitch is used to secure lining or interlining to curtain (drapery) fabric and lining to interlining. It is a loose blanket stitch. Its purpose is to ensure that two layers of fabric hang together in identical folds but at the same time it must still be possible for them to move slightly and not drag against one another. Leave the thread between the stitches fairly slack and place the stitches at 5–7.5cm (2–3in) intervals (Fig 4).

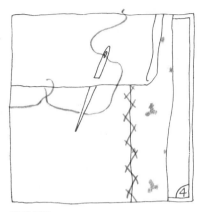

SEAMS

As with stitches, different seams have different purposes, depending on fabric, position and expected wear.

Flat seam

This is the simplest seam of all. Place the two pieces of fabric right sides facing and tack (baste) with raw edges level. Machine stitch in a straight line, parallel to the edge (Fig 1). Press the seam open with one seam allowance at each side (Fig 2). The raw edges can be finished off with zig-zag stitch to prevent fraying or, on a very fine fabric, the edges turned under and machine stitched.

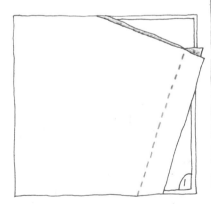

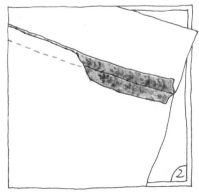

Flat fell seam

This is an extremely hard-wearing seam which is reversible and makes a neat finish.

Place the two pieces of fabric right sides together; tack (baste) along the seam line. Machine stitch along the tacking (basting). Press the seam open then press both seam allowances to one side. Trim the underneath seam allowance to half its width (Fig 3). Turn the upper seam allowance over the trimmed one and tack (baste) (Fig 4). Top stitch close to the edge. Press flat.

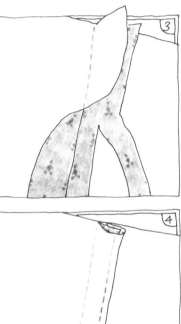

French seam

This is also a hard-wearing seam because it encloses the raw edges. It is not as decorative as the flat fell seam but is useful on transparent fabrics or those which fray easily.

Place the two pieces of fabric wrong sides together; tack (baste) with the raw edges level, 6mm ($\frac{1}{4}$in) from the edge. Machine stitch along the tacking (basting). Trim the seam to 3mm ($\frac{1}{8}$in) as shown in Fig 5. Press the seam open then tack (baste) 6mm ($\frac{1}{4}$in) from the first seam with the fabric folded right sides together and machine stitch along the tacking (basting)

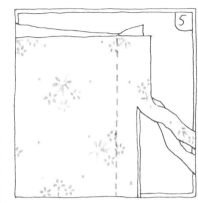

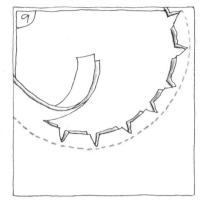

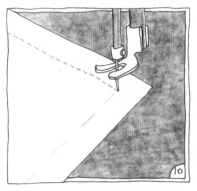

(Fig 6). Press the seam with the allowances to one side (Fig 7).

Curved seams

Once a curved seam has been stitched using a flat seam, it should

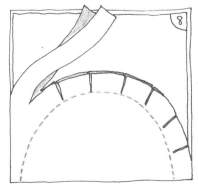

be trimmed to 6mm ($\frac{1}{4}$in) from the stitching. On an outside curve, clip into the allowance at evenly-spaced intervals so that the fabric can open out to lie flat. Take the clips as close as possible to the stitching without, of course, cutting through the seam (Fig 8).

On an inside curve, notch the allowance to get rid of excess bulk (Fig 9). The notches close up so that the fabric can lie flat.

Turning corners

To make a right-angled corner in a seam, machine stitch into the corner and, leaving the needle in the fabric, lift the presser foot of the machine and swivel the fabric round until the foot is aligned with

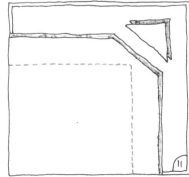

the continuation of the seam (Fig 10). When the seam is completed, clip away the corner as shown in Fig 11 to get rid of excess bulk.

To make a V-shaped seam, work in the same way, pivoting the fabric at the corner. When you have completed the seam, trim the corner diagonally in both directions as indicated by the dotted lines in Fig 12.

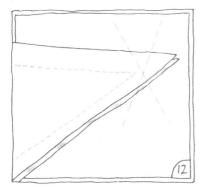

When adding a border to a rectangle, first strengthen the inside corner with a line of stitching just inside the seam allowance round the corner. Clip into the corner, close up to the stitching (Fig 13). The border can then be added by stitching the right sides together

in the usual way, taking the needle right to the corner. Then, with the needle still in the fabric, lift the presser foot and pivot the fabric until the foot is in line with the continuation of the seam (see Fig 10).

Alternatively, and more simply, just turn the seam allowance on the border to the wrong side all round and press, then carefully top stitch the border to the centre panel (Fig 14).

Matching patterns

It is very important that you match obvious patterns along straight seams especially on curtains. One of the advantages of the extra work is that if it is well done, the seam is far less obvious than it would have been on a plain fabric. Turn under the seam allowance on one of the pieces of fabric and press. Lay the second piece of fabric flat, right side up, and place the folded edge, also right side up, against the seam line on the second piece, matching the pattern. Pin it in place with the pins at right angles to the seam.

Tack (baste) the pieces together by knotting the thread on the wrong side of the fabric at the right-hand end of the seam. Bring the needle to the front of the fabric close against the folded edge of the other piece. Insert the needle into the fold, exactly level with its position in the first fabric. Slide it along the inside of the fold for about 12mm ($\frac{1}{2}$in) before bringing it out again. Insert it into the unfolded fabric exactly level with where it emerged from the fold. Take a 12mm ($\frac{1}{2}$in) stitch in

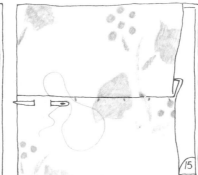

the fabric, bringing the needle out close to the fold again (Fig 15). Continue in this way for the length of the seam, always checking that the pattern is exactly matched. Finish off the tacking (basting) securely.

Turn the fabric pieces right sides together and machine stitch along the tacking (basting) line.

Piped (corded) seams

Cord. Uncovered piping (cable) cord can be stitched directly over the right side of a seam. Choose a thread which matches as closely as possible the colour of the cord.

Pass the needle through the cord, taking it between the twists so that the thread is embedded in the furrows, and into the fabric at right angles. Return the needle through the seam a short stitch-length along and back through the cord as before, to emerge between the twists (Fig 16).

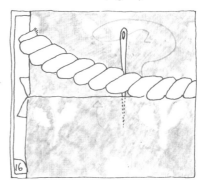

Covered piping (cording). Cut or make up bias binding to the required length, either 2.5cm (1in) wide or 5cm (2in) wide, depending on the thickness of the piping (cable) cord. Cut the cord to the same length.

Place the cord down the centre of the wrong side of the bias strip and fold the binding in half. Tack (baste) close to the cord (Fig. 17). Using either a piping foot or a zipper foot, machine stitch over the tacking (basting). Trim excess binding to match the allowance on the seam on to which the piping (cording) is to be applied.

Place the piping (cording) between the two pieces of fabric which are to be seamed together, right sides

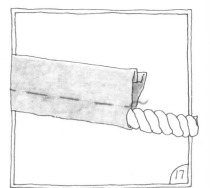

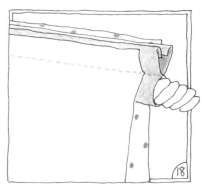

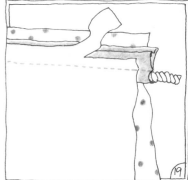

facing, the raw edges matching. Stitch along the seam line which should be as close as possible to the cord (Fig 18).

On bulky fabric such as quilting, it may be easier to stitch the piping (cording) to the seam line on one piece of fabric first before joining the two pieces together.

Always layer the seam allowances afterwards to keep bulk to a minimum (Fig 19).

When piping (cording) is to be applied to a continuous seam, it has to be joined. To do this smoothly, first stitch together the bias strips and unravel the cord at each end by about 2.5cm (1in) as shown in Fig. 20. Cut each strand

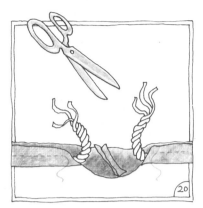

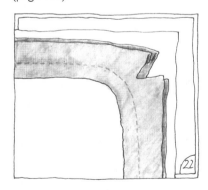

to a different length and weave them loosely together (Fig 21) before enclosing them in the bias binding in the usual way.

When the piped (corded) seam turns a corner, always stitch along a gentle curve (Fig 22) and notch the binding seam allowance as shown.

To use cord to give a ribbed surface to fabrics, see Cording (page 155).

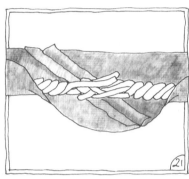

MITRED CORNERS

The neatest way of working hem corners is to mitre them. Borders and edgings also look better with a mitred corner.

Hems

With wrong side of fabric facing

you, turn in and press the first fold of the double hem. The size of this turning will depend on the article in question and on loose-lined curtains there is only a single side turning but the method is the same.

Turn in and press the second foldline along each edge. Press and open out these second folds (Fig 1).

Fold the corner diagonally so that the second foldlines match up as shown in Fig 2 and press. Trim the corner between these matching points (Fig 3). Fold both edges in place and slip stitch the diagonal seam. Work towards the corner, taking the needle straight across from one side to the other then sliding it down inside the fold

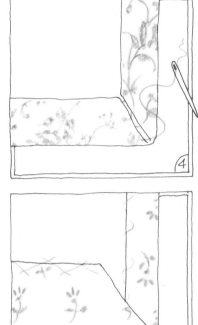

before bringing it out again and taking it straight across to the other side (Fig 4). Finish off securely on the hem allowance near the corner, making sure the thread goes through one thickness of fabric only and does not show on the front of the fabric.

On items like curtains, the mitres will not be of the same depth (Fig 5). Where they do correspond, slip stitch them together leaving the remainder on the deeper mitre secured only at the hem.

Edgings

Any edging such as a lace or scalloped edge which is being added to cushions, pillows, curtains or a bedcover will lie better with a mitred corner.

Stitch the edging in place to about 7.5–10cm (3–4in) from the corner (Fig 6). The edging must extend well beyond the corner. With tailor's chalk, draw a diagonal line across the edgings as shown in Fig 6. Trim them 6mm ($\frac{1}{4}$in) outside this line. Place the two edgings right sides together and stitch along the chalk line (Fig 7). Press the seam open and zig-zag the raw

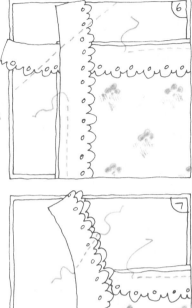

edges to neaten (Fig 8). Complete the seams joining the edging to the main fabric.

Appliquéd borders

To mitre the corner of any border which is top stitched to the main fabric, first turn in and press a 6mm ($\frac{1}{4}$in) fold to the wrong side along each inside edge of the border strip. Top stitch it to the main fabric to about 15cm (6in) from the corner. The border should project well beyond the corner (Fig 9 p 152). With tailor's chalk, draw in a diagonal line as shown in Fig 9. Trim each border to 6mm ($\frac{1}{4}$in) outside this line. Place the two borders right sides

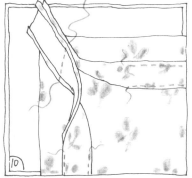

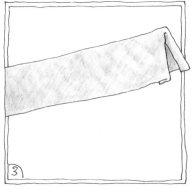

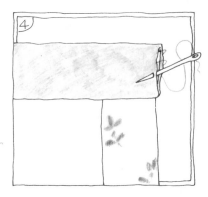

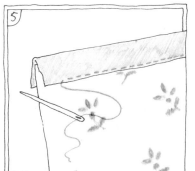

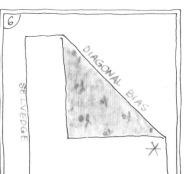

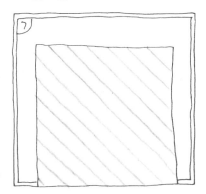

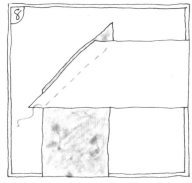

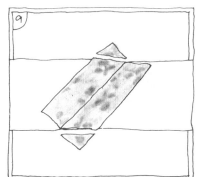

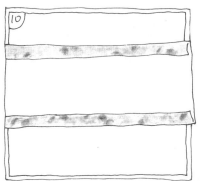

together (Fig 10) and stitch along the chalk line. Press the seam open. Tack (baste) the border in place at the corner and complete the top stitching (Fig 11).

EDGES

Apart from the simple hem, there are several decorative ways to finish off a raw edge.

Binding

Binding is a simple way to finish off raw edges and is especially useful on quilted fabric. Always use bias binding (see below) on a curved or diagonal edge.

Most mass-produced straight binding has finished edges. Simply fold the binding in half (Fig 1) and press. Encase the raw edge in the fold (Fig 2) and pin and tack (baste) it in place.

Finish the raw ends of the binding by turning them in (Fig 3) and slip stitching them together (Fig 4).

Stitch as close as possible to the edge of the binding (Fig 5) ensuring that the edges are caught in on both sides.

If the binding is cut from fabric and cut on the straight of the grain, make it up as for bias binding (see below).

Bias binding

It is possible to buy ready-made bias binding in a variety of colours and widths. However, by making your own you have a variety of colours and fabrics to choose from and more scope.

Lay the fabric flat and fold over one corner diagonally (Fig 6), ensuring that the corner starred is an exact right angle. The foldline, at a 45 degree angle to the straight of the grain, is what is known as the 'bias' and when pulled, will stretch like elastic. Mark the ends of the foldline with pins. Open out the fabric and mark the diagonal with tailor's chalk and a ruler or straight edge.

Draw lines across the fabric, parallel with the first one (Fig 7) and spaced at intervals 12mm (½in) wider than the binding required. Remember, too, that the finished width of the binding is halved once it has been applied. Cut the fabric along these parallel lines.

To join the bias strips into a continuous length, place the ends of two strips, right sides facing, at right angles to one another (Fig 8) and stitch 6mm (¼in) from the edge. Press open and trim the surplus at the corners (Fig 9).

With wrong sides of the binding facing, turn in 6mm ($\frac{1}{4}$in) and press along the long edges (Fig 10).

To apply the binding, fold it in half, wrong sides together, and place it over the edge to be bound. Mark the position of the turned-in edge with a pin (Fig 11).

Open out the binding and place it, right sides together, with the main fabric, placing the top folded edge of the binding on the pin mark (Fig 12). Keeping the raw edge of the binding an equal distance from the raw edge of the main fabric, then stitch the binding along the fold.

Fold the binding over the raw edge to the wrong side of the main fabric and slip stitch in place (Fig 13), just covering the machine stitching.

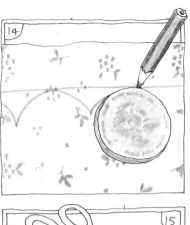

Scalloped edge

For a large scallop, see instructions for making a paper pattern for Scalloped Heading Curtains (see page 113).

For a tiny scallop, bound with satin stitch, mark a straight line parallel to the edge of the fabric, using pencil or tailor's chalk. Then, draw the scallops on the fabric using a large coin such as a 2p piece (quarter) as a template and placing the top of each curve on the line (Fig 14).

Work satin stitch along the outline then trim the fabric close to the stitching, taking care not to cut into the stitching. Curved nail scissors may make the job easier (Fig 15).

RUFFLES

Ruffles are a soft, luxurious way of decorating the lower edges of all sorts of soft furnishings. Although they look purely decorative, their added weight will improve the hang of curtains or tablecloths. You can use matching or contrasting fabrics.

Simple ruffle

The simplest way to make a ruffle is to join strips of fabric together along their short edges to make a continuous length. It should measure from one-and-a-half to two times the finished length, plus 2.5cm (1in) for turnings and the finished depth plus 2.5cm (1in) for turnings. Stitch the ends together for a continuous ruffle or turn in the ends and slip stitch them in place for a straight ruffle. Make a double 6mm ($\frac{1}{4}$in) hem on the lower edge.

Make two lines of running stitch 6mm ($\frac{1}{4}$in) and 12mm ($\frac{1}{2}$in) from the top edge. Draw up the gathering threads to fit, arranging the gathers evenly.

Pin the ruffle right sides together on the main fabric with the pins across the seam. Tack (baste) along the 12mm ($\frac{1}{2}$in) gathering thread

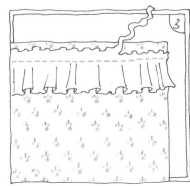

and machine stitch in place (Fig 1). Finish the raw edges with zig-zag stitch through both thicknesses and press the seam towards the ungathered fabric (Fig 2). Alternatively, trim the ruffle to 6mm ($\frac{1}{4}$in) (Fig 3) and turn the ungathered seam allowance over it in a double hem to make a self-bound edge (Fig 4).

Double ruffle

This is made in the same way as the simple ruffle but eliminates the need for a lower hem. It also makes the ruffle reversible which is particularly suitable for a valance on a four poster bed, for example, where it will be seen from both sides.

Once the length has been cut, this time to twice the finished depth plus 2.5cm (1in) for turnings, either join the ends or hem them as before.

Fold the strip in half lengthways (Fig 5) and make the lines of tacking through the double thickness.

The top edge can be finished off as before, either with zig-zag stitch through all thicknesses or with a self-bound edge.

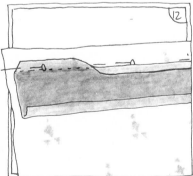

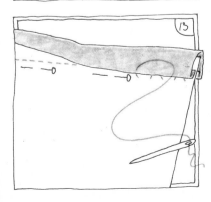

Double-sided ruffle

This is gathered along the centre and top-stitched to the main fabric.

Cut the strips as described above either adding 2.5cm (1in) to the depth for a double 6mm ($\frac{1}{4}$in) hem top and bottom or cutting to the exact finished depth and then binding the edges.

Join the strips with French seams (see page 149) and finish off the top and bottom edges.

Make one line of gathering stitches along the centre of the ruffle. Draw it up to fit and pin it to the main fabric, both with right sides upwards. Tack and machine stitch along the gathering line (Fig 6). Alternatively, place the line of gathering off-centre, which will give a small ruffled heading with the main ruffle below (Fig 7).

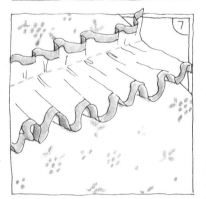

For an extra frothy look, cut the fabric to two-and-a-half or even three times the finished length of the ruffle.

Pleated ruffle

Make up a strip of fabric to twice the finished length of the ruffle, plus 12mm ($\frac{1}{2}$in) turning at each end, joining the strips with flat seams pressed open. The depth should be the finished depth plus 2.5cm (1in) for the lower hem and 12mm ($\frac{1}{2}$in) for the top turning. Make a double 12mm ($\frac{1}{2}$in) hem along the lower edge.

Lay the fabric flat, wrong side uppermost, and, with pins or tailor's chalk, mark the width of each pleat along the fabric (Fig 8). Fold A to C, D to F and so on, taking the next foldline to the next-but-one all along (Fig 9). Pin the pleats in place then tack along the top, 6mm ($\frac{1}{4}$in) from the edge, to secure. Finish off the short ends with a double 6mm ($\frac{1}{4}$in) hem.

Place the ruffle right sides together with the main fabric, raw edges matching, and stitch 12mm ($\frac{1}{2}$in) from the edge. Finish off as for a simple ruffle.

Box pleats

Box pleats are used on valances (skirts) along the lower edges of loose (slip) covers or bedspreads or as curtain pelmets (drapery valances).

Multiply the finished length of the valance (skirt) by three and add 2.5cm (1in) for turnings (seams). The depth of the valance (skirt) is measured from the base of the mattress or chair to just above floor level. Add 2.5cm (1in) for the lower hem and 12mm ($\frac{1}{2}$in) for the top turning (seam). Turn up and press the lower hem before making the pleats.

Generally speaking, 10cm (4in) is a convenient width for the pleats but the final decision depends on the exact finished measurement. The outer edge of the end pleats must line up with either the corners of the chair or bed or the ends of the curtain valance (Fig 10). For example, on a chair measure each side (Fig 11) and divide it into equally-sized pleats which are as near to 10cm (4in) as possible.

To help fold the pleats accurately,

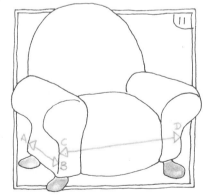

cut a piece of stiff card to the length and width of one finished pleat. Lay the fabric flat, wrong side up, and with tailor's chalk or pins, mark out the pleats using the card as a template (Fig 12). Fold line B to line A and line C to line D and so on (Fig 13) all the way along the valance (skirt). Make sure that

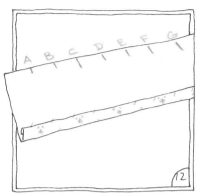

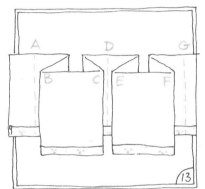

any seams in the fabric are hidden, where possible, behind a pleat. Tack (baste) and press the pleats in place. Turn in and slip stitch the side edges and press.

SPECIAL EFFECTS

These techniques can be used to add extra richness and texture to fabric surfaces.

Appliqué

Ardent home sewers usually keep a 'rag bag' so that when it comes to designing an appliqué cushion or bedspread, they have a good choice of colours and patterns. Of course, for a special design you may need to buy new fabric or special patchwork packs or look around for end of roll scraps in fabric store sales.

First draw out the design, then cut out the different shapes in coloured paper — pink for petals and green for leaves for instance. Pin them in place to see whether the design works and, if not, you can move the pieces around to find one that does. When you have worked out your design, you can use the paper cutouts as patterns for the shapes (Fig 1).

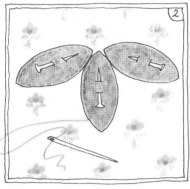

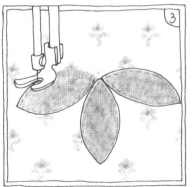

Pin each paper shape to the fabric and cut it out with an extra 3mm (⅛in) all round. Cut the same shape out of medium-weight Vilene (non-woven interfacing).

Pin each shape, together with its Vilene backing, in place on the background fabric. Tack (baste) round the shape through all thicknesses, as close to the edges as possible (Fig 2). With the machine set to zig-zag, satin stitch over the raw edges (Fig 3). Satin stitch uses up a lot of thread, so make sure you have plenty of the correct colour before starting.

To give the appliqué a richer texture, cut terylene wadding (polyester batting) slightly smaller

than the appliqué shape and place it between the Vilene (interfacing) and the backing fabric. Apply the shape as before.

Borders

To edge a curtain or a cushion, cut out a border on the straight grain of the fabric to the required width and length.

With the wrong side of the fabric facing, turn in 6mm (¼in) and press along the long edges (Fig 4).

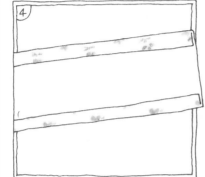

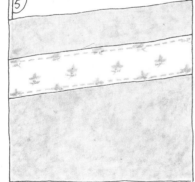

Pin the border, right side up, to the right side of the curtain or cushion and tack (baste) along both edges (Fig 5). Machine stitch close to the edges.

To mitre the corners of a border, see Mitred Corners (page 151).

Cording

This technique is often used to give cushion covers or bedspreads an interesting texture. Usually it is in parallel rows, equally spaced, and the rows are always on the straight of the grain. Some sewing machines have a special cording foot but, if not, the same effect can be produced with a very slender piping (cable) cord.

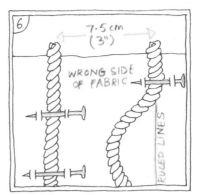

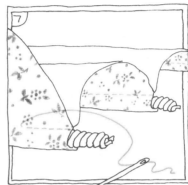

Using tailor's chalk and a straight edge, mark out the lines of the cording on the wrong side of the fabric, usually about 7.5cm (3in) apart. Cut cord to fit each line and lay it on the fabric positioned centrally over the line and pin it in place (Fig 6) with the pins at right angles to the cord. Turn the fabric over and pin the cord again from the right side of the fabric and again with the pins at right angles. Remove the pins from the wrong side.

Wrap the fabric round each cord and, with right sides facing, tack (baste) the fabric close to the cord (Fig 7). Using a piping (cording) or zipper foot, stitch along the lines of tacking (basting).

Machine patchwork

The secret of success with machine patchwork is to cut the pieces very accurately and to keep to a very strict seam allowance.

To make up the pattern in Fig 8, for example, draw out the pieces on the fabric with pencil before cutting them out carefully. On the wrong side of each piece, pencil in the 6mm (¼in) seam allowance all round, using a ruler.

Always pin and tack all the sections together, making sure that everything lines up as it should before pressing the tacked seams. Finally, stitch the pieces together. Test first to ensure that the tension on your machine is correct, otherwise the seams will pucker.

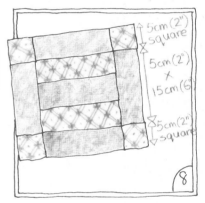

LAURA ASHLEY SHOPS

UNITED KINGDOM

12 New Bond Street
BATH
Tel: 0225 60341

14/16 Priory Queensway
BIRMINGHAM
Tel: 021 233 1499

80 Old Christchurch Road
BOURNEMOUTH
Tel: 0202 27572

104/106 Queen's Road
BRIGHTON
Tel: 0273 27431

14 Trinity Street
CAMBRIDGE
Tel: 0223 51378

5 High Street
CARDIFF
Tel: 0222 40808

1a Queen's Circus
Montpellier
CHELTENHAM
Tel: 0242 45500

17/19 Watergate Row
CHESTER
Tel: 0244 316403

66 Purley Way
(Sainsbury's Homebase)
CROYDON
Tel: 01 684 8250

43/45 Lothian Road
EDINBURGH
Tel: 031 229 5135

137 George Street
EDINBURGH
Tel: 031 225 1121

215 Sauchiehall Street
GLASGOW
Tel: 041 333 0850

404 Byres Road
GLASGOW
Tel: 041 339 5911

Old Cloth Hall
North Street
GUILDFORD
Tel: 0483 34152

North Leeds Shopping Centre
(Sainsbury's Homebase)
Kings Lane
LEEDS

30 Great Oak Street
LLANIDLOES
Powys
Tel: 05512 2557

7/8 Harriet Street
LONDON SW1
Tel: 01 235 9797

71/73 Lower Sloane Street
LONDON SW1
Tel: 01 730 1771

75 Lower Sloane Street
LONDON SW1
Tel: 01 730 5255

183 Sloane Street
LONDON SW1
Tel: 01 235 9728

157 Fulham Road
LONDON SW3
Tel: 01 584 6939

35/36 Bow Street
Covent Garden
LONDON WC2
Tel: 01 240 1997

28 King Street
MANCHESTER
Tel: 061 834 7335

8 Nelson Street
NEWCASTLE
Tel: 0632 615 195

3/5 Dove Street
NORWICH
Tel: 0603 26533

58 Bridlesmith Gate
NOTTINGHAM
Tel: 0602 53366

26/27 Little Clarendon Street
OXFORD
Tel: 0865 52477

65 Wyle Cop
SHREWSBURY
Tel: 0743 51467

Unit 5 King Edward Court
WINDSOR
Tel: 07535 59560

REPUBLIC OF IRELAND

7 Dawson Street
DUBLIN 2
Tel: 001 714 247

UNITED STATES OF AMERICA

Main Level
Lenox Square
3393 Peachtree Road
ATLANTA
Georgia 30326
Tel: 404 231 0685

Pratt Street Pavilion
Harbor Place
BALTIMORE
Maryland 21202
Tel: 302 539 0500

203 Beachwood Place
26300 Cedar Road
BEACHWOOD
Ohio 44122
Tel: 216 831 7620/21

83 Newbury Street
BOSTON
Massachusetts 02116
Tel: 617 536 0505

6–26 Watertower Place
835 N Michigan Avenue
CHICAGO
Illinois 60611
Tel: 312 951 8004

South Coast Plaza
33 Bristol/San Diego Freeway
COSTA MESA
California 92626
Tel: 714 545 9322

The Galleria
FORT LAUDERDALE
Florida

Riverside Square
Rt 4/Hackensack Ave
HACKENSACK
New Jersey 07601
Tel: 201 488 0130

Macy's
Herald Square
NEW YORK

714 Madison Avenue
NEW YORK
New York 10021
Tel: 212 371 0606

Oakbrooke Mall
OAKBROOKE
Illinois

9 On the Square
Suburban Square
Ardmore
PHILADELPHIA
Pennsylvania 19003
Tel: 215 896 0208

1827 Union Street
SAN FRANCISCO
California 94123
Tel: 415 922 7200

The Mall at Short Hills
SHORT HILLS
New Jersey 07078
Tel: 201 688 5910

3213 M Street N W
Georgetown
WASHINGTON DC
20007
Tel: 202 338 5481

85 Main Street
WESTPORT
Connecticut 06880
Tel: 203 226 7495

CANADA

Laura Ashley Edmonton
P.O. Box 225
West Edmonton Mall
8770 170th Street
EDMONTON
Alberta

2110 Crescent Street
MONTREAL
Tel: 514 284 9225

136 Bank Street
OTTAWA
Tel: 613 238 4882

Les Galeries de la Capitale
5401 Boulevard des Galeries
(Store 213)
QUEBEC G2N 1N4
Tel: 418 627 5826

18 Hazelton Avenue
TORONTO
Tel: 416 922 7761

213 Carrall Street
VANCOUVER
Tel: 604 688 8729

AUSTRALIA

The Gallerie
Gawler Place
ADELAIDE 5000
Tel: 08 223 6548

179 Collins Street
MELBOURNE
Victoria 3000
Tel: 03 63 3506

6 Collins Place
Collins Street
MELBOURNE
Victoria 3000
Tel: 03 63 5548

City Arcade
Hay Street Level
PERTH 6000
Tel: 09 321 2391

74 Castlereagh Street
SYDNEY
New South Wales 2000
Tel: 02 232 2829

EUROPE

Austria
Weihburggasse 5
VIENNA 1010
Tel: 222 529340

Belgium
Frankrijklei 27
ANTWERP
Tel: 3231 343461

32 rue de Namur
1000 BRUSSELS
Tel: 02 51 29206

81/83 rue de Namur
1000 BRUSSELS
Tel: 02 51 28639

Denmark
Gronnegade 10
1107 COPENHAGEN
Tel: (01) 15 20 80

France
4 rue Joseph Cabassol
13100 AIX-EN-PROVENCE
Tel: 42 27 31 92

2 place de Palais
33000 BORDEAUX
Tel: 56 44 10 30

1 Quai Tilsitt
69002 LYONS
Tel: 78 37 40 11

37 place Bellecour
69002 LYONS
Tel: 78 37 18 19

94 rue de Rennes
75006 PARIS
Tel: 548 43 89

66 rue des Saint Pères
75007 PARIS
Tel: 544 15 96

22 rue de Grennelle
75007 PARIS
Tel: 544 63 04

34 rue de Grennelle
75007 PARIS
Tel: 548 84 48

95 avenue Raymond Poincaré
75016 PARIS
Tel: 704 41 73

4 rue de Faisan
67000 STRASBOURG
Tel: 88 35 23 26

50 rue Boulbonne
31000 TOULOUSE
Tel: 61 21 38 85

Italy
4 Via Brera
20121 MILAN
Tel: 02 808 477

The Netherlands
Singel 439/441
1012 WP
AMSTERDAM
Tel: 020 228087

Singel 417/419
1012
AMSTERDAM
Tel: 020 268538

Bakkerstraat 17
6811 EG
ARNHEM
Tel: 085 430250

Markt 21
5611 EC
EINDHOVEN
Tel: 040 435022

Brugstraat 22
9711 HZ
GRONINGEN
Tel: 050 140167

Papestraat 17
2513 THE HAGUE
Tel: 070 600540

M Smedestraat 9
6212 GK
MAASTRAICHT
Tel: 043 50972

Oude Gracht 141
3511 AJ
UTRECHT
Tel: 030 313051

Switzerland
8 rue Verdaine
1204 GENEVA
Tel: 022 2134 94/022 2833 40

21 Augustinergasse
ZURICH
Tel: 01 221 1394

West Germany
4000 DUSSELDORF
Hunsrückstrasse 43
Tel: 0211 327009

6000 FRANKFURT/MAIN
1 Goethe Strasse 3
Tel: 0611 288791

2000 HAMBURG
Neuer Wall 73/75
Tel: 040 371 173

8000 MUNICH
Sendlingerstrasse 37
Tel: 089 2608224

MAIL ORDER DEPARTMENTS
UNITED KINGDOM MAIL ORDER
Box No. 1
Mail Order Department
Laura Ashley Ltd
Carno
Powys
Wales SY17 5LG

REPUBLIC OF IRELAND MAIL ORDER
Laura Ashley Ltd
7 Dawson Street
Dublin 2
Republic of Ireland

USA MAIL ORDER
Laura Ashley Inc
Mail Order Department
55 Triangle Boulevard
Carlstadt
New Jersey 07072

FRANCE MAIL ORDER
Vente par Correspondance
Département A1
198 Avenue du President Wilson
93210 La Plaine St Denis

HOLLAND MAIL ORDER
Laura Ashley Postorders
Oudegracht 141
3511 AJ Utrecht

GERMANY MAIL ORDER
Laura Ashley Postversand
Hunsruckstrasse 43
4000 Düsseldorf

SWITZERLAND MAIL ORDER
Laura Ashley S.A.
Augustinergasse 21
8001 Zurich

BELGIUM MAIL ORDER
Vente par Correspondance
32 rue de Namur
1000 Bruxelles

ITALY MAIL ORDER
Laura Ashley SRL
Via Brera 4
2012 Milano

DENMARK MAIL ORDER
Laura Ashley APS
Gronnegade 10
1107 Kobenhavn K
Danmark

INDEX

Note: Page numbers in *italics* refer to
    illustrations.
Page numbers in **bold** refer to
    instruction pages.

A

157

ACKNOWLEDGMENTS

Special thanks are due to Sasha de Stroumillo of Laura Ashley Limited for styling many of the photographs and for giving so much of her time in the preparation of the book; and to Monica Sudek for providing patterns and making up many of the furnishings featured.

The publishers would like to thank the following individuals and organizations for their kind permission to reproduce material in this book:

PHOTOGRAPHS
Laura Ashley Limited 8–9, 22 above, 24 above right, 25, 45 below, 60 below, 61 above, 64 above, 74, 80 above, 85 right, 87 right, 89, 90 below, (Nick Ashley) title pages, 6, 7 above, 8–9, 13, 14–15, 23, 39 above, 41, 55 above, 61 below, 62 left, 63 below, 64 below, 66 below, 78, 80 below, 90 above, 94 below right, 95, (Jean Dalban) 26 below left, 54, 55 below, 62 above right, 65 above left and right, 83, 88 below right, (Mike Hancock) 51 below, 52 below, 53, 57 left and below right, 65 below left and right, 75, 86 right, 88 below left and above right, (Stefano Massimo) 39 below, (Arabella Campbell McNair Wilson) 7 above right and below, 14, 17 above left, 20, 20–1, 21, 26 above, 26 below right, 27–35, 37, 43, 45, 47 below, 48, 49, 51 above, 52–3, 56, 58, 60, 62 below right, 66 above, 67, 72, 73, 76, 77, 79 left, 81 below, 82, 84 left, 85 below left, 87 above and below left, 88 above left, 91, 94 above right, 96, (James Mortimer) 24 left, 38, 85 above left, (George Mott) 22 below, 36, 36–7, 39 above, 86 above.
Camera Press Limited 71; Carina 47 above; Philip Dowell 90–91, 92 below; Henry Fullerton 46; Louis/Shevre Associates (Elliot Blatt) 11 below right, 40; Derry Moore 63 above; Meredith Corporation (Bradley Olman) 44, (Thomas Hooper) 69; Malcom Robertson 11 above left, 57 above right; Schöner Wohnen 12; Syndication International 24 below right, 50; Elizabeth Whiting and Associates 9, 10, 11 above right, 15, 16, 16–17, 17 above right, 18, 19, 42, 59, 70, 79 above and below right, 81 above, 84 right, 92 above, 92–3, 94 left.

ARTWORK
Sue Thompson 98–123, Lynn Breeze 124–155.

ROOM DESIGN
Antony Childs, Inc. & Laura Chester 11 below, 40; Betty Hammell Robrecht 46; Johnny Grey 18; Virginia Wetherall 11 above right, 18 right, 19, 59.

STENCIL DESIGN
Felicity Binyon/Elizabeth McFarlane 11 above, 18 right, 19; Margaret Colvin 87 above; Mary Macarthy 87 below.

PDO 82-0464